P9-EDR-717

Philosophy Beside Itself

Philosophy
Beside Itself
On Deconstruction
and Modernism

Stephen W. Melville

Foreword by Donald Marshall

Theory and History of Literature, Volume 27

University of Minnesota Press, Minneapolis

The University of Minnesota gratefully acknowledges assistance
provided by the Andrew W. Mellon Foundation for publication of
this book.

Published by the University of Minnesota Press
2037 University Avenue Southeast, Minneapolis MN 55414.
Published simultaneously in Canada
by Fitzhenry & Whiteside Limited, Markham.
Printed in the United States of America.

Library of Congress Cataloging-in-Publication Data
Melville, Stephen.
  Philosophy beside itself.

  (Theory and history of literature ; v. 27)
  Bibliography: p.
  Includes index.
  1. Deconstruction. 2. Derrida, Jacques—Contributions in
criticism. I. Title. II. Series.
  PN98.D43M45 1986   801'.95   85-14025
  ISBN 0-8166-1437-7
  ISBN 0-8166-1438-5 (pbk.)

Excerpt from *L'Ecorce et le noyau* by N. Abraham and M. Torok
(pp. 337-39), © 1978 Flammarion, translated and reproduced with
the permission of the publisher.

The University of Minnesota
is an equal-opportunity
educator and employer.

for Ruthie

Theory and History of Literature
Edited by Wlad Godzich and Jochen Schulte-Sasse

Volume 1. Tzvetan Todorov *Introduction to Poetics*

Volume 2. Hans Robert Jauss *Toward an Aesthetic of Reception*

Volume 3. Hans Robert Jauss
Aesthetic Experience and Literary Hermeneutics

Volume 4. Peter Bürger *Theory of the Avant-Garde*

Volume 5. Vladimir Propp *Theory and History of Folklore*

Volume 6. Edited by Jonathan Arac, Wlad Godzich,
and Wallace Martin
The Yale Critics: Deconstruction in America

Volume 7. Paul de Man *Blindness and Insight:
Essays in the Rhetoric of Contemporary Criticism*
2nd ed., rev.

Volume 8. Mikhail Bakhtin *Problems of Dostoevsky's Poetics*

Volume 9. Erich Auerbach
Scenes from the Drama of European Literature

Volume 10. Jean-François Lyotard
The Postmodern Condition: A Report on Knowledge

Volume 11. Edited by John Fekete *The Structural Allegory:
Reconstructive Encounters with the New French Thought*

Volume 12. Ross Chambers *Story and Situation: Narrative Seduction
and the Power of Fiction*

Volume 13. Tzvetan Todorov *Mikhail Bakhtin: The Dialogical Principle*

Volume 14. Georges Bataille *Visions of Excess: Selected Writings,
1927–1939*

Volume 15. Peter Szondi *On Textual Understanding and Other Essays*

Volume 16. Jacques Attali *Noise*

Volume 17. Michel de Certeau *Heterologies*

Volume 18. Thomas G. Pavel *The Poetics of Plot: The Case of English Renaissance Drama*

Volume 19. Jay Caplan *Framed Narratives: Diderot's Genealogy of the Beholder*

Volume 20. Jean-François Lyotard and Jean-Loup Thébaud *Just Gaming*

Volume 21. Malek Alloula *The Colonial Harem*

Volume 22. Klaus Theweleit *Male Fantasies, Volume 1. Women, Floods, Bodies, History*

Volume 23. Klaus Theweleit *Male Fantasies, Volume 2. Male Bodies: Psychoanalyzing the White Terror*

Volume 24. Hélène Cixous and Catherine Clément *The Newly Born Woman*

Volume 25. José Antonio Maravall, *Culture of the Baroque: Analysis of a Historical Structure*

Volume 26. Andrzej Warminski *Readings in Interpretation: Hölderlin, Hegel, Heidegger*

Volume 27. Stephen Melville *Philosophy Beside Itself: On Deconstruction and Modernism*

Contents

Foreword by Donald Marshall   xi

Preface   xxv

1. On Modernism   3

2. A Context for Derrida   34

   Hegel: Realizing Philosophy   37

   After Hegel (I): The Disposition of Philosophy   45

   After Hegel (II): Philosophy Beside Itself   60

   After Hegel (III): The Philosopher's Death   71

3. Psychoanalysis and Deconstruction   84

   Questions of Tradition and Method   84

     Psychoanalysis of Philosophy: The Status of "Freudian Concepts";

      Philosophy and Psychologism; Freud and Hegel   84

     Odds and Evens: The Argument with Lacan   88

     Psychoanalysis and Philosophy: Critical Realism;

      De-idealization; *Mise-en-abîme*   93

     Contre-bande: The Opposition; the Legacy; *Anasémie*;

      the Exorbitant   97

   [Questions of Style]   106

   Open Questions   113

4. Paul de Man: The Time of Criticism   115

5. Psychoanalysis, Criticism, Self-Criticism   139

Notes   159

Bibliography   173

Index   183

Foreword
Donald Marshall

In 1912, Arnold Schönberg composed *Pierrot Lunaire*, a musical setting of "thrice seven" poems by the French poet Albert Guirard. The texts assemble a conventional symbolist environment, through which move characters from the *commedia dell'arte* engaged in vaguely ritual actions of indeterminate import but with overtones of hostility to the order and monuments of ordinary bourgeois culture. They are, in short, "dated." But Schönberg's music remains irreducibly strange even after three-quarters of a century (this fact has seemed to some Schönberg's chief excellence). And the "method of composing with twelve tones" goes even further. For that method can no longer be simply defined against a reigning orthodoxy, and yet its methodicalness is inaudible even for the trained ear. Any amateur can hear an organizing key, but not even an expert could write out the tone row from hearing a serial composition. Something so natural, a convention so deeply in accord with our actual makeup that all the accumulated training of modern life has not reduced its power as a norm against which strangeness is experienced, is here violated, producing instantly the effect of "the modern." (To be sure, Schönberg remarked that his music was not modern, just badly played.) Such an experience of undiminishing "modernity" resists the historian of art's commitment to describe a series of "period" styles and discern the law or logic of their succession. And yet Schönberg himself saw the "twelve-tone method" as the culminating point in the historical progression of music and as the origin for a new era in that progression.

Just this ambiguity—establishing an opposition between the historical (or any other mediation) and the immediacy of an absolute present (or of an autonomous, self-standing object), and then oscillating between these poles—defines, according to Paul de Man, "modernity" as a value, not just as a shifting and contingent historical moment. My parentheses imply that the opposition between history and a posited absolute present lies close to, is even the same as, an opposition between two kinds of consciousness, one directed toward objects and constituted by tacit influences and components, the other fully and rigorously self-constituted. I mean to assert an equivalence between "modernity" and the kind of consciousness called in philosophy "critical." We have no obvious label for its opposite, but the temptation to call it "ordinary" has not often been resisted. Ordinary consciousness may be naive or sophisticated, but critical consciousness is sophisticated or it is nothing. Its discoverer—or inventor—according to the usual account, is Kant, and his characterization of a consciousness aware of its own conditions of possibility and limits has seemed to provide the model for "modernity" in every field of the mind's exertions, from science to the arts. To say that "modernity" in philosophy and in thought generally "begins" with Kant is, of course, paradoxical, since the point of such a consciousness is to escape just that sort of contingency. What may be said (is sometimes said; would have been said by Kant himself) is that Kant laid bare what had been there all along, not exactly the "essence" of consciousness, or its "foundation," but how it appeared to itself when it was, so to speak, at home. The therapeutic and cathartic effect of setting one's house in order impelled and still sustains the quest for self-awareness and self-justification. Reformulating modernity as critical consciousness in this way lets us see the peculiar ambiguity of both Marxism and psychoanalysis. On the one hand, consciousness is lured into forfeiture to the everyday and blindly subjected to historic forces (manifested as ideology) and to its own unacknowledged desires (manifested as repression). But, on the other, it can struggle against these degradations and seek—even if only in an endlessly deferred and utopian form—a world beyond class struggle (and the history it generates) and beyond repression and its analytic dissolution.

The connection of modernity, critical consciousness, and deconstruction is as difficult and obscure as possible. A preference of taste is manifest in, for example, Derrida's respectful tone—one could speak of an "endorsement," in all its senses—when he writes about Artaud or Blanchot. One might surmise that Derrida and even de Man respond to Rousseau much as Kant himself did, a surprising elective affinity described well by Ernst Cassirer. Yet no one could be more alert than Derrida and de Man to the self-effacing (in a double sense) claims of critical consciousness to pure self-constitution. The taste for "modern" writers justifies itself on the principled ground not of their achievement of critical consciousness, still less of their solving the antinomy between its possibility and impossibility, but of their awareness that that antinomy is inescapable. Are we to take this awareness as a triumph of critical consciousness because it is an awareness, or as a defeat, because it is awareness of an inescapability?

The antinomy certainly cannot be figured as an opposition between the self-deluding pretenses of philosophy and the life-enhancing complexities of literature: it is not a "romantic" protest. If literature enjoys an advantage here, it is that a writer is, before anything, a writer, wedded to the action of writing in a way that constantly threatens to obtrude itself on him. As de Man remarks, one can imagine a thinker who never writes, like Socrates, but not a writer who never writes. Calling a writer a philosopher or a poet merely distracts from the question, whether he or she has lost sight or not of being a writer. The labor or gift of keeping in view what it is to be a writer characterizes the particular form of critical consciousness we call simply "criticism." I do not mean the ancient activity of assessing the success of a written work according to a canon of rules or models or according to the effect one suspects it may have on readers or other writers. In its modern sense, criticism is an effort to see just how a writer keeps (or fails to keep) writing in view. A distinction between "writer" and "critic" would be equally distracting. Nor would it be easy to sustain the more inviting distinction between writing and reading.

In undertaking to investigate the relations between deconstruction, criticism, modernism, psychoanalysis, and history, Stephen Melville has not written a conventional, has written an unconventional "introduction" to deconstruction. It is not simply his intelligence which invites the qualification. But by isolating issues that arise at the origin of modern thought in and around Kant and then thinking these along through Hegel and the absorption of Hegel into French intellectual life in the 1930s, Melville makes of "deconstruction" what Stanley Cavell achieves with skepticism: it becomes not just an odd system of notions, but what it makes sense for an intelligent and thoughtful (in every sense) individual to say from a certain position within history or the history of thought. In this sense, the book is not simply propaedeutic, intended to lead up to the study of something; nor is it simply an exposition of a school and its leading figures. It is an introduction in a more important sense, as one might speak of the introduction of Derrida into American criticism and ask how this was accomplished, what made it possible, and what were its consequences. But I want to hold to the idea of an "introduction" in the full range of its implications, for our almost immediately negative reaction to that idea leads directly, I think, into the central issues Melville faces.

A book is like a city, and not every reader is native to its complexities. One wouldn't automatically praise those who refused to draw a map or give a clear direction to a visitor on the ground that the city itself was a unique experience one ought to master for oneself. Yet distrust of every mediation runs deep in modern intellectual life. Paraphrase has been called a heresy by a critic who does not take religious language lightly. An introduction offends by producing a miniature of the book itself, implying that a thin thesis seeks liberation from layers of discursive fat or that the introducer finally stated what the author was too tongue-tied to utter. In Schönberg's *Moses und Aron*, God startles the hermitic/hermetic Moses with the mission to proclaim Him. When Moses protests his tongue is "ungelenk," inflexible, God makes his brother Aaron his mouthpiece. There follow all the predictable ill consequences of representing the unrepresentable to an excitable populace. Modernism could almost be defined as a conviction that any book can never be explained.

Yet it is a plain fact of language that any utterance can be paraphrased. Understanding would be paralyzed if we could only ritualistically recite the *ipsissimi verbi* and never take them up into our own words. It is doubtful enough that we can think anything that cannot be put into words, and incredible that what has been put into words once cannot be put into other words. The ideology of anti-paraphrase expresses a perverse *Selbsthass* on the part of criticism: every comment obtrudes into the pure and immediate relation of the reader to the "poem itself." Publishing such comments is even worse, explicable only in economic terms as a necessity of academic employment, or even worse in psycho-moral terms as a lust for fame achieved by the subreptive, parasitic expropriation of another's "genuine" creative, original work. Even Derrida and Paul de Man have incautiously expressed moral indignation at paraphrasing, at explaining, at faithfully summarizing—at all the sins of introducing. In the preface to *On Christian Doctrine*, Augustine was already driven to defend training commentators and preachers of the Gospel against those who claimed that anything but insight straight from the Spirit was illegitimate and futile.

Augustine's answer is, we would say, political. Let those on speaking terms with the Holy Ghost rejoice, but let them not deny more ordinary mortals access to a saving word. There is a Parnassian and finally rather nasty tone to this scorn for aids to the audience. Not everyone's education assures him or her of immediate membership in the charmed circle of those who read with understanding; not everyone has consulted the oracle in Paris. Shall not these be fed? Even if we concede the harried reader may cut a corner and let the introduction supplant the introduced, by what right do we let a moral condemnation cover over the accelerating speed and volume which are precisely the temporal and technological characteristics of modern culture that ought to invite reflection? In this insistence on an originary, immediate contact between author and reader, between reader and book, are we not living out the hermeneutics and the politics of the Reformation?

An introduction puts a book in a nutshell—or takes the nut out of the shell. The contradictory reversibility of the metaphor tells the tale. The introduction is outside the book, yet its inmost essence, where its real core emerges. It is essentially preliminary, but a preliminary essential. This relation Derrida calls "supplementarity." At once outside and inside, the introduction violates and erases the threshold: when you read the introduction, have you already begun to read the book or not? Where does the book "really" begin? Between the title page and the text, the introduction is a part and not a part, in but not of. The introduction is a parasite, one who feeds at another's table, but earns his keep by making lively conversation, making conversation lively. It is an advance man, a warm-up act, a pro-phet. Yet its perversion of the bordering, defining threshold goes further. Everyone has had the experience of reading a brief comment on some book and finding it incomprehensible until one has read the book itself. De Man and Derrida supply this experience in abundance, and only when you have read closely the text of Freud or Plato or whoever is under examination do you comprehend the explanation. Readers may expect that they will read Melville to understand deconstruction and Derrida. They may find, to their chagrin, that they must read deconstruction and Derrida to understand Melville. By a curious reversal, Derrida becomes the introduction to Melville. This is to say that a genuine introduction, an essential introduction must already itself participate in what it introduces. Hegel's *Phenomenology of Mind* begins with an introduction that leads us up to the real philosophical thinking. But, as Melville says, it is only from the perspective of that completed thinking that one can grasp the necessity for this way in. An introduction to philosophy must itself be philosophical. These are the dialectics of all literary imitation, and equally of any commentary ambitious to enter the circle of predecessors commented on. Derrida is in the line straight from Hegel, for whom the historical "introduction" to philosophy was itself philosophy and in fact the philosophy which was the outcome of philosophical history. We never come to the history of philosophy or culture "from the beginning"—even if we could locate the beginning. As the theorist of narrative Gerald Prince once remarked, "We read because we have read." Always in the midst, the later is our constant introduction to the earlier. Thus Derrida is metaleptic, turning his later into an earlier. How many readers come to a text *after* reading Derrida on it, and hence coming to it through him?

The power of an introduction *before* we have read the work it introduces is just that it is fascinating but unintelligible: to use a term Melville takes from Michael Fried, the art historian, it is "absorptive" and hence unreadable. If the risk of staging a work is that theatrical representation, however brilliant, is artificial, not simply true, the risk of absorption is the loss of critical distance, especially when the assumption that what we see is the genuine article is unchecked by familiarity with the original thus represented. To be sure, if we must read what the introduction explains in order to understand the introduction, the lazy reader's project of saving labor is frustrated. But, meanwhile, the introduction owes its success to its being *fascinating*. There exist strange books comprising an author's introductions to other books, which are now sometimes of interest only because this author once introduced them—think of Poe's marginalia and reviews. Since understanding and therefore "truth" isn't in question, the fascination must be a fascination of style: how could anyone learn to talk this way? The glimpsed prospect, the promised land is the possibility that if I read Derrida or whatever the introducer has read, then I too may learn to talk like this. We get a sort of ventriloquism, a speaking not from the brain, but from the belly (style is the man; you are what you eat), a concern less with what is said than with how it sounds (or feels) to say it. An introduction thus seems to tap independent sources of interest: one may read it with no intention or no impulse remaining to read further. Yet in supplanting, it doubly "rips off" the authorial identity of what it introduces, stealing both what it says and how it says it. An introduction rouses some of the same disapproval as plagiarism and every effort to gain intellectual credit for someone else's work.

Just to the degree an introduction transcends its secondariness, it opens the full complexity of historical time. How many were led to read Hegel and other monuments of the philosophical tradition by an interest in, a wish to understand, Lacan or Derrida? Reading this way is doubly *nachträglich*, "after the fact": one understands Hegel in the light Derrida throws on him, but one also understands Derrida in the light Hegel throws on *him*. When Kant's critics accused him of taking all his ideas from Leibniz, Kant replied that the charge was true enough, but that it was only when he had written his books that it became possible to see that Leibniz had said *that*. To have seen what one's great predecessors made it possible to say is highly creditable. Of course, one may question the legitimacy of such a proceeding: it seems the weakness of Aristotle's summaries of the metaphysical opinions of his predecessors that he makes them all answer *his* questions, lead up to *his* solutions. We have been told that we must efface ourselves, leap imaginatively into the world of our ancestors, think their thoughts uncontaminated with anachronism. It seems cynical to say that history is written by the winners. But in fact this only means that what matters to history is what has had and continues to have consequences. Even if we temporarily bracket ourselves in order to guess what the "original audience" understood (a notion full of unexamined abstraction, as Hans-Georg Gadamer says), we do so only in the service of historical integration at a larger level, not as an end in itself.

The only sensible choice is to write history in relation to its results, its outcomes. Supplementarity applies in the history of ideas too. If one cannot really understand Derrida without reading Hegel, then Hegel is at once outside and inside Derrida, a supplement made necessary by Derrida himself. To "introduce" the past, one must actually return to it. Derrida is introduced (in)to Hegel and Hegel is introduced (in)to Derrida. It is not clear what "earlier" would mean in such a case, nor does Melville shrink before the speculative possibility of weighing "Derrida's influence on Hegel." We cannot understand the history of ideas without thinking, without ourselves having ideas, and we must therefore necessarily turn to those among us who have ideas and stimulate thinking. What "intellectual" history teaches us—and it is true of all history—is that historical time is anything but linear. T. S. Eliot's "Tradition and the Individual Talent" is no less powerful merely because it has ceased to be the common reference point for a generation of students of literature. What Kant or Hegel or Heidegger means must constantly be readjusted in the light of what thinkers like Lacan or Bataille struggle to make of them. This is just what tradition is—not a linear series of fixed opinions safely encrypted, but a mobile dance of vampire-like figures that, by feeding on the blood of the living, not only gain new life for themselves, but welcome their victims into perpetual fellowship.

The process may be made to sound less mysterious than this chiasmus of earlier and later seems: if we write the *history* of art, we must still write the history of *art*; and our idea of what art is is itself the outcome of history and the point at which history is forever open. There is no escape from this abyss, and there had better not be. To be out of it is to be outside both history and our idea of art which emerged from it. Where would that put us? Derrida himself has no illusions about ignoring or escaping history. He works like frost, levering open the granite blocks of monuments along their edges and fissures. If Derrida owes his life to the great writers whose parasite and parodist he has become, they owe their living on to his unflagging interest in them.

The further paradox of filling in the background Derrida claims for himself is that in Melville's introduction, Derrida never quite arrives, and we never quite arrive at him. Our interest cannot but grow as we pass from Kant to Hegel to Heidegger to Lacan and Bataille—with so great a weight of tradition, surely some revelation is at hand. And yet just when we get to Derrida, we suddenly swerve into Paul de Man and Barbara Johnson and Shoshanna Felman. This curiously elided figure, known only in what he compels into the position of predecessors, adversaries, and *sequelae*, never appears at the outer edge, the border or shore where past attains a peak and stares with wild surmise over its future. Nor does he figure as the father of waters, the discovered source, or a root diversely engra(ph)ted. Derrida thus (dis)figured exemplifies his own critique of Heidegger. Against any idea of *Ereignis*, of history conceived as the event in which we make the past our own, Derrida disclaims "personality," all attempts to make ourselves responsible for the endless improprieties of the past. This is not to say that Derrida is *ir*-responsible, only that history is never anything we could own, and hence never lives in history books, but is only something done and still doing. Those who think history never repeats itself are as wrong as those who think it never does anything else. Those who think that through history they can know the future are as wrong as those who think that through history they can know the past in order to have done with it. We are not outside history as the masters or mere victims of its movement, nor as spectators in a darkened theater before its futile panorama. *Ni Marx, ni Ranke.*

To write an introduction is to recognize that time is out of joint. For Melville, the exploration of how we are in and out of history is central to what is "modern" in modern culture, and deconstruction's centrality lies in its prolongation of precisely this exploration. That Melville unostentatiously uses the resources of deconstruction to put before us its past makes his a thoroughly modern introduction. History is the reality that everything we do—and writing is action of a kind purer perhaps than any other—is other (more and less) than us, than our intentions. Modernism is just the self-consciousness we feel in the presence of this basic fact. For unlike our heroic ancestors, we have no confidence in history. It is not a stage on which we seek applause or submit to hisses, not a court where we can be saved or damned. Even the fame which tempted the noble mind (or tempted the ignoble mind to rise above itself) seems to us pure illusion or at least worthless.

Philosophy attempts to escape history by acts of pure self-reflection. What differentiates these attempts from earlier transcendentalisms is the maintained relation to what it flees from. Critique gets to the border of historical experience and tries to live on that border line, never stepping over it. This ambition has finally talked itself out of itself. In Husserl's return to the category of the life-world, in Wittgenstein's return to "forms of life," the most rigorous forms of reflection undo themselves, often explicitly as therapy against the pride of reason. Literature's resources for waking from the nightmare of history are perhaps even more devious. Originality, novelty, the absolutely outrageous are efforts to break the chains of history, but they show that history had first to be conceived as chains. Myth, symbol, and the varied appropriations from religion are not only attempts to capture religion's cultural role, but a project to discover for literature resources proper to it yet able to rival the success of its chief antagonist, science, in escaping history. Even allusion, borrowing, and parody are devices to evade historicality by establishing a decontextualized immediacy. But the most paradoxical move by which both philosophy and literature try to escape their own history and therefore themselves is by turning each to the other. Deconstruction is the exemplary no-man's-land where this purely modern warfare, truce, and incessant exchange of prisoners between philosophy and literature is carried on.

One might suppose that modernism's resistance to history would make it congenial to America. A country could scarcely be more thoroughly contemporary than the United States. But the American is wrong to think modernism means a break with the past. The European knows that modernism rather seeks *Lebensraum* in a world where the dead crowd out the living, where monuments of the past are so thick on and under the ground that digging a new foundation is ineluctably archaeological. A culture cannot break from a past it never had. The immigrants did not simply forget their heritage; they never had any. They were, in Eric Hoffer's richly ironic phrase, "the scum of the earth," the huddled masses excluded from the history of their "homelands." Politically conscious educators had no difficulty filling this blank slate with the mythic shapes of the Founding Fathers. The children of immigrants, drawing pictures of turkeys and playacting Pilgrims and Indians, forgot even the deliberateness of their parents' assimilation to the New World. As a consequence, when American academics want to teach their students modernism, they must first infect them with the cultural disease of which it is either the cure or else the most virulent strain. Lionel Trilling despaired to find his students dutifully studying and blandly accepting the most harrowed, anguished expressions of modernist consciousness. For the American, modernism is not the sign of alienation and cultural despair in the face of historical catastrophes. On the contrary, through modernism America triumphantly accedes to its rightful status as a world culture in the "American century." It is the end of provincialism, the end of childhood. Americans domesticate modernism by regarding it as something with a quite smart European accent, mental furniture harmonious with cheap trips abroad and fond recollections of croissants for breakfast. Nausea in Kalamazoo is a cousin far removed from Bouville. American kitsch voraciously absorbs modernist cliches, which become a standard background, a universalism unconstrained by local history.

I am speaking, of course, about the political implications of deconstruction. I intend something other than partisan politics: neither deconstruction nor modernism more generally has as origin or destination a political program or party affiliation. Ingenious attempts have been made to connect deconstruction with current politics: decolonization has shifted the relations between center and periphery or margin, and deconstruction shows us how to analyze these relations; as the most rigorous form of modernism, deconstruction shows the nature of all forms of modernization; because everything is a text, the textual operations of deconstructive reading are immediately political and applicable to all institutions; by exposing at the most general level the ruses of authority and the deceptive and self-deceptive linguistic maneuvers of ideology, deconstruction unmasks the claims of neutrality and objectivity by which interested power structures underwrite their legitimation. Such arguments on inspection seem like merely verbal maneuvers, all puns and metaphors. Equally ingenious reasoners demonstrate that on its own showing, deconstruction makes no difference: at best it merely invites us to examine metaphysical presuppositions and at worst it leaves us in a state of demystified resignation to structures and operations that it asserts are as delusory as they are unavoidable. But this analysis seems abstract: the political significance of an idea rarely coincides with what its advocates think or claim for it, nor with what merely follows logically from a systematic formulation of it, especially one gleaned by an adversary from diverse writings for the purpose of criticizing it. The controversy seems to be whether deconstruction—taken as exemplary of modernist thought—issues in effective action or only in some state of mind. The questionableness of that contrast ought to alert us that something is fishy in the whole debate. Both sides seem too sure they already know what politics is. They miss the point insofar as the challenge of deconstruction is not to decide which political camp it belongs to, but in what terms we are to think of politics at all.

In meeting this challenge, Derrida and de Man have not given us much help. At the end of a profoundly intelligent essay on "Literary History and Literary Modernity," de Man writes: "To become good literary historians, we must remember that what we usually call literary history has little or nothing to do with literature and that what we call literary interpretation—provided only it is good interpretation—is in fact literary history." So far, so good, but one can only feel a certain embarrassment when he adds the concluding sentence, "If we extend this notion beyond literature, it merely confirms that the bases for historical knowledge are not empirical facts but written texts, even if these texts masquerade in the guise of wars or revolutions." This is boilerplate rhetoric from a modernist manifesto, an anarchism at once cryptic and timid, uttered in the manner of jesting Pilate. One feels how little de Man really cares about historical knowledge, empirical fact, wars, or revolutions, and how little serious thought he has given any of them. Nor has Derrida done much better, whether darkening counsel with equivocations on "property," "representation," and "copyright," or muddying the waters of feminism. I think this rhetoric in bad taste, leaves a bad taste, but my point is not to reproach de Man and Derrida for not doing what they never intended to do. It is simply that if we wish to ask about "modernism and politics" or even "deconstruction and politics," we are on our own and can't expect simply to read off what to think from their pronouncements.

I have no intention of pursuing this question in general terms—I don't think it makes much sense in such terms. I want to stick instead to some more local surmises about modernism and deconstruction in America. This topic is political in Gerald Bruns's sense, that deconstruction and modernism must, like everything else, make their way in the world. Gerald Graff argues for a hidden convergence between modernism and consumer capitalism. Of course modernist culture in this country thinks of itself as anti-establishment. But this delusion covers a divided self: adversary in style and rhetoric, in substance a reliable ally of everyday order, because what it dreams is already the unacknowledged reality. A country where a television series can star a talking horse can only pretend to be shocked by Surrealism. This seems persuasive, largely perhaps because it pursues a Marxist demystification of an ideology's "objective" social correlates and class interests. But, on reflection, it may seem no less merely metaphorical than some deconstructors' notion that "subverting" a text is the same thing as "subverting" an economic system. We might expect more insight from examining the lives and thoughts of actual individuals. Julia Kristeva's change of heart about America is suggestive: from Paris, it had seemed the archetypal imperialist, rigid conservator of a materialistic domination of the world, that is, the projected embodiment of everything "bourgeois" in her own culture. After her residence in New York, it showed itself as just that disseminated society of which modernism dreams. But, again, conclusions could only follow systematic collection and analysis of facts, and I know of no such venture yet undertaken. We may be on firmer ground to consider the more relevant convergence noticed long ago by Charles Feidelson in *Symbolism and American Literature*. The peculiar parallelism he finds between the premises of, say, Melville's *Pierre* and Gide's *The Counterfeiters* explains, among other things, the sympathetic reception of American literature by some European modernists. This suggests a complex genealogy: a culture which diverges from its parent, like separated twins, after pursuing an indigenous evolution, bears an uncanny family resemblance at a reunion some generations later. The ambiguous relation of deconstruction to New Criticism may be even more pertinent. Literary modernism made its way into the world of academic literary study as New Criticism, not without struggle. I am certainly not alone in finding that New Criticism paved a broad, smooth highway to deconstruction—which certainly does not mean they are the same thing. Virtually the dying words of Paul de Man were a bitter defense of New Criticism against its cultured despisers. The difference between New Criticism and deconstruction lies much more in the conflicting rhetoric of their mutual self-representations and accusations than in any substantive reality when they close in on a text. American academics nurtured on New Criticism oscillate between finding deconstruction an echo, even a parody, of familiar notions and finding it an ungrateful offspring of modernism whose tooth is turned against the parents who taught it to speak. This is a familiar scene in the drama of politics: the young zealots struggle with the old guard for control of the revolution. The tragic conflict is not between enemies, but between allies who cannot recognize each other or the older and younger son of the same father. The sharpest pain is not defeat, but the fear that the convictions one has served with dedication have been usurped and turned into accusations by those one trusted to be their heirs: see Stanley Cavell on *King Lear*.

Because of this problematic immediacy—uncanny homeliness in an impressively alien dress—Americans have a responsiveness to a thinker like Derrida that has made him rich. The potential for misunderstanding is all the greater, and Derrida has himself been surprised, sometimes even offended, at how he reads in America, at Americans' tendency to think he simply means what he says. Some Americans seem quite unaware of and others have no appetite for the laborious route by which Derrida actually got to his position—the slow work through Kant and Hegel and Heidegger, the tortured labyrinth of European leftism and psychoanalysis, the respectful weighing of grotesques like Bataille and Artaud. As a result, Derrida is perhaps more alarmed by the Americans with whom he succeeds than by the Europeans unpersuaded of any of his ideas. With them he feels at home, for they see that he occupies a known, even a respectable position, one they can acknowledge in their thinking, neither raging against it, nor epigonized by it.

Under these circumstances, the need for a formal introduction is unavoidable. One can have no faith in those who dismiss the social barrier that keeps strangers in silence side by side in an elevator, as though the realities that barrier acknowledges could be swept aside by an ideology of spontaneous bonhomie. There is a false camaraderie in those who think one can just "strike up" a conversation, without acknowledging the implied commitment to and risk of mutual consequences and without needing a mediating third party, who stands between us precisely to bring us together and then stand back. One must not presume too much on a common background and a common outlook. Despite a rare success, such casual encounters always border on a moment of madness, a language not embroidered on a durable web of social connections.

We need an introduction to Derrida because he is undeniably foreign. He doesn't "speak our language," though he is steadily mastering it. An introduction permits or gives permission to two people to converse. According to Aristotle's conception that our mutual conversation is what makes us political animals, such an introduction is a profoundly political act. One of Melville's aims is to make Derrida conversible, that is, to situate him within the world of talk we occupy. If we are to hear what Derrida says, he must learn to talk our language. But the irreducible reciprocity of all introductions reminds us that the strain and profit of meeting someone is that we must learn to talk our language too. We are never masters of our language once and for all, but relearn it, as it were, whenever we speak. We want to keep up our end of the conversation. That is why the introduction of Stanley Cavell into this book is so apt, for he is the most accomplished of our philosophical conversationalists. Cavell's tact at hearing what we mean when we speak teaches us that in conversation we do not wish simply that our partner be an echo of ourselves, nor do we even seek a mere exchange of experiences and opinions. In conversation, we acknowledge a claim: the point of talking with Derrida is gained by having Derrida be and sound like Derrida. Otherwise, why talk with him at all? The great art of introduction is not the bare bringing together, but finding the few well-chosen words whose offering starts a conversation that can continue of itself. Such a never-stabilized circulation of positions is for most of its American enthusiasts the excitement of deconstruction.

In venturing the model of conversation, I want to take up a final topic, the notorious "difficulty" of modernist art, and at the same time return, without resolving it, to the antinomy or self-reversals between history and modernity with which I began. Let me first put the best possible face on the matter. A genuine conversation does not just echo received opinion, but ruptures historical ties to let us gain a present glimpse of what we speak of. Yet it also calls into being a lasting relation between its partners, whether of alliance or opposition. The clearer insight they may gain of what matters most must be put into the words they can mutually bring, and all words, Plato points out, block the very view they open. This is the ineluctable condition not just of language, but of our finitude: autonomy and heterogeneity, acknowledgment and critique, tradition and modernity stand together. The absoluteness of a conversation's present aims to originate a fresh point of departure in the wider world. It thus makes us aware, as Melville says, of "the ways we do and do not belong in time and in community." For Plato, insight into the good, achieved in utopian moments of conversational inquiry when ordinary time and commitments were in suspension, served not abstracted contemplation, but the nurturance of a capacity to return to the world of contingency with mastery, instead of blind submission. Deconstruction sets into play the same shuttling movement of mind.

The unsettling question is whether in fact any such return is possible. If there is no appeal to ordinary language or ordinary experience *against* modernism (because modernist thought *as critical* is aware of premises blindness to which is what makes ordinary experience ordinary), can there be any return from the critical self-consciousness of modernism to anything we could recognize as "ordinary" experience? Is the discourse of modernism possible never face-to-face with ordinary language, but only, so to speak, behind its back? Theodore Adorno insists that true art is irreducibly oppositional. Heidegger could find only in *Angst* the phenomenological moment when the question of existence could obtrude itself on the everyday and seem to offer an answer the everyday itself could acknowledge. Walter Benjamin sought in urbanization and industrialization the new social experiences under whose pressure traditional forms took on the distinctiveness of modern art, sometimes with, usually against the artist's knowledge and intentions. We now find fantastic Schönberg's vision of a time when children would whistle his music. Literary interpreters make an industry of showing that "pre-modern" writings always exhibit a modernist aspect under intense scrutiny, but the demonstration is often so difficult to keep in mind that it seems rather the interpreter's obsession than anybody's experience. Some artists now dare to suggest that modernism was somehow a huge mistake and that "high" art needs to recover contact with the "popular" mind or achieve its alienations at most by invoking the contrasting ordinariness of past or ethnically divergent traditions. If philosophy anticipated modernism with Kant, then it seems already to have attempted a return to "ordinary" language. That return is prolonged in the revival of moral philosophy. Even the much-debated resurgence of political conservatism may reflect a widening sense that we cannot make ourselves or the social order objects of a fully explicit, critical consciousness. It may even be too hopeful to say that the "lesson" of modernism has somehow been absorbed: it was essential to modernism that it not be able to be "absorbed," and the versions of it which have been vulgarized have somehow missed its essence. Yet no one wants to leave modernism just hanging there: a vast museum of works no one can live with. The risk is that we will seem to ourselves to have been not up to the rigorous demands of modernism, once more slackly preferring the *salon* to the *refuses*.

There can probably be no answer to this dilemma. Whether in domestication modernism and deconstruction have their heart torn out or whether permanent revolution is simply the last tyrannical delusion of the bourgeois aesthete may in fact be an opposition falsely posed. One could only welcome a reformulation that did not seem merely evasive. The terror of modern physics is not that the theoretical formalisms don't work or don't allow the physicist to work, but that what the physicist accomplishes may be uninterpretable, may lie beyond any human power of understanding. In *The Savage Mind*, Claude Lévi-Strauss argues that "non-representational painting adopts 'styles' as 'subjects'. It claims to give a concrete representation of the formal conditions of all painting. Paradoxically the result is that non-representational painting does not, as it thinks, create works which are as real as, if not more real than, the objects of the physical world, but rather realistic imitations of nonexistent models. It is a school of academic painting in which each artist strives to represent the manner in which he would execute his pictures if by chance he were to paint any." And yet, as Geoffrey Hartman has remarked of Derrida's *Glas*, there can be no going back from this self-consciousness. If in Stanley Cavell's term we genuinely acknowledge modernism, we may have to say that it puts us in the impossible position of being unable to go on or go back or just stay put. It is not easy to say why anyone should tolerate being put in such a position, but the defensive hostility modernism still arouses strikes me as evidence that it has its grip on a real fact. What that fact is perhaps can't be said otherwise, but modernism shows it can be said this way. What more has anyone a right to ask?

Preface

The writings of the French philosopher Jacques Derrida have been unquestionably the single most powerful influence on critical theory and practice in this country over the past decade and more. But this influence has been curiously mediated. Until just a few years ago, very little of Derrida's work was available in translation. American philosophers have, with few exceptions, taken little or no interest in Derrida's work, and the whole business of reception, translation, and commentary has been left to the literary critical community.

The Yale literary critic Paul de Man has played an essential role in this reception. His seminal 1971 book, *Blindness and Insight: Essays in the Rhetoric of Contemporary Criticism*, provided one of the first and still most lucid accounts of Derrida's project and, in effect, established the foundations of the enterprise of deconstructive criticism in terms of which Derrida's work continues very largely to be received. It is then of special interest to remark that this moment of reception has the form of a critique and that the appropriation of Derrida to literary criticism goes hand in hand with a certain rejection or correction of him. A more nuanced account of this extremely complex moment is one of the central objects of this book.

Derrida has appeared to us, for the most part, as a figure already caught up in and defined by essentially literary critical kinds of activities and interests. It is a striking feature of our reception of him that it has involved very little writing of the kind that normally accompanies such work—books and essays with titles like "Derrida and Hegel," or "Derrida and Kant," or "Jacques Derrida and the Heritage of Surrealism," or "Derrida's Quarrel with Psychoanalysis," and so on. The case of "Derrida's Quarrel with Psychoanalysis" is instructive. There has been a fine, compelling, and influential essay written on the topic—Barbara Johnson's "The Frame of Reference: Poe, Lacan, Derrida"—but the title alone betrays its interests and points toward the difficulties that finally undo it: the essay is conceived as an exercise in deconstructive literary criticism and somehow (exactly how will be one of the subjects of chapter 5) manages to lose track along the way of the quarrel with which it means to be explicitly concerned. Johnson's conclusion discusses the reasons she finds herself unable to decide who is saying what and whether or not there is in fact any disagreement between the participants in the apparent argument; but something has to be wrong here—both on the face of it and for deep philosophic reasons. The very terms through which Johnson addresses Derrida's text block any access to its properly philosophic motives.

With this invocation of the "properly philosophic," a certain "deconstructive" objection to the drift of these remarks may find its focus. Deconstruction, the objection runs, is a subversion of philosophic property and propriety (this is why it has become so quickly entangled with literature and its criticism). The attempt to contextualize it, to drag its texts back into the confines of a received tradition and problematic, is to domesticate it, to neutralize it, to undermine or deny its deepest motives. It is to be less than rigorous with a writing that depends everywhere on its rigor. My response must be that there is a point at which rigor betrays itself and becomes evasive rather than enabling. I will be arguing that we cannot grasp Derrida's improprieties unless we first grasp his property, and I will be arguing this because I will be arguing as well that until and unless we grasp his philosophic ambition, we remain fundamentally unable to see his significance for criticism.

I have put the argument of this book rather harshly. But I am myself very much a product of Derridean subversions—neither fully critic nor fully philosopher, at once uneasily and joyously adrift between departments and disciplines—and would have it no other way. Derrida's work *is* subversive, profoundly so—so profoundly that nothing is obvious either in advance or after the fact about what does and does not neutralize it, where it has and has not been domesticated, or what approaches to it are or are not rigorous. What I insist—what I think I have learned from Stanley Cavell—is that there is no way around the question of criteria, and it is upon that question that my argument turns. The embeddedness of the question of criteria within what would otherwise appear a considerably more straightforward argument is characteristic of enterprises we call modernist, and the argument I am making about Derrida, about his philosophic property and impropriety, is that he is a profoundly modernist philosopher. The first task of this book will be to fill in the sense and interest of this formulation.

Earlier versions of this book devoted themselves very largely to making good on—"supplying" I suppose I should say—the deficits in Derrida's reception—offering things that could count as "Derrida and Hegel," "Jacques Derrida and the Heritage of Surrealism," and "Derrida's Quarrel with Psychoanalysis." This ambition made for an extremely unwieldy manuscript, traces of which still litter the present work. I am delighted that the past few years have brought about a situation in which I no longer feel the need for such gross quasi-historical excursions. Vincent Descombes's *Modern French Philosophy* has taken magnificent care of the first of my headings and done nicely by the second as well.[1] Crucial aspects of the second are also addressed by Michele Richman in her book-length study of Georges Bataille.[2] Although there is still considerable room for straightforward exegetical work on Lacan, his writings are increasingly available and increasingly common property. Anthony Wilden's early eassay on Lacan continues to provide a useful introduction, as does Sherry Turkle's *Psychoanalytic Politics*.[3] There remains a great deal to be done: Derrida's relation to Kant is of increasing centrality and has been very little discussed in any context; his relation to Maurice Blanchot is crucial, and translations of Blanchot's criticism as well as his *récits* are badly needed.[4] The list, of work needed and of work done, can be extended quite a distance and has grown with every draft of this book.

In the meantime the present work has been freed to a somewhat more streamlined and systematic exposition, beginning with an attempt to fill out the notion of philosophic modernism, passing through an exploration of Derrida's work—very much along the lines of his quarrel with psychoanalysis—and closing with a consideration of the appropriation of that work to literary criticism. Jacques Derrida's achievement has been to find a new and necessary way to assert, in detail, that the task of philosophy is criticism; our work will be done when we have found a way to acknowledge this achievement, a way to bring a certain recognition of criticism back home, to the extent that criticism allows itself such domesticity.

* * *

Despite its baggy shape, this book has a rather narrow focus: first on the relation of Derrida's philosophic work to an overridingly Hegelian context and then on de Man's criticism considered as an appropriation of this work. I hope, naturally, that my choices here will be their own argument, but I cannot help noting two other ways in which I might have proceeded.

—By presenting Derrida in such a thoroughly Hegelian context, I have been led into a systematic neglect or disparagement of Kant that is based upon what is, finally, neither a particularly deep nor a particularly generous reading of him.

The story can be told differently: sooner or later it will have to be, because Kant remains a central node and test for modern philosophy—as he remains also a central point of appeal for our understanding of our various romanticisms.

—My relatively restricted concern with the texts of Derrida and de Man left me little room to recognize the work of other writers arguing along similar or parallel lines. The number of people taking what amounts to a second look at Derrida and at de Man grows almost daily (and in many instances these are in fact first looks only now gaining a public forum). More or less arbitrarily I would want to point to writings by the late Eugenio Donato, Rodolphe Gasché, Frank Lentricchia, Joseph Riddel, Samuel Weber, Christopher Fynsk, Stanley Fish, Christopher Norris, William Ray . . . as the manuscript was going through its last revisions Suzanne Gearhart published a stunning piece in *Diacritics* and Henry Staten's important *Wittgenstein and Derrida* appeared while the manuscript was being edited. As will be readily apparent, this list represents no emergent school or position—but it does signal a renewed willingness to grapple with the novelty and difficulty of things and texts Derridean, a new willingness to receive or re-receive that work.

* * *

The book has incurred considerable debts along its way and only the most pressing can be discharged here. The foremost is certainly to Françoise Meltzer at the University of Chicago. Ted Cohen and Paul Ricoeur of the Philosophy Department there also contributed greatly to the final shape of the manuscript. More diffuse debts are owed to Kenneth Northcott and Richard Strier.

Much of the material has been worked through at some length with one or another member of an institution known intermittently and informally as La Groupe de Recherche de Gnu (the Gnu critics). The lives and fates of its members have been as various as such intellectual lives and fates now are, and so it seems particularly urgent to acknowledge the help and criticism of Richard Eldridge, Lorna Gladstone, Paul Gudel, and Andrew Parker.

Other readers of the manuscript in one or another of its stages have offered useful criticism; I would want to single out especially Robert Knapp at Reed College and Donald Marshall of the University of Iowa. I would like also to thank the Mrs. Giles Whiting Foundation for its timely financial support.

* * *

There is a last debt, undischargeable. It is of course to the late Paul de Man. There are pages in what follows that may make mine seem a hard acknowledgment of his influence—but it is such an acknowledgment nonetheless and I would not wish it to be thought anything else. The shape of our literary critical and theoretical concerns is very largely the shape he has given them—and will continue to give for some time to come. His achievement has been immense.

S. M.
Syracuse

Philosophy Beside Itself

Chapter 1
On Modernism

Speaking at Johns Hopkins University in 1967, Jacques Derrida introduced his work to the English-speaking world in the following way:

> Perhaps something has occurred in the history of the concept of structure that could be called an "event" if this loaded word did not entail a meaning which it is precisely the function of structural—or structuralist—thought to reduce or suspect. But let me use the term "event" anyway, employing it with caution and as if in quotation marks. In this sense, this event will have the exterior form of a rupture and a redoubling.[1]

The simultaneous reliance on and evasion of notions of "history" and "event" evident in this passage is deeply characteristic of Derrida's writing. This writing emerges always within a history it would subvert and takes its sense from that history even as it would undo that history's claims to mastery over sense: to the extent that his writings can be seen as moments within that history, they have fallen short of their goal—and yet if they cannot be seen as such, they fail equally and inversely. Derrida is thus double-bound, his words necessarily at war with themselves, struggling to exempt themselves from the very grammar in which they are caught up and by which they mean. Inevitably they are qualified, hedged with quotation marks, "written under erasure," submitted to what a late essay on psychoanalysis refers to as "ploys of designification."

Such devices and evasions are not without a philosophic pedigree of their own. Their nearest precedent is in Heidegger's various neologistic plays with

"Sein"—Seyn, Seyn—and there is a clear sense in which Derrida's various "graphemes" are revisions or translations of Heidegger's, just as the term "deconstruction" with which he names his project is a revision or translation of Heidegger's terms *Destruktion* and *Wiederholung* (usually rendered "destruction" and "retrieve"). Somewhat further in the background is Nietzsche with his aphorisms and fragments—his refusal to mean philosophically. The dominating figure still further in the background is Hegel, whose work is, in this respect, a sustained argument for the absolute propriety of "history" and "event" and who thus seems exempt from the problems that increasingly complicate the texts of those writing in his wake. Yet Hegel's sustained excursus on the prosody of the speculative proposition in the "Preface" to the *Phenomenology of Spirit* seems a first version of the difficulty posed by writing for Nietzsche and Heidegger and Derrida—just as that text's assertion of truth as a "Bacchanalian whirl in which no member is sober" seems the first echo of what Nietzsche would later claim as news.

Setting Derrida's remarks about the "event" at stake in his writing into this context gives those remarks a properly problematic edge. Is this contextualization a neutralization of the subversive force of Derrida's writing, and thus a reduction of that practice to what Derrida dismisses as "un épisode moderne de la reproduction philosophique"? Or is it a gesture toward one of Derrida's deepest points, that, as he puts it in an essay in which he takes a careful distance from Heidegger, "the text of metaphysics is *comprehended*. Still legible; and to be read. It is not surrounded but rather traversed by its limit, marked in its interior by the multiple furrow of its margin."[2] What does it mean that one can come to have this kind of question – that the difference between the domestication and the preservation of deconstruction can seem so infinitely narrow?

Derrida's "épisode moderne de la reproduction philosophique"–referred to elsewhere in the same essay as "la reproduction auto-critique" and "l'autocritique interne de la philosophie"—may well recall the powerful vision of modernism advanced in this country in the fifties and sixties in relation to the visual arts and especially associated with the writings of Clement Greenberg.

> I identify Modernism with the intensification, almost the exacerbation of this self-critical tendency that began with the philosopher Kant. Because he was the first to criticize the means itself of criticism, I conceive of Kant as the first real Modernist. . . . The Enlightenment criticized from the outside, the way criticism in its more accepted sense does; Modernism criticizes from the inside, through the procedures themselves of that which is being criticized.[3]

This is the Modernism Derrida fears being co-opted by. It is also, as will become apparent, a version of modernism which, depending as it does on a strong distinction between inside and outside, Derrida's tools are particularly well designed to dismantle. However, rather than submit Greenberg's definition to any easy simulacrum of deconstruction, I prefer to explore its ambiguities a bit as a prelude to Derrida.

As Greenberg develops his essay, "Kantian self-criticism" is glossed as a demand for the "rational justification" of "every formal social activity." This is a demand before which it is possible to fail: "We know what has happened to an activity like religion that has not been able to avail itself of 'Kantian' immanent criticism in order to justify itself," Greenberg writes; and what we know, presumably, is that religion has been unable to justify itself as the bearer of a particular and autonomous truth, and so has withered away. Having no self to criticize, it vanished under the force of the Enlightenment.[4]

On this view, "self-criticism" names an effort to find the irreducible rational kernel of one's activity. In Greenberg's words:

> The task of self-criticism became to eliminate from the effects of each art any and every effect that might conceivably be borrowed from or by the medium of any other art. Thereby each art would be rendered "pure" and in its "purity" find the guarantee of its standards of quality as well as independence. ("Modernist Painting," p. 68)

The scare quotes around the forms of "purity" might warn us against thinking that we know what is at stake in them; they might well be taken to mark a place at which Greenberg is less than happy with the way he finds himself putting things. If we do take the notion of purity to be transparent here, we are likely to have little trouble seeing where this view will lead. Each art will have to be said to possess its own irreducible essence, and the modern history of each art will be that of its progressive paring away of the inessential as it moves toward an increasing awareness and display of the essential kernel:

> It was the stressing, however, of the ineluctable flatness of the support that remained most fundamental in the process by which pictorial art criticized and defined itself under Modernism. Flatness alone was unique and exclusive to that art. The enclosing shape of the support was a limiting condition, or norm, that was shared with the art of the theater; color was a norm or means shared with sculpture as well as with the theater. Flatness, two-dimensionality, was the only condition painting shared with no other art, and so modernist painting oriented itself to flatness as it did to nothing else. ("Modernist Painting," p. 69)

The development of modern art is, on this view, convergent with that of modern science, so that "Modernist art belongs to the same historical and cultural tendency as modern science." But with this Greenberg's view comes into apparent conflict with itself—or, more exactly, appears to discount wholly its own distinction between the spirit of Enlightenment and the spirit of Kantian self-criticism. Greenberg seems to be setting aside the very distinction on which he would found his position.

Self-criticism is the term on which Greenberg insists, but it is also the term that seems, in the end, to get somehow lost. And it seems to get lost in, so to speak, the scare quotes around "purity." When we discount them and take "purity" at something like face value, we find it naming the rational kernel of art, a kernel that may be revealed in time (because not everything can happen at once, or because we are confused in our perceptions or misled, or stupid) but that is not in any essential respect historically determined.

If, on the other hand, Greenberg does mean, deeply, his distinction between two modalities of criticism and is therefore properly nervous about his use of the word "purity," the distinction will have to be worked out in a way that is essentially historical. This version of things will not be organized around some central and essential truth, but by a continuing and continuously difficult attempt to find, in Greenberg's phrase, "the way to stronger, more expressive art." (This version of Kant makes him Nietzsche's precursor.)

We can start developing this picture by looking at the brief historical assertions from which Greenberg's essay takes off:

> We know what has happened to an activity like religion that has not been able to avail itself of "Kantian" immanent criticism in order to justify itself. At first glance the arts might seem to have been in a situation like religion's. Having been denied by the Enlightenment all the tasks they could take seriously, they looked as though they were going to be assimilated to entertainment pure and simple, and entertainment itself looked as though it were going to be assimilated like religion, to therapy. The arts could save themselves from this leveling down only by demonstrating that the kind of experience they provided was valuable in its own right and not to be obtained from any other kind of activity. ("Modernist Painting," pp. 67-68)

The account of the emergence of modernism begins here not from a concern for the purity or rationality of the particular arts, but from a concern with the value of art at all (and this concern appears as a reaction to and against Enlightenment criticism). It is as if art suddenly found itself in a situation in which it became aware that it was capable of losing itself altogether—becoming "mere" entertainment, devoid of larger relevance or authority—and so moved to reoccupy its own proper and wholly aesthetic ground as more or other than mere decoration. Thus Greenberg writes: "The essence of modernism lies, as I see it, in the use of the characteristic methods of a discipline to criticize the discipline itself—not in order to subvert, but to entrench it more firmly in its area of competence."

There are, of course, two stances one may take toward this kind of perceived threat of loss and assimilation. If we take it that this perceived threat is in fact nonexistent, the version of Greenberg we have already sketched will follow. The movement toward aesthetic autonomy is nothing more than a reactive reentrenchment, a shedding of the inessential and a reappropriation of the central kernel of art. In this view there is no room for anything that would deserve to be called modernism (except as a style like another style within the sequence of styles that would be the history of art). The idea that art must retreat into some more restricted region of purely aesthetic activity, surrendering moral authority as the cost of renewed security, is simply confused: there was never any need for such reentrenchment since the danger was never real. The history of modern art reduces to an unhappy episode, the confused attempt of art to maintain itself in a logical and aesthetic space that would be magically closed to all extraaesthetic contingency and so would be incapable as well of generating any history beyond the simple fact of progression. We are free on this view to imagine a "postmodernism" in which art would reassume its full moral and spiritual authority as it wakes from its bad dream and realizes it need never have shed that authority in the first place. The entire story is one of error, of overestimation of the force of the rational criticism of the Enlightenment. The notion of self-criticism proves radical only in its emptiness and absolute irrelevance. "Purity" names precisely nothing.

Clearly, however prone Greenberg may be to misread himself, he is not trying to say this, and if we are to understand his position fairly and fully we are going to have to explore the other option. We are going to have to see what happens if we take it that the perceived threat is (in some sense: we shall see that it is difficult to pin this sense down) correctly perceived. Such an account can begin only from the assumption that art is in fact something capable of being "assimilated to entertainment pure and simple." The threat can be real only if art is understood from the outset to be the sort of thing that can go astray in this way.

We want, then, to say that it is an essential possibility of art that it can mistake itself in a certain way. In so doing, we rule out any radically aestheticist position from the very beginning, and this means that we are going to be able to use notions like purity only if they are somehow bracketed; we have in effect already built an impurity into our notion of art in a way that cannot be overcome. At the same time, because we have begun from an effort to take a certain kind of threat seriously, we are forced to speak of something like "purity" as a central project for or aspiration of art. And with this double handling of "purity," we have installed a contradiction at the heart of modernism and so given it a dialectical motor capable of generating a real history operating in something other than logico-aesthetic space—a space organized by a desire to continue the enterprise of art and not a desire to offer "theoretical demonstrations."

It should be noted that part of the power of this second reading of Greenberg lies in its ability to map out within itself the very terms in which it (Greenberg) is tempted to misread itself (himself). Greenberg can be said to oscillate between a tendency to participate in or accede to the purifying impulse within modernism, and another, more critical and complex tendency. Both positions can be seen at work in his essay—but the first appears to preclude the second, while the second, critical, position can place the participatory moment as a necessary temptation. (This is of course to be expected, since we constructed this second reading precisely in order to recover a central function for Greenberg's "self-criticism.")

Greenberg's ablest student in this regard is undoubtedly the critic and art historian Michael Fried. His series of brilliant and persuasive articles on the emergence of modernist painting is an exemplary fleshing out of this second Greenbergian position.

Fried argues, in a series of articles on Diderot now gathered together in his book *Absorption and Theatricality*, that the abstract threat of the reduction of art to entertainment is realized for French painting in the rococo.[5] It is in the paintings of, for example, François Boucher that art sees how it is that it might lose itself: it catches a glimpse of a possible future, and that future is purely— merely—decorative. One does not want to speak here of any cataclysmic Death of Art. It is not the case that one fears that the activity of painting will somehow cease; instead, that activity will cease to be one that matters. Painting will simply become the creation of vaguely pretty objects, panels of pleasant wallpaper, things to be glanced at and passed by. Painting would simply cease to be an art (would cease to be able to be the bearer of the values we associate with, say, the works of Rembrandt or Van Eyck or Poussin) and this could happen—would happen—in silence and invisibility. A world in which painting had become mere decoration would no longer even know how the Old Masters might have mattered except as decoration (accompanied perhaps by some vague imputation of inarticulate monumentality). (And if we are to have a fear for Jane Austen or Henry James, Samuel Johnson or Lionel Trilling, it will have to be a fear of this sort: a fear that they will be lost in plain sight, not behind some flood of critical articles, but—as it were—on the very surface of that flood.)

There are, I think, real problems involved in trying to think or work through the sense in which this vision can be said to be of a real possibility, but it is important that these difficulties not block our recognition of the stakes in play. The fear we attribute to the world of art is not bizarre; it is based on the way things of culture increasingly do appear to die, to cease to count, in our world: not with a bang, but a whimper. It is, among other things, fear of Muzak. We can respond to this, recognize it—even as we hold on to our reservations about the sense we can make of it as a real threat to the world of art.

Within the admittedly vague limits of these reservations, we can see that rococo is telling—revealing—a fundamental truth about art, and this truth is that it exists for a beholder: that art will be decoration and answerable only to the beholder's pleasure, the vagaries of taste, unless it can master its relation to that beholder and make itself count for him or her. Rococo raises the question of the aesthetic as such (and opens accordingly the possibility of "aestheticism" for modern art and theories of it).

Rococo painting—whether one finally finds it "decorative" or not—registers or responds to the emergence of a new public for painting, forces a recognition of that public, of the publicness of painting in general, and so also of the "primordial convention that paintings are made to be beheld." It thus engenders a complex problematic of aesthetic autonomy. It becomes of utmost importance to painting that it be able to find a way to say that what happens with a person standing before a painting is fundamentally different from what happens with a person looking at wallpaper or gazing through a window. This project appears, in the first instance, as a repudiation of something fundamental and ineluctable—the fact that paintings exist for a beholder. That this is precisely a repudiation of something that cannot be repudiated in that way determines the structure of the ensuing history: such a denial cannot but betray the recognition on which it is founded.[6] It is at this level that we can recover and justify our reservations about the reality of the threat art perceives for itself. The account we will want to have in the end will have to be able to steer its way between our recognition of the fate art fears and our knowledge that this fear is also a denial of the necessary conditions under which art always labors. This means that we have to ask continually how seriously we can take this fear, not as a rhetorical question but as a real and difficult question that nonetheless cannot even ensure its own final seriousness. It is the insistence of this question that has become central for criticism now.

I have said that for painting rococo raises the question of the aesthetic as such. The consequent attempt to (re)establish the autonomy of the aesthetic can be posed initially in terms of a problem of purification—but the attempt at purification has become necessary only because painting has already glimpsed (and would suppress) its openness to and implication in the "impurity" of the extraaesthetic. The problem at first appears to be simply semantic—a matter of getting things (aesthetic and nonaesthetic) properly sorted out—but it can appear at all only because of a prior structure that might be called grammatical insofar as its full explication demands our parsing out the implications and transformations of the sentence, "Painting does (not) exist for a beholder." It is the "not" that precludes, in the long run, any simple semantic solution for the art of painting.

The initial problem as we have laid it out is that painting finds itself imperiled by its own possibility of becoming mere decoration, and this means that it can assert its aesthetic autonomy and purity only by refusing to admit this possibility of going astray. It has to think its own possibility of failure as itself already an *aesthetic* failure. Painting that fails is not to be understood as "non-art"— because then painting that succeeds would have to be understood on the basis of its openness to non-art and so would be unable to guarantee its proper aesthetic autonomy. Painting fails by failing to be painting, by being some *other* art. The threat of the "merely decorative" is reconstrued as a threat of "theatricality" and so a threat that remains itself properly aesthetic. Theater is the name within an autonomous aesthetics for that which succumbs to the desire to exist for its beholder. Painting no longer runs the risk of not being art; some paintings, however, fail to be painting.

It will come as no surprise that the development of this position in practice is accompanied by certain difficulties. If, for example, theatricality is to name the possibility of painterly failure, and if it is not itself to become simply another term for the extraaesthetic, it must be understood in some relation to the "real drama" of the stage, a drama which would then figure as the master term for successful painting—which would then be not painting, but another art: unless we say that this drama has been realized on no stage, that the stage can learn its (proper) drama only from painting—as Diderot does.

Clearly, there is a sort of game being played in which a claim to autonomy and "purity" is being negotiated through a system of transformations and displacements that aims not only to relegate a certain (inner) threat to outside the enterprise proper, but even to relegate that place in which the threat can appear to outside the discipline: not only is painting not liable to fall into mere decoration, the threat itself bears not on painting but on the stage.

We should note here that, because of the way in which the issues of painting (as a particular art) and aesthetics (in general) are intertwined, the system we are explicating prescribes not only an impulse toward "pure painting" but also an impulse toward a "total painting"—some synthesis of all the arts under painting. Such double prescriptions are one of the constants of modernism. It is worth seeing that in Mallarmé, for example, the impulse toward a radically purified poetry and the impulse toward a "Book" that would be the poetic transumption of all art can—and, in a sense, must—coexist. This necessity belongs to the grammatical linkages that tie a given artistic discipline to the larger problem of the autonomy of aesthetics *überhaupt*, and that tie a given art to those other arts through which it determines and articulates its "proper" possibilities. It is again the "not" that ties everything together.

All of this can be said to end in the disengagement of a properly aesthetic goal for painting: a successful painting is one that (dramatically) masters its beholder, stops her in her tracks and draws her into its frame, does not allow her to behold it simply as an object hanging on the wall. Now, within the field of representational painting, not all subjects are equally apt to promote this absorption of the viewer—a landscape or a still life, for example, invites—at least at first glance—external viewing or beholding in a way that a picture of a family gathered around the bed of a dying patriarch or of an engraver bent over his work does not. The latter subject matters already have a considerable ability to draw us into participation (we face the paintings as, in effect, already a part of the group around the bed; we find ourselves looking over the engraver's shoulder and sharing his concentration). The restructuring of the painterly field in terms of a polarity of absorption and theatricality leads not only to a certain set of "lateral" distinctions between the arts (the distinction that sets "bad art" and "non-art" together under the heading of "theatricality"), but also to a "vertical" distinction within painting, organized by the master theme of absorption and articulating itself as a hierarchy of genres. One of Fried's essays on Diderot and the problem of theatricality begins expressly from a question about the renewed emphasis on problems of genre and hierarchy.

Any particular hierarchy will be subject to continuing critique—and any "genre" can appear to be the (more or less naturally) adequate vehicle for serious painting. A painting like Greuze's "La Piété filiale" (Filial piety) will quickly come to seem sentimental and "literary," playing on and *to* extra-aesthetic responses in its viewer and so hurling him or her out of the instant of the frame and into some larger narrative that is summed up in the painter's moment. The very realization of this possibility of absorption reveals itself as inherently theatrical (and looking at Greuze now we have, I suspect, little trouble seeing this theatricality—what is difficult for us is to see how such a work could ever have appeared as other than, even anti-, theatrical). So now it is perhaps the solitary figure turned away from the viewer and absorbed utterly in his work that seems to invite our absorption; but in so soliciting our attention it implicitly places us as voyeurs and so once more as beholders and viewers . . . so now it may be historical subjects absorbed in the fullness of their action that demand our attention (and claim to be able to bear it), seeking to realize as explicit tableaux the integral drama that remains unrealizable for the stage. . . . The sequence appears arbitrary, answering to no logic given in advance or through the essence of painting. In large measure Fried's task has been to show the critical logic that makes the history of art here something other than mere and arbitrary sequence—but also something other than a simple unfolding of truth in time.

Insofar as all of these efforts aim at the realization of an artistic purity that is predicated on a denial of theatricality and a denial of the beholder, they are doomed to critique and to failure. There is no way to absorption because absorption is, in the last analysis, a lie. In this dialectic of absorption and theatricality, absorption may appear as the master theme but theatricality is the only real term. The dialectic, as it were, limps along on one leg—and this leg is supposed to be the bum one, the one to be expunged from the whole and healthy body of pure and absorbing painting. In this history we have neither a simple and progressive purging of the inessential from some final truth of painting (as in Greenberg) nor the (in some ways more inviting) dialectical development of painting toward its truth, but instead something like the retrospective dialectical responsiveness of painting to its failure to be autonomous and free of extra-aesthetic contingency.

This last statement brings into view a new aspect of the development we are considering. The history of the field polarized the terms theatricality and absorption *would be* self-enclosed, *would be* purely a history of painting—thus analyzable entirely in terms of the movement of painting toward ever more absorptive—ever more successful and more fully painted—works. But even as theatricality is the term that would ensure the distinction between the aesthetic and the nonaesthetic, it is also the term that reinserts the nonaesthetic at the very heart of what would be pure art. (To put this another way: we have said that theatricality names at once "bad art" and "non-art" undecidably. It puts both terms into play. In discussing paintings or objects claiming to be paintings one will want to use both but will frequently find oneself unable to use either comfortably, and it is through this "confusion" that it seems possible to mark off a region that would be an autonomous art: Duchamp's work makes its claim on our attention by the way it plays on this confusion).

All of this means that an adequate history of art during this period will necessarily involve reference to extraaesthetic contingency. But this reference will, in its turn, be necessarily constrained by its relevance to or visibility for the issues that the history of art has generated for and out of itself. In Fried's analysis, the move from the historical tableaux of David to the political action paintings of Couture is a move responsive to the contingencies of French political history; and it is because French politics are thus made part of the problematic of painting that Manet is able to pose the issues of his painting in terms of "Frenchness" in a way that allows him to recover a certain contact with the larger tradition of Western painting.[7] We might note that it is because this history in effect made itself as a history of French painting—and not simply because it is peopled with French painters—that the history Fried finds of interest is always to be described as a history of French painting. This is very different from some "preset" dialectical development in which the spirit of France (say) has its own bit to contribute to the working out of the overall pattern. To the extent that there is an overall pattern, it is there as the product of a certain persistent movement toward autonomy that must continually take account of those other histories from which it cannot simply disimplicate itself.

We ought to be able to see now that within the history of modernist painting the problem raised by the attempt to distinguish aesthetic and nonaesthetic complicates itself not only into a question of genre and subject matter, but also into questions about what is and is not proper to—internal to—the history of painting, and—finally—into questions about the continuity and discontinuity of that history.

One wants, for example, to say both that new paintings—new claims to the absorption of the beholder—are implicit or explicit denunciations of the (theatrical) work that has preceded them, and that they are possible and comprehensible only on the basis of that work. In this history each work is making a claim to autonomy and to the adequate realization of what painting ("as such") really is. But the claim itself can only be explicated through reference to those other works that the claim itself would disallow. There is tension between an impulse to novelty unburdened by any past and the necessary implication, rootedness, of that impulse in a certain history—or between the desire of painting to see itself as deployed simply in a logico-pictorial space of problems and solutions, and the obvious fact of its historicity. This tension is the historical reflection of the tension we have seen at work in the attempt to institute a radical distinction between aesthetic and nonaesthetic.

Fried summarizes much of this history as follows:

As I see it and have tried to demonstrate in previous studies, the evolution of painting in France in the nineteenth century up to and including Courbet is largely to be understood in terms of the dialectical unfolding of a problematic of painting and beholder which emerged as an issue for French artists and critics as early as the mid 1750s and which received its classic formulation in Diderot's writings on drama and painting of the 1750s and 1760s. The fundamental question addressed by Diderot concerned the conditions that had to be fulfilled in order for the art of painting to successfully persuade its audience of the truthfulness of its representations. . . . I have elsewhere summed this up by saying that Diderot's conception of painting rested ultimately upon the supreme fiction that the beholder did not exist, that he was not really there, standing before the canvas.[8]

To this point we have been exploring the consequences for painting of its project of pure absorption as it is prescribed by this frame, and in this exploration we have always come back to the way in which the project is complicated and even disrupted by the fact that its foundation is, in the end, a fiction, a denial. It should be intuitively clear that such an enterprise can only become ever more difficult, the denial ever more extreme. Fried finds it coming to a crisis in the work of Gustave Courbet. Here the struggle against the facts of beholder and beholding becomes a battle against the very identity of the artist himself: "The self-portrait was at the outset a privileged genre for Courbet because his struggle against his own identity as a beholder found there a natural—a counterconventional—home." As Courbet's painting develops out of this struggle it comes ultimately to "aspire to abolish the impersonal or objective conditions constitutive of the very possibility of spectatordom'' (that is, it aspires to realize in fact the terms of Diderot's supreme fiction). This cannot but force a crisis, a turning point, within the development of modernist painting, and Fried locates this turning point in Manet:

> In Edouard Manet's seminal masterpieces of the first half of the 1860s, Courbet's enterprise is reversed in almost all respects. Most important, Manet seems intuitively to have recognized that Courbet's attempt to abolish the very possibility of spectatordom was doomed in every instance to (ontological not artistic) failure, or at any rate that success in that attempt was literally inconceivable, and that it was necessary to establish the beholder's presence abstractly—to build into the painting the separateness, distancedness, and mutual facing that I have associated with the painting-beholder relationship in its traditional or unreconstructed form—in order that the worst consequences of theatricalization of that relationship be averted.

This is, radically, an event in the development of modernist painting—an event in a way that the move from David to Couture or from Couture to Courbet is not. These latter transitions at least offer the possibility of being thought of purely in terms of a logico-pictorial matrix. The event Fried wants to localize in Manet is not simply a further move within such an apparent abstract matrix, but a transformation of the terms that engendered such an appearance in the first place: Manet's painting—as Fried's essay "Manet's Sources" argues—is predicated on an explicit pictorial acknowledgment of the fact and presence of the beholder. Such an acknowledgment is to be sharply distinguished from any dialectical overcoming of the opposition between "theatricality" and "absorption." These terms are not surpassed but redistributed in such a way that the absorptive project can and must be recognized as itself inherently theatrical—so that the only way to whatever can exist in the place "absorption" set out to name is through an explicit acknowledgment of the theatricality of such an undertaking. The attempt to create pure and absorptive (nontheatrical) works is now bound to appear "merely theatrical."

One is tempted to say that what has happened here is that painting has finally come into its truth, has appropriated for itself its proper field or problematic—except that this problematic is precisely that of painting's essential impropriety, its essential—if profoundly difficult—possibility of losing itself. "Theatricality" can no longer serve as some external dumping place for the failures of painting because it is now a term internal to painting itself. By the same token, one will no longer be able to maintain some sort of implicitly absorptive concern with, for example, the hierarchy of genres separate from the outer darkness of the theatrical. (But, of course, this was always true; it was only that one had *thought* that one could maintain such a separation—the event we are examining has the form of an acknowledgment and not that of the emergence of a new truth or new knowledge of the real situation or essence of painting.) The contradiction or system of contradictions at the heart of the world of painting has been acknowledged in such a way that the claim of a given painting on its audience (a claim it now, in effect, admits to making) can no longer be explicated solely out of that painting alone (it cannot be said to be simply and in itself absorbing), nor can its value be determined in simple contrast to other and merely theatrical works. Rather, the claim a given painting makes on us can only be fully articulated through its relation to other paintings. Fried can, for example, advance his claim for Morris Louis only by distinguishing that work from the theatricality of the work of Donald Judd or Tony Smith—and these works are thus themselves already implicitly recovered from the darkness to which the label of theatricality might appear to condemn them.[9]

We might say that Diderot advanced a theory that would ideally have allowed him to stroll through a gallery being arrested by some paintings and not by others; presumably all the arresting pieces could then be gathered into one place and that place would be a collection of works that were at once "art" and "good art." We have now moved into an area where this is explicitly impossible. Nothing—as we may find ourselves protesting—can be kept out of a museum—which now becomes the place or one of the places where the struggle to sort out art and non-art, good art and bad art, is necessarily fought out in complex and ultimately undecidable ways (and, again, Diderot's gallery was never possible, but Diderot could not say this).[10]

We might also say that the central questions in this newer frame are no longer on the order of "What is art?" but "How is art?" I want to call this a shift from semantics to grammar.

A part of what has to be said here is that this acknowledgment radically alters the way one can think or talk about the history that preceded it. This history can no longer appear (as, we may be tempted to say, it did to itself) as simple and progressive but must show itself instead as organized by its denial of the beholder. It is not clear whether one wants to claim that some new and deeper level of coherence has been discovered—a level at which what had appeared as merely accidental now answers to a new necessity that is the real organizing principle (of the text, of the history)—or to claim that a certain disruption of any principle of system or coherence has occurred, so that the history of painting from Greuze to Courbet seems to be traversed everywhere by gaps and faults. At different times and in varying circumstances one or the other of these claims will tend to take the lead—one and the same painting may need to be said to count for us in its novelty and as a "breakthrough," or in the way it develops and prolongs some of the deepest tendencies of the strongest art of the past 200 years. . . . . The grammatical structure at work here is a reflection of the grammatical tensions we have seen in the opposition of theatricality and absorption.

This is the structure of "radical self-criticism," and such criticism is different from either knowledge of the self in its inmost essence on the one hand, or the utter dissolution of the self on the other. These latter are recognizable as temptations that belong to the project of "radical self-criticism" or as possibilities through which such a project may have to understand itself in certain circumstances. But if they are taken up as independent stances, we will be inclined to condemn them as "theatrical" (with all the recognitions and acknowledgments that condemnation must entail).[11]

Such "radical self-criticism" is also clearly different from any search for abstract purity. The search for purity may have a certain justice as a description of the history from Diderot to Courbet (as sketched by Fried)—but even here its usefulness, its ability to understand the paintings in question—is extremely limited; the history *as a history* is comprehensible only on the basis of our recognition of the deeper complications that prescribe both the search for an abstract purity and its necessary failure. The two terms of "radical self-criticism" together circumscribe the historicity of modernist art.

"Self-criticism" can be "radical" only if it genuinely places its self at stake and holds itself in this condition of being at stake, assuming neither the positive guarantee of that self's inviolable autonomy nor the negative guarantee of its nonexistence; and this means that self-criticism is radically and inevitably *critical*—one can paint only out of the history of painting and the particular concrete paintings that matter for and constitute that history. For the art critic or historian, the confrontation with a given painting is necessarily an explication of that history within which the painting in question exerts its claim on us. For the painter who would explicitly acknowledge the situation of painting (for example, Manet), this acknowledgment necessarily takes a form that can be described either as an appropriation of the great paintings of the past or as criticism of them. One can see a parallel logic at work in Greenberg's descriptions of surrealism: the tension between a movement of return and a more "revolutionary" moment of parody belongs properly to such an attempt to reopen the possibility of art.[12] The critic who writes from the position of a Greenberg or a Fried cannot simply "exclude" anyone from the history of art; exclusion belongs to the way the issues are set up for modernism: so that one will, on the one hand, always want very much to find that artifact (dadaist or minimalist or conceptual . . .) that lies definitively beyond the limits of art (and one will be led inevitably to assert such exclusions); and one will, on the other hand, be equally inevitably led to acknowledge that this "far side" of art always lies within art itself (so that one's exclusions will always be given in terms of theatricality, and such an exclusion is, finally, no exclusion at all).[13]

But then it will also be true that one can no longer offer the sorts of historical accounts one might like. One cannot pick out cleanly the "true" or "central" line of development except by including in that account a number of works that one wants to exclude from that central line. One cannot lay down an orderly sequence of steps in the progressive solution of certain problems given—more or less—in the nature of art, as the real problems of painting. And, by the same token, one will be hard put to find some simple origin for such a set of problems. One may want to attribute the origin of modernism to Diderot and the painters of the mid-eighteenth century, but one will also want to attribute this origin to Manet. This cannot be settled by breaking the history into a first phase and a second, because the first is only comprehensible on the basis of the second, and the second does not supplant or otherwise do away with the first—instead, it persists within it in such a way as to present one with the temptation to break "modernism" into orderly phases—"traditional" and "antitraditional," "modern" and "postmodern." This original tension is overcome only at the cost of doing away with the problematic itself. What is needed is a way to think about how this tension works, what notions of time and event it puts into play.

This tension within modernist painting ends by breaking its apparent historical bounds—the development of painting from neoclassicism to the present. It forces Greenberg's description of the Old Masters as "using art to conceal art"—a description that does not condemn them to painterly irrelevance and error but stresses the way they are both again and newly visible for us. The modernist project is importantly a conservative one, motivated by a desire to ensure the production of works of art that can matter to their audience, can exert a claim on that audience, in the same way that the Old Masters do; but this also means that the success of modernist painting will entail a reevaluation of the great art of the past, or, perhaps more accurately, a new recovery of the value of the great art of the past. It is altogether too easy to call this a reduction of the Old Masters to their modernist rereading and revision; these painters are valuable not simply because they somehow manage to be modernist despite themselves, but also and primarily as they are masters and as their works are the standards that set in motion the modernist enterprise—as they are the source from which it draws its inspiration and strength. These same objects may, however, also be or seem to be the bearers of what has become the "merely tasteful" and as such come to represent that which must above all be purged from serious painting.

The relations between the modern and the traditional are satisfactorily caught neither by an insistence on rupture nor by a counterinsistence on continuity. Stanley Cavell, whose writings on modernism have emerged in close dialogue with Fried's work, has offered the following:

> The essential fact of (what I refer to as) the modern lies in the relation between the present practice of an enterprise and the history of that

enterprise, in the fact that this relation has become problematic.
(*MWM*, p. xix)

This formulation, tying together the thing and its grammar, "the modern," and "what I refer to as the modern," is of surprising simplicity and equally surprising complexity. Of particular significance in the present context is the way it seems to cut the modern away from any historical particularity—if "the modern" is an event, that event is primarily grammatical and not—not easily—chronological. "Modernism" seems almost to invade history, transforming that field in such a way that every point within it is able to bear the weight both of radical rupture with the past and of resolution of continuity with it. "Modernism" becomes properly capable of finding itself wherever it looks, even as it thus finds itself only in division against itself.

Such logic returns us to the "exterior form"—rupture and redoubling—of the "event" announced by Derrida at Hopkins. Our business from here on will be with the "inner form" and philosophic particularity of this "event."

I am suggesting that we see Derrida in something like the way Fried sees Manet or Morris Louis—as a figure deeply involved in a history and a discipline that has become complex and problematic, to the point of being deeply, internally, at war with itself. It should be apparent from what we have seen of Fried's work that the critic of modernist art cannot escape his own implication in the logic of that modernism. He cannot, for example, mean "theatricality" quite the way he perhaps would like (as radically exclusive of certain types of work) without undercutting his own ability to valorize the works he does want to call art—without, that is, falling into a certain theatricality himself. Such criticism is thus obliged to a project of radical self-criticism, an undertaking that is at least implicitly a reflection on its own condition. In general, Fried has been content simply to mark the place where such further reflection becomes necessary:

> Moreover, the notion that there are problems "intrinsic" to the art of painting is, so far as I can see, the most important question begged in this essay. It has to do with the concept of a medium and is one of the points philosophy and art criticism might discuss most fruitfully, if a dialogue between them could be established. Similarly, an examination of the "grammar" (in the sense Wittgenstein gives to this word in the *Philosophical Investigations*) of a family of concepts essential to this essay—e.g., problem, solution, advance, logic, validity—would be more than welcome.[14]

Stanley Cavell's definition of modernism means to be responsive to these issues, and the notion of grammar to which we have had recourse in the preceding pages is itself a crude and unsystematic derivation from Cavell and Wittgenstein. It is now time to look more directly at Cavell's writings on modernism and philosophy. It is through this work that we will make our first approach to the meaning of modernism in philosophy, and so to the sense of the claim I am making for Jacques Derrida.

Cavell's work plunges us immediately into the complex field of the "oblique and shifting relations between an art, and its criticism, and philosophy" (*MWM*, p. 223). This is a space in which the relations of the various disciplines to their proper pasts and to each other are always problematic, necessarily critical, and always caught up within the terms of radical self-criticism. It is the region we enter when we say that the problem with Greenberg's essay on modernist painting is that it finally fails to take seriously its dependence on a philosophic "model" that *is* a demand for its own submission to self-criticism—and therefore something other than a simple model.

In Cavell's case, this exploration of oblique and shifting relations is not separable from his meditation on philosophic modernism itself; and this meditation, in its turn, can be no more sure of exactly where it begins and ends than a modernist painting can be sure of its claims to be painting or to be art. Cavell writes that two of the essays in *Must We Mean What We Say?*—essays on *King Lear* and on *Endgame*—may be thought to be pieces of literary criticism or of applied philosophy, while the remainder "are (at least closer to being) straight philosophy."

> I wish to deny this, but to deny it I would have to use the notions of philosophy and of literature and of criticism, and the denial would be empty so far as those notions themselves are unexamined and so far as the impulse to assert such distinctions, which in certain moods I share, remains unaccounted for. In wishing to deny that some of these essays are philosophical and others not, I do not deny that there are differences among them, and differences between philosophy and literature or between philosophy and literary criticism; I am suggesting that we do not understand these differences. (*MWM*, pp. xvii-xviii)

A similar problem has grown up around Derrida's writings as they have been received in this country—although the impulse has been to take this work as already both philosophy and criticism rather than to insist on their distinction. Throughout the following chapters I will tend to insist on such distinctions and on the necessity of trying to come to some understanding of them—without losing touch with the impulse to blur over such distinctions, an impulse "which in certain moods I share."

Cavell's insistence on finding a way to hold open the question of the relation between philosophy and literary criticism so as to understand both the possibility of their coincidence and the necessity of their distinction is implicitly also an insistence on posing the question of modernism in philosophy. It entails our taking a more partial stance toward two other distinctions:

If I deny a distinction, it is the still fashionable distinction between philosophy and meta-philosophy, the philosophy of philosophy. The remarks I make *about* philosophy (for example, about certain of its differences from other subjects) are, where accurate, on a par with remarks I make about acknowledgment or about mistakes or about metaphor. I would regard this fact—that philosophy is one of its own normal topics—as in turn defining for the subject, for what I wish philosophy to do. (*MWM*, p. xviii)

I do assert a distinction throughout these essays which, because it may seem either controversial or trivial, I want to call attention to from the beginning—a distinction between the modern and the traditional, in philosophy and out. My claim is not that all contemporary philosophy which is good is modern; but the various discussions about the modern I am led to in the course of these essays are the best I can offer in explanation of the way I have written, or the way in which I would wish to write. (*MWM*, p. xix)

The denial of the distinction between philosophy and metaphilosophy precludes the displacement of the question of philosophic modernism into mere epistemological regress and enforces our taking seriously the challenge latent in Kant's "explicit recognition that the terms in which the past is criticized are specific to one's own position and require justification from within that position" (*MWM*, p. xix). This cuts off at its source the sort of confusion we have seen at work in Greenberg's essay (Greenberg in effect thinks to offer a loosely metaphilosophical report on Kant's philosophical position). What Cavell calls a recognition, Greenberg reports as a discovery—a truth about the limits of disciplinary work roughly parallel to the truth of physics, and so capable of overseeing the self-critical project of the various arts. It is this tacit assumption of the distinction between philosophy and metaphilosophy that enables Greenberg's slide from a notion of "philosophy, which is critical by definition" to the assertion that "Kantian self-criticism finds its perfect expression in science rather than in philosophy"—a slide in which what is lost, what becomes incoherent, is precisely the central notion of self-criticism.

To deny the distinction between philosophy and metaphilosophy is to rule out as well any picture in which philosophy figures as a form of science—and with this any picture in which the fundamental stakes are stakes of knowledge. It is this that sets up, for example, Cavell's sustained engagement with the argument between skeptic and anti-skeptic. This argument takes itself to be about knowledge, but can neither understand nor resolve itself until it is reconceived of terms of acknowledgment. The confrontation with skepticism—both about the world and about other minds—is central to Cavell's work. An understanding of this centrality will feed directly into Cavell's notion of philosophic modernism and so open into our exploration of Derrida's work.

At the heart of this confrontation is a question of criteria—a question the approach to philosophy through ordinary language is particularly well suited to raise. What ordinary language can teach us, according to Cavell, is not—not primarily in any case—that certain philosophic questions arise only through mistakes about—abstractions from—our ordinary use of language, but rather that all utterances—even philosophical—mean from within their human use. The appeal to ordinary language is not an appeal to truth or authority, but an appeal, as it were, to our selves—to what Cavell calls "the specific plight of mind and circumstances within which a human being gives voice to his condition" (*MWM*, p. 240). The appeal thus operates not as a means to or a guarantee of knowledge, but as a way of reminding ourselves what kind of thing will count for us in response to the questions we raise. Such an appeal does not drive a wedge between ordinary usage and its philosophic etiolations; rather it reminds us of their solidarity, so that one can take the burden of the appeal to be either that one must seek that place from which the saying of what one wants to repudiate as extraordinary, abusive, far-fetched, catechristic, is in fact ordinary (how the skeptic can mean what he or she says) or that one must learn just how extraordinary what we ordinarily say finally is (how Austin's Finney manages to get everything just right as he recounts the scalding of his patient).[15] However we proceed through this choice we end with our philosophy and our selves, our words and our plight, facing one another. As Cavell puts it:

> The way you must rely upon yourself as a source of what is said when, demands that you grant full title to others as sources of that data—not out of politeness, but because the nature of the claim you make for yourselves is repudiated without that acknowledgment: it is a claim that no one knows better than you whether and when a thing is said, and if this is not to be taken as a claim to expertise (a way of taking it which repudiates it) then it must be understood to mean that you know no better than others what you claim to know. (*MWM*, pp. 239-40)

The very possibility of making this kind of appeal implies a stance toward skepticism, but, as Cavell stresses,

> the appeal to ordinary language cannot directly repudiate the skeptic (or the traditional philosopher generally) by, for example, finding that what he says contradicts what we ordinarily say or by claiming that he cannot mean what he says: the former is no surprise to him and the latter is not obviously more than a piece of abuse. What the appeal can and ought directly to do is to display what the skeptic does or must mean, even how he can mean what he says. (*MWM*, p. 240)

The moment we approach the skeptic no longer by thinking to refute him, but by asking *how* he can say *that*, the ground shifts beneath the traditional arguments. The classic antagonists reveal themselves to be complicitous with one another, agreed in advance that a self or feeling is properly an object of knowledge (and therefore also one that can be found to be "unknowable"). The skeptic and the anti-skeptic are united in the belief that a feeling is something one has first of all privately, so subject equally and indifferently to expression or concealment. They read, together, the utterances "I know I am in pain" or "I know you are in pain" as if they are epistemological statements, judgments in need of *that* sort of grounding—in certainty, transparency. In fact, Cavell argues, the case is just the reverse: what the skeptic has discovered is that there is no such grounding available for such utterances and that this is a fundamental fact about what it is to be human:

> there *are* special problems about our knowledge of another; *exactly the problems the skeptic sees.* And these problems can be said to invoke a special concept of knowledge, or region of the concept of knowledge, one which is not a function of certainty. This region has been pointed to in noticing that a first person acknowledgment of pain is not an expression of certainty but an expression of pain, that is, an exhibiting of the *object* of knowledge. (*MWM*, pp. 258-59)

The problem for Cavell is that as the skeptic and his would-be confounder trade their arguments about the knowability of selves and feelings, they lose, together, the experience the skeptic means to offer for registration—transforming an experience of our separateness (the "terrible or fortunate fact, at once contingent and necessary, that *I* am not in that [your] position") into an epistemological problem, "a metaphysical fact [into] an intellectual lack" (*MWM*, pp. 259, 263). Cavell's impulse is to redeem these facts from our reduction of them to matters of cognition, epistemology, and what we have come to call "psychology"—our faith in the psyche as the radically private object of our knowledge.

This impulse is attuned to the deepest motives of modern philosophy. Both Anglo-American and Continental philosophers find their way into the twentieth century only by passing through a critique of "psychologism," whether in Frege or in Husserl. In Cavell's case, however, the screw is turned tighter still:

> We know of the efforts of such philosophers as Frege and Husserl to undo the "psychologizing" of logic (like Kant's undoing Hume's psychologizing of knowledge): now, the shortest way I might describe such a book as the *Philosophical Investigations* is to say that it attempts to undo the psychologizing of psychology, to show the necessity controlling our application of psychological and behavioral categories; even, one could say, show the necessities in human action and

passion themselves. And at the same time it seems to turn all of philosophy into psychology—matters of what we call things, how we treat them, what their role is in our lives. (*MWM*, p. 91)

We do well here to note the resonances of this with a passage from one of Derrida's essays on the psychoanalytic writings of Nicolas Abraham (with whom we will be concerned at greater length in a later chapter):

> Nicolas Abraham sought . . . an effective passageway through phenomenology . . . a reinterpretation of its content . . . and of its method. . . . These were the conditions for a critical break with every sort of presupposition or naiveté, whose traces psychoanalysis itself, even today, is still unevenly maintaining. A break, in particular, with every sort of psychologism.[16]

The result in both cases is, in ways that may look radically different, a concern with "what we call things, how we treat them, what their role is in our lives."

Derrida and Cavell stand together at a major crossing in modern philosophy, a point at which what seemed philosophy's search for its own pure and proper ground apart from any psychology or psychologism is radically complicated by what can appear either as philosophy's invasion of psychology (as if to protect psychology from its own internal tendency to psychologism) or as philosophy's coming to acknowledge psychology as something inevitably internal to itself (and so not simply dismissible as an accidental and exterior encrusting "-ism"). The obvious question here is, "What can Cavell mean in speaking of the need to undo the 'psychologizing of psychology' "? This does not appear to be, on the face of things, a bad thing: what would psychology look like if it were "depsychologized"?

I suppose the simplest answer to this would be that it would not look quite like psychology. In particular, it would not look like that disciplinary thing that lies just alongside but clearly outside, for example, logic; the world—the human world in any case—would no longer break in two along that line of division. Things would no longer parse easily into the merely psychological and the logical. This might mean, for example, that what we find funny might be not simply a matter of opinion, personal perspective, or point of view, but rather a matter of what is funny. Some things aren't funny no matter who laughs at them, and those who do laugh at such things are not so much expressing their selves or their opinions as they are displaying their being apart—for better or worse—from the conventions that compose our nature. This laughter demands a psychology in a way shared laughter does not; a psychology that stands on this foundation is one that begins precisely in a forgetting of what binds us together. Such a psychology is already a psychologism, a reduction of the psyche to its privacy or claims to privacy—a locking of that psyche in its garden and so an enforcing of it within that "picture." Cavell's diagnosis follows directly from his understanding of Wittgenstein's diagnosis of the philosopher:

> He finds that someone has become obsessed with a "picture" of the way he imagines the world or the mind must be; or supposes himself to be communicating a piece of information when in fact no one could fail to know what he says (hence no one could be informed by it). Such a person—any person at such a moment—is lost not in parable but in fact; he has lost not the depth of his words, but their surface, their ordinariness—not their power to save, but their power to record; he is out of touch not with his individual existence but with his common human nature.[17]

The skeptic, along with his psychologizing opponent, arises just at that point at which the fact of our "common human nature" to be registered is that of our separation from one another. When this effort at registration turns, behind its own back, into a search for an epistemologically grounded reconstruction of that common human nature, then that nature has already been deeply lost, and we can find our way back to it by collapsing and conflating the distinctions our quest for certainty brings in its wake:

> [Wittgenstein] also says that language, and life, rests on conventions. What he means is, I suppose, that they have no necessity beyond what human beings do. He does not mean, for example, that we might all convene and decide or vote on what our human forms of life shall be, choose what we shall find funny or whether we will continue finding loss or comfort where we do. If we call these arrangements conventional, we must then also call them natural.

The argument about skepticism is thus not simply an argument within philosophy. It is an argument that makes plausible a certain purifying separation of disciplines and thus spills over into issues one might otherwise be tempted to call "metaphilosophical." The position of skepticism within modern philosophic thought is of a piece with the disciplinary position of philosophy itself. To stand, as Cavell would, in a new relation to the argument between skeptic and anti-skeptic is to stand in a new relation to the discipline itself.

In this transformed field—a field in which philosophy admits to its inevitable entanglement with psychology (its dealing with questions that it is essentially human to have)—philosophy is free to recognize once again within itself an impulse that can be called therapeutic. And what this therapy would address is our tendency to take ourselves for psychological, or for epistemological, as objects of knowledge in either case, rather than the living beings we, more or less, actually are.

A consequence of this in Cavell's writings is that a certain notion of therapy, loosely derived from psychoanalysis, and a certain understanding of the nature of the philosophic response to skepticism flow together, most visibly in Cavell's rapprochement of Wittgenstein to Hegel:

That is, of course, Wittgenstein's sense of the way philosophical problems end. It is true for him, in the *Investigations* at any rate, this happens when we have gone through a process of bringing ourselves back into our natural forms of life, putting our souls back into our bodies. . . . That a resolution of this sort is described as the solution of a philosophical problem, and as the goal of its particular mode of criticism, represents for me the most original contribution Wittgenstein offers philosophy. I can think of no closer title for it, in an established philosophical vocabulary, than Hegel's use of the term *Aufhebung* . . . as an ideal of (one kind of) philosophical criticism—a criticism in which it is pointless for one side to refute the other, because its cause and topic is the self getting in its own way—it seems about right.

. . . It is my impression that many philosophers do not like Wittgenstein's comparing what he calls his "methods" to therapies; but for me part of what he means by this comparison is brought out in thinking of the progress of psychoanalytic therapy. The more one learns, so to speak, the hang of oneself, and mounts one's problems, the less one is able to *say* what one has learned; not because you have *forgotten* what it was, but because nothing you said would seem like an answer or a solution: there is no longer any question or problem with which your words would match. (*MWM*, pp. 85-86)

This confluence is of but intermittent interest to Cavell—his philosophic center lies in Kant not Hegel—but is absolutely central for Derrida's work, and our approach to Derrida will be very much in terms of it, in terms especially of the problematic play of identity and difference, philosophy and psychology, at work between Hegel and Freud. It is enough here, however, to remark how Cavell's notion of acknowledgment—opening on one side into an image of therapy—opens on another into a version or reading of what Hegel calls "the labor of the negative." The achievement of acknowledgment is deeply bound to its failure—and its *radical* failure, the denial of acknowledgment, inevitably gives itself away, leaves its mark:

A "failure to know" might just mean a piece of ignorance, an absence of something, a blank. A "failure to acknowledge" is the presence of something, a confusion, an indifference, a callousness, an exhaustion, a coldness. Spiritual emptiness is not a blank. —Just as, to say that behavior is expressive is not to say that the man impaled upon his sensation must express it in his behavior; it is to say that in order not to express it he must suppress the behavior, to twist it. And if he twists it far or often enough he may lose possession of that region of the mind which the behavior is expressing. (*MWM*, p. 264)

Here we are as close as Cavell ever comes to explicitly Freudian formulations, close enough for us to say that for Cavell a theory of repression will make sense only insofar as it is a theory of how a certain failure of acknowledgment comes to pass.

The contrast between knowing and acknowledging has another interesting feature. If the issue is one of knowledge, you have, in respect to your pain, an apparently privileged relationship from which I am excluded; but when the issue is one of acknowledgment, I stand in a position no better and no worse than your own. Finitude lies not simply between us, but within us. Cavell's essay "Knowing and Acknowledging" thus ends:

Here is the source of our gratitude to poetry. And this sense of unknownness is a competitor of the sense of childish fear as an explanation for our idea, and need, of God. —And why should the mind be less dense and empty and mazed and pocked and clotted—and why less a whole—than the world is? At least we can say in the case of some mental phenomena, when you have twisted or covered your expressions far enough or long enough, or haven't yet found the words which give the phenomenon expression, I may know better than you how it is with you. I may respond even to the fact of your separateness from me (not to mention mine from you) more immediately than you.

To know your pain is to acknowledge it, or to withhold the acknowledgment. —I know your pain the way you do. (*MWM*, p. 266)

In such a passage one sees the way in which a doubleness of language and of voice insists even into what appears to be—what wants to be—a conclusion, a resolution of the controversy that has presumably set the two voices against one another in the first place. Even in this brief passage, it becomes increasingly difficult to sort out where one voice ends and the other responds—or to tell which voice is Cavell's and which that of another. We can take the last paragraph to employ two voices—and yet they here appear to say the same—and yet again each demands that it be heard somehow distinctly. The grammar of such disruption is the grammar of the acknowledgment it would accomplish.

Cavell's "other voice" arises from his concentration on the problem of other minds as it emerges through skepticism about material objects and in tragedy, and as it calls for an act of (philosophic) acknowledgment. Such an acknowledgment must, Cavell argues, be an explicit recognition of the way in which the skeptic can mean what he says—of the way in which his apparently outrageous assertions are in fact ordinary statements once one recognizes when and where one is tempted to them. Philosophic acknowledgment of the recurrence of philosophic skepticism demands recognition of the skeptic in one's self. So Cavell writes, "Wittgenstein's interlocutors, when he writes well, when he is philosophically just, express thoughts which strike us as at once familiar and foreign, like temptations," and so also Cavell comes to put such interlocutors at work within his own writings.

Acknowledgment and its tendency to lose itself in—or as—epistemology is thus a central theme in Cavell's work, and it is one that bears not only on questions internal to philosophy but also on the structure of the field itself. Not only are Cavell's remarks about philosophy "on a par with remarks I make about acknowledgment," his remarks about acknowledgment are, in the end, remarks about philosophy as well. It is in these terms that we should understand Cavell's refusal to accept or deny a distinction between philosophy and literary criticism: such a distinction is not something to be known, but something to be acknowledged—and it is not clear what this might mean. Certainly such an acknowledgment is not just a matter of submission to the truth about the distinction, for this would make the distinction nothing more than an object of knowledge and Cavell's determined muddling of it a product of ignorance or contrariety. But neither is it a simple recognition of the disciplinary facts of life, because if it were there would be no problem for Cavell to raise. One of the things we want to be able to say about acknowledgment is that it figures somewhere between knowledge and recognition, and our use of it should be one that lets us acknowledge the way in which, at various times, we want to use these words as well.

But if acknowledgment can carry the weight of articulating a problem of philosophical autonomy, we should expect to find it reappearing when we turn to the distinction Cavell does want to assert between the modern and the traditional (in philosophy and out). We have in fact already glimpsed it in the redescription of Kant in terms of an "explicit recognition" instead of an epistemological discovery, and we need now only put that redescription in its proper place. For Cavell, the fact that the relation of past and present has become problematic for philosophy is most clearly evident in the writings of Wittgenstein and Heidegger:

> Innovation in philosophy has characteristically gone together with a repudiation—a specifically cast repudiation—of most of the history of the subject. But in the later Wittgenstein (and, I would now add, in Heidegger's *Being and Time*) the repudiation of the past has a transformed significance, as though containing the consciousness that history will not go away, except through our perfect acknowledgment of it (in particular, our acknowledgment that it is not past), and that one's own practice and ambition can only be identified against the continuous experience of the past. (This new significance in philosophical

repudiation itself has a history. Its most obvious precursor is Hegel, but it begins, I believe, in Kant. For it is in Kant that one finds an explicit recognition that the terms in which the past is criticized are specific to one's own position, and require justification from within that position). (*MWM*, p. xix)

We can specify the traditional mode of repudiation as (loosely) epistemological—taking the form of asserting (or proving) someone to be wrong, or right, but partial and so ultimately mistaken. Certainly one culminating moment in the history of this mode of repudiation is Wittgenstein's *Tractatus* with its determination to tell the (relatively uninteresting) truth about things with as little fuss as possible. In the later Wittgenstein the repudiation of the tradition implicit in the Tractarian correction of philosophy is transformed through the appeal to ordinary language—an appeal that opens out into a demand that one struggle to meet the tradition as something radically inevitable—or, for example, to meet the skeptic not only or primarily as someone who has made a mistake but as someone who, in a sense, one already is—someone whose meanings cannot but be acknowledged. Heidegger's existentialism and project of "the destruction of the history of philosophy" have, on the surface, a very different look; but Cavell's remark that "Heidegger's consciousness that our deepest task, as philosophers and as men, is one of getting back to a sense of words and world from which we are now away" (*MWM*, pp. xix-xx) touches precisely at the juncture of the two bodies of work.

What differentiates them is, of course, the split between Anglo-American and Continental that has come to be one of the more obvious features of contemporary philosophy. Because Heidegger and Wittgenstein belong to such different traditions, their modernisms are articulated very differently. In general, the Anglo-American exploration of philosophic modernism, as exemplified by Cavell, finds its starting point in Kant, and particularly in Kant's opposition to Hume and to skepticism; it is the recurrent moment of skepticism that carries the weight of the tradition of the past (so Cavell writes that "one could say that in a modernist situation 'past' loses its temporal accent and means anything 'not present.' Meaning what one says becomes a matter of making one's sense present to oneself" [*MWM*, p. xix]). The Continental tradition is more inclined to find its problem in Hegel and his positing of the history of philosophy as a history of Spirit—with the result that "past" here regains its "temporal accent." It is across this difference that one can call Cavell's attempt to acknowledge the skeptic and Heidegger's effort to destroy/retrieve the history of philosophy "the same."

"Repudiation" names a new difficulty in getting at what may be very old truths; its new significance is at work in Greenberg's assertion that the problem of the Old Masters in modernist painting is not one of overcoming but of recovery:

> Nothing could be further from the authentic art of our time than the idea of a rupture of continuity. Art is, among many other things, continuity. Without the past of art, and without the need and compulsion to maintain past standards of excellence, such a thing as Modernist art would be impossible. ("Modernist Painting," p. 77)

"Authenticity" appears as the stake in our relation to our past (as it does also for Heidegger). "Sincerity" and "authenticity" are of course catchwords of our modern selves and times. The terms that are set against them within the grammar of the modern can be said to cluster around the notion of "fraudulence"—the name with which we will perhaps denounce Carl Andre laying down a row of bricks in a London gallery or by means of which we will perhaps try to point toward the empty core we may see behind the rhetorical flights of a John Barth or a Donald Barthelme or an Alain Robbe-Grillet . . . they may well be the terms by which we would denounce Derrida's work.

Cavell has argued at length that this risk of or openness to fraudulence is more crucially defining of the modern than the apparent positive terms of sincerity or authenticity or demystifying truth telling insofar as it is the omnipresent possibility of fraudulence that determines our countervailing valorization of authenticity.[18] This is not a simple possibility—not just the possibility of our being duped by someone else, someone of malicious intent. The risk to which Cavell points cuts much deeper: it is the risk that inheres in (for example) his own inability to decide the questions he raises about his essays on *King Lear* and *Endgame*—could it be that these are not philosophical writings? And if so, has Cavell put a fast one over on us? on himself? Could Cavell have known this? And if so, could he have done something else? What would it mean to call (for example) such essays "fraudulent," "counterfeits of philosophy," "not the real thing"? How can fraudulent art, or philosophy, be exposed?

The last of these is Cavell's question in his essay "Music Discomposed." He goes on to answer it (in part) as follows:

> Other frauds and imposters, like forgers and counterfeiters, admit *clear* outcomes, conclude in dramatic discoveries—the imposter is unmasked at the ball, you find the counterfeiters working over their press, the forger is caught signing another man's name, or he confesses. There are no such proofs possible for the assertion that the art accepted by a public is fraudulent; the artist himself may not know; and the critic may be shown up, not merely as incompetent, not unjust in accusing the wrong man, but as taking others in (or out); that is, as an imposter.

The only exposure of false art lies in recognizing something about
the object itself, but something whose recognition requires exactly the
same capacity as recognizing the genuine article. . . . You often do
not know which is on trial, the object or the viewer: modern art did
not invent this dilemma, it merely insists upon it. (*MWM*, p. 190)[19]

"The artist himself may not know": this is the crucial depth to the possibility
of fraudulence and describes the risk that is inherent in Cavell's writings on *Lear*
and *Endgame* or, more recently (perhaps more obviously), in his work on and
claims for the movies. All of this writing is (holds itself) open to the charge of
fraudulence, and this charge is not one Cavell can refute through more argument
or the production of proofs. The charge is met or not met, refuted or not refuted,
in his writing—the way the same charge is refuted or not refuted on the canvas
of a (modernist) painting. And we will want even to say that some works may
stand convicted precisely by their inability or refusal to pose the possibility that
they are in fact fraudulent (exactly as we want to call "theatrical" those works
that fail to pose the question of their own theatricality).

It is, I take it, significant about modernism and its "permanent revolution" that its audience recurrently tells itself the famous stories of
riots and walkouts and outrages that have marked its history. It is as
though the *impulse* to shout fraud and storm out is always present, but
fear of the possible consequences overmasters the impulse. Remember
Saint-Saëns: He said the Emperor had no clothes, and then history
stripped him naked. The philistine audience cannot afford to admit the
new; the *avant garde* audience cannot afford not to. This bankruptcy
means that both are at the mercy of their tastes, or fears, and that no
artist can test his work either by their rejection or their acceptance.
(*MWM*, pp. 205-6)

The assertion that the avant-garde cannot afford not to admit the new cap-
tures, I think, something deep in our fears of it: that modernism opens up a
course that leads inevitably to an indiscriminate acceptance of all that claims
novelty, that with modernism one buys willy-nilly a background ideology of
progressivism that ultimately undercuts any moral sensibility whatsoever.

But it matters more to see that Cavell is here working again at the grammar
of our modernism, seeking to show where and how its crises arise and what
demands they impose on us. That, for example, modernism must work without
any ability to appeal to the authority of its audience points to the way in which
the work of the modernist must (if it is to be anything) conceive itself in and
test itself against its own history; it points also to the way in which modernist
works will present themselves inevitably as fighting against their audience
(including the artist himself insofar as he participates in that audience) and

against its taste—fighting in the name of the morality or integrity of the discipline and the tradition that has formed those tastes.

It is only through this having of "history as a problem, that is, as a commitment" (*MWM*, p. xxii) that the modernist can authorize himself, find his proper authority. The rest we condemn as "merely modernizing" and bent solely on novelty—except that we can never pin this distinction down, in ourselves or in others. The critic is as fully at risk as the artist himself:

> He is part detective, part lawyer, part judge, in a country in which
> crimes and deeds of glory look alike, and in which the public not
> only, therefore, confuses one with the other, but does not know that
> one or the other has been committed: not because the news has not got
> out, but because what counts as one or the other cannot be defined
> until it happens; and when it has happened there is no sure way he can
> get the news out; and no way at all without risking something like a
> crime or glory of his own. (*MWM*, p. 191)

We have come a long way from Greenberg's statement that "nothing could be further from the authentic art of our time than the idea of a rupture of continuity." We have come far enough that, although we now know what this wants to say and know also the ways it is precisely and powerfully correct, we now know also that we have to rewrite it to read: nothing could be further from *and more familiar to* the authentic art of our time than the idea of a rupture of continuity. The history of modernism is in effect everywhere haunted by this idea and, through it, develops itself as a continuous betrayal of its audience and itself, a betrayal of the standards of taste in the name of those standards (or in the name of their conditions of possibility).

> What looks like "breaking with tradition" in the successions of art is
> not really that; or is that only after the fact, looking historically or
> critically; or is that only as a result not as a motive: the unheard of
> appearance of the modern in art is an effort not to break, but to keep
> faith with tradition. It is perhaps fully true of Pop Art that its motive
> is to break with the tradition of painting and sculpture; and the result
> is not that the tradition is broken, but that these works are irrelevant
> to that tradition, i.e., that are not paintings, whatever their pleasures.
> (Where history has cunning, it is sometimes ironic, but sometimes
> just.) (*MWM*, pp. 206-7)

With this we are returned once again to considerations of the ways in which modernism is and is not an event, and of the ways in which this "event" transforms the terms in which we can construe history—so that history appears as a continuity that is traversed at every point by discontinuity and disruption, permanent revolution.

It may be that we can now feel the grammatical sense behind what might be called the "modernist imperative"—the way in which the modernist must say "must" without being able to know whether or how he or she really means it. If I say, "Philosophy must now put itself into question if it is to maintain itself as philosophy . . . ," I am, I think, not giving orders nor am I attempting to exclude from philosophy all work that does not "put itself in question" (except of course that I am attempting precisely that)—it is more nearly the case that with this "must" I commit myself to philosophy, its history and its discipline, in the only way that I can, which is: at risk and with no authority beyond that commitment and the conviction it may compel. The force of such a "must" does not lie in me, but elsewhere. In this it is a little like a promise, dependent on an uptake it can only secure elsewhere—a risky imperative.

I am then at risk here. I am in the position of arguing for the Emperor's clothes. The robes that count here are the robes of a certain tradition and a certain problematic developed within it, handed down by it: to claim Derrida as significantly a modernist philosopher entails placing him within a tradition—Continental, philosophic—and describing him as powerfully responsive to it.

Success in this enterprise carries its own risks. The figure of the Emperor, and the interest we take in establishing his truth, is one Derrida has addressed within his texts—in, especially, the introduction to—or pretext for—his polemic with Lacanian psychoanalysis, "The Purveyor of Truth." I leave it to other readers and writers to make something of this knotting of figures, controversy, and argument. Derrida has also registered more direct dissent from the project I appear to be (may in fact be) engaging. I will simply recall here the strictures of "Où commence et comment finit un corps enseignant?" (Where begins and how ends a teaching body?).

> If deconstruction had rested at a simple semantic or conceptual deconstitution, which it has never done except in the eyes of those who benefit from seeing nothing there, deconstruction would have formed nothing more than a—new—modality of the internal auto-critique of philosophy. It would have risked reproducing philosophic propriety, the self-relation of philosophy, the economy of traditional questioning.[20]

I recall also another passage from the same essay:

> Always interminable in this sense, and in order not to reduce itself to a modern episode of philosophic reproduction, deconstruction cannot associate itself with a liquidation of philosophy.[21]

If deconstruction can be said to aim at some kind of revolution (and clearly it does) it is important to see that this is a revolution that in one sense will have always already happened and in another sense will always be still to come, but in which one will never participate as if in some present event. Reproduction and rupture risk one another, and I risk both in advancing my claims for Derrida. To attempt to proof myself against such risk would be to lose everything.

And I may of course be wrong about the Emperor. History stripped Saint-Saëns naked and is no doubt not done yet. Time, as we say, will tell.

But my question is: *What* will time tell? That certain departures in art-like pursuits have become established (among certain audiences, in textbooks, on walls, in college courses); that *someone* is treating them with the respect due, we feel, to art; that one no longer has the right to question their status? But in waiting for time to tell that, we miss what the present tells—that the dangers of fraudulence, and of trust, are essential to the experience of art. (*MWM*, pp. 188-89)

Among the things we do not, in the end, know is what nakedness—or clothing—is. This vision of the way in which time can tell—nothing—and so can only return us to—perhaps maroon us in—a present that is built of nothing but risk, dangers either of fraudulence or of trust—this vision may well seem uncomfortable. What Cavell is saying is that there is, however, no other way to the experience of art (or, now, of philosophy): we have no choice then but affirmation—can do no better than affirm that affirmation—within—and without—our history.

Chapter 2
A Context for Derrida

We begin then, once again, in and from the double bind constituted by and constitutive of Derrida's philosophic position.

The double bind, like so many of the terms by which one would describe Derrida's position, has itself come to work as a figure within it.[1] And as with most of Derrida's terms, what begins its life as the name of a concept ends, in his hands, differently—as a word or a trace or a gramme (more "concepts" that Derrida has retrieved from themselves, or destroyed). The double bind translates itself into French, miming its sound and its sense, as *"double bande"*—and so translated it unfolds a new complexity of sense, touching on sexuality (*bander* is slang for having an erection) and on wounding and healing (*bandage*) and on the reproduction of voice (*bande électromagnétique*). As it thus unfolds, it at once deepens and displaces the crisis it would appear to name; even the double bind in which a certain errance of sense places us is itself in errance, adrift— exiled from itself.

The double bind: when it is stretched to the limit, what threatens is cramp; it encorpsulates without containing [*se cadavérise à vide*] between two incompatible desires, condition of the possibility (and) impossibility of the erection. The game is thus paralyzed by the very indecidability that also opens its field.

But if this double bind is ineluctable (in me as idiom and/or outside of me), *there must be*—an entirely other *there must be*—somewhere, no last word. Without this it would arrest, paralyze, or petrify itself, immediately, I mean even before it stops itself, since, yes, it will arrest itself in any case. It must be that beyond the untiring contradiction of the double bind, an affirmative difference—innocent, intact, gay—succeeds in being absent without leave, escapes with a leap and laughingly signs that which it lets go, that which it makes and unmakes, *en double bande*.[2]

The second paragraph turns on its idioms:

Mais si cette double bande est inéluctable (en moi comme un idiome et/ou hors du moi), *il faut*, un *il faut* tout autre, que quelque part elle ne soit pas le dernier mot. Sans quoi ça s'arrêterait, se paralyserait, se méduserait, immédiatement, je veux dire avant même que ça s'arrête, car, n'est-ce pas, ça s'arrêtera de toute façon. Il faut que áu-delà de l'infatigable contradiction du *double bande*, une différence affirmative, innocente, intacte, gaie, en vienne *bien* à fausser compagnie, échappe d'un saut et vienne signer en riant ce qu'elle laisse faire et défiler en double bande.

The double bind in which we find ourselves is then as proper a frame as any for Derrida's writing—and as such demands both its violation and its preservation (this demand risks Hegel, then). Inside and outside, possibility and impossibility, will be its privileged *topoi*.

If it is indeed here that we are to find ourselves, then while we may be tempted to say that there is no way into Derrida's work (we may be particularly tempted to this if we see Derrida's work as a radicalism always threatened with domestication), we must say also that we are already within that work (and saying this will perhaps register our sense that Derrida is writing about nothing other than the world). Subscribing to this double necessity, we encounter Derrida's texts not as objects of knowledge, but as moments both of acknowledgment and in need of acknowledgment. This I would suggest would be to grasp that "différence affirmative" which signs "en riant ce qu'elle laisse faire et défiler en double bande."

Stanley Cavell, continuing his meditation on the ''new significance of philosophical repudiation,'' has written:

Hegel, I am told, said that he was the last professor of philosophy. I think I know what he would have meant—that he was the last man to feel that he could speak evenly about every way in which the philosophical impulse has found expression, the last with the natural conviction that his own work was the living present of philosophy's history, able to take that history for granted. And that would mean that philosophy, as it has been known, is past. (*MWM*, p. xxiv)

Two features of the remark seem to merit special attention: (1) If the passage is to be granted its fullest force, "professor" must be understood not simply as a title or particular institutional position, but in its first and most active sense—"one who professes something . . . who openly declares his sentiments." The tension between these two senses shows something of the way in which, for both Cavell and Derrida, a problem about the profession of philosophy is also a problem about the philosophic profession . . . however one distributes the weight of these phrases. (2) Cavell's remark is cast in the subjunctive—as if he is giving us what Hegel would have meant if he could have meant it, although he could not. This, I take it, is a tacit recognition of the grammatical structure of modernism: had Hegel been able to mean what Cavell takes it he would have meant, then he—Hegel—would have been something other than the last professor of philosophy. Instead, and at best, Hegel could end only by finding himself, too late, to have already been the last professor:

> One word more about giving instruction as to what the world ought to be. Philosophy in any case always comes on the scene too late. As the thought of the world, it appears only when actuality is already there cut and dried after its process of formation has been completed. . . . When philosophy paints its grey in grey, then has a shape of life grown old. By philosophy's grey in grey it cannot be rejuvenated but only understood. The owl of Minerva spreads its wings only with the falling of the dusk.[3]

Rupture and redoubling: an "event" has already passed, invisibly, between Hegel and himself. The Hegelian project opens by promising to put an end to that night of philosophic confusion in which all cows are black; but it ends here, grey on grey, at dusk, with the night still to come.

Beginning here, with the last professor of philosophy, we find ourselves at once too near to and too far from Derrida, as if we have found ourselves, too quickly, outside the work of history. We might say that we have already made, "as some may be tempted now, an assured value of indecidability—which is to double-bind oneself to the point of paralysis or tetanus."[4] A certain double bind has in effect become a simple truth of philosophy, belonging to a certain apparently reflexive moment within philosophy, but not capable of placing philosophy itself in question. From this position one can no longer understand how it is necessary for philosophy that it place itself in question (how the fact that philosophy is one of its own normal topics is defining for it): we cannot now understand the imperative/promise of "un il faut tout autre."

We have seen that Cavell is inclined to attribute the emergence of philosophic modernism to Kant (while recognizing the ways in which Hegel may look to be a better candidate to some). It may be that what has to be said here is that Kant so philosophized that there could be no strong post-Kantian philosophy that did not begin by explicitly posing philosophy itself as a problem. That is, in making the position of the philosopher a part of his philosophic problem, Kant implicitly demanded that philosophy henceforth see itself as situated within a larger disciplinary context and as needing to give an account of that situation. It is this legacy that Hegel saw and claimed. The problem with our earlier attempt to grasp "the last professor of philosophy" is that it clove too closely to the initial Kantian matrix, problematizing only the position of the philosopher while continuing to assume the ability of philosophy as a discipline to master the difficulty (more or less) unproblematically. Within this frame a certain "double bind" appears as the "true" result of a moment of self-criticism in the same way that one understanding of self-criticism in the work of modernist painting can claim to find an (absorptive) "truth" of painting behind the extravagant outer garments of theatricality.

It is in Hegel that the connection between the position of the philosopher and the position of philosophy itself is explicitly developed. This takes the form of a phenomenology of spirit, a narrative articulation of the relation of the philosopher to philosophy, and so of philosophy to itself. The *Phenomenology of Spirit* will provide our primary context for Derrida.[5] The notion of a "context" for Derrida returns us again to the deconstructionist demon of "domestication." There is nothing I can do to insure that my contextualization is not a domestication; sooner or later, inevitably, it will be something of the sort. At the same time, it may be helpful to entertain the notion that contextualizing Derrida in terms of the Hegelian *Phenomenology* amounts to a description of the double bind within which Derridean philosophy finds itself— "between" the *Phenomenology*—and by which it finds itself torn. This context is a structure at once of appropriation and of shear.

Hegel: Realizing Philosophy

We can begin by setting the stage for Hegel. The first generation of philosophers following Kant tended to see their task as one of reassembling certain terms set too radically asunder in Kant's philosophy—self and world, subject and object, sense and understanding. What was needed and sought after was some *tertium quid* with which to reestablish the broken unity of experience. In practice, this third term ended either by reproducing within itself the split it was intended to breach or else by sliding off to one side or another of that split (becoming, as it were, a "bigger," "meta-" subject or object that simply subsumed all of Kant's distinctions). Philosophically considered these are weak efforts, too visibly in the service of certain desires and so forced to misread Kant's texts in very specific ways. In general, the essential tendency of these efforts can be described as an attempt to reinstall the Sublime of the *Critique of Judgment* at the heart of the *Critique of Pure Reason*; this pastiche has come to be a major influence in English and American literary theory, arising first in Fichte, then in Novalis and the Schlegels in Germany, and passing through Coleridge and Carlyle in England.

The general impulse behind these various projects can be said to prefigure Hegel's dialectic of overcoming (*Aufhebung*), but his radically post-Kantian problematic emerges first of all from a critique of such attempts to find some unifying Absolute within the Kantian framework. This critique begins from the recognition that such attempts to reassert the unity of experience invariably finish in mere opposition to the articulation of experience:

> Dealing with something from the perspective of the Absolute consists merely in declaring that, although one has been speaking of it just now as something definite, yet in the Absolute, the A = A, there is nothing of the kind, for there all is one. To pit this single insight, that in the Absolute everything is the same, against the full body of artic- ulated cognition, which at least seeks and demands such fulfillment, to palm off its Absolute as the night in which, as the saying goes, all cows are black—this is cognition naively reduced to vacuity. (*PG* 16)

It is on this basis that Hegel is able to turn in a different direction and to begin from an explicit acknowledgment of the problem of positionality. This acknowledgment demands in its turn a critique of those elements in Kant that would still deny the priority of such a problematic.

The picture Hegel sets out to break down in the "Introduction" to the *Phenomenology of Spirit* may be put as follows: philosophy aims at "the actual knowledge of what truly is"; to gain this knowledge philosophy must—before it undertakes its proper business with "what truly is"—ensure that its way of knowing is indeed legitimate and reliable. The picture advances a distinction between the preliminary critique of the epistemological "tool" and the more authentically philosophical use of that tool.

It is of course true that what matters to us in Kant (and what we insist on referring to as his philosophy) is nothing more or other than the mere and preliminary critique. To the extent that Kant recognizes a certain doubling of philosophy and what is (would be) preliminary to it, we can, with Cavell and Greenberg, attribute to Kant the foundations of philosophic modernism. But to the extent that Kant continues to maintain this distinction between "philosophy proper" and something prior to it, less "real" but nonetheless necessary, we are more inclined to locate these foundations elsewhere, in a structure we can call the post-Kantian.

The effect of this distinction is to reduce our temptation to pose modernism through a certain rhetoric of purity; the relocation of modernism within the "post-Kantian" shifts the burden off "purity" and toward "integrity," or away from questions of scientific knowledge and toward those of disciplined and disciplinary activity.

In the instrumental picture of knowing that Hegel finds at work in Kant, *we* are *here*; it is *there*; some tool or medium must bridge the gap between; and we must be sure of that tool or medium first of all—or else ''we might grasp clouds of error instead of the heaven of truth'' (*PG* 73). Our basic impulse here is to protect ourselves against skeptical attacks on our unbridled speculation. Such an impulse dovetails easily with Greenberg's reading of the Kantian project as an attempt to reentrench philosophy within its (purer) self. Within this picture, if we know what our tool does to what it grasps or if we know how the intervening medium refracts it, we should be able to correct for the truth of the object,

> for this would enable us to eliminate from the representation of the
> Absolute which we have gained through it whatever is due to the
> instrument, and thus get the truth in its purity. But this "improvement"
> would in fact only bring us back to where we were before. If we
> remove from a reshaped thing what the instrument has done to it, then
> the thing—here the Absolute—becomes for us exactly what it was
> before this [accordingly] superfluous effort. On the other hand, if the
> Absolute is supposed merely to be brought nearer to us through this
> instrument, without anything in it being altered, like a bird caught by a
> lime-twig, it would surely laugh our little ruse to scorn, if it were not
> with us, in and for itself, all along and of its own volition. (*PG* 73)

For Kant, philosophy seems a terribly difficult enterprise, hedged about with dangers and traps for the unwary. Best first build up a stronghold one can count on ("entrench it more firmly in its area of competence") and then make forays therefrom. Hegel, in contrast, assumes that the world lies before him for the taking; philosophy is there, obvious, waiting. There is work to be done.

> If the fear of falling into error sets up a mistrust of Science, which in
> the absence of such scruples gets on with the work itself, and actually
> cognizes something, it is hard to see why we should not turn round
> and mistrust this very mistrust. Should we not be concerned as to
> whether this fear of error is not just the error itself? (*PG* 74)

This is not to say that there are no problems involved in doing philosophy or that the philosopher does not (cannot) make mistakes. It simply says that philosophy is done by doing and not by preparing, that if one devotes all one's effort to laying out the conditions of possibility for philosophy either one will never get to its actuality or one will end by finding that one is in fact already doing philosophy and the preliminary effort was therefore unnecessary from the outset.

These Hegelian formulations can be see to point at once toward Wittgenstein's appeal to ''what we ordinarily say when . . . '' and toward Heidegger's complex meditation on our distance from and proximity to the world and Being. Each undertakes a complication and closer grasp of what lies before us; each can lay a claim to being (or trying to be) profoundly "realistic"—committed to what is *there*, "the actual knowledge of what truly is." This is, as we shall see in chapter 3, a commitment shared by Derrida.

These concerns with obviousness, with our proximity to and distance from the world, are intimately entangled with questions about beginnings and especially about the beginning of philosophy, the way in which one—you or I or he or she—comes to philosophy. As we shall see shortly, this is, for Hegel, the demand for a phenomenology; in Heidegger, it is the problem of *Dasein*—human being as it is always already caught up in ontology, tied to Being; in Cavell, it is the question of audience. In Derrida such questions are posed, among other ways, through his involvement with GREPH (Le Groupe de Recherches sur l'Enseignement Philosophique, an organization founded by Derrida and others to examine the place and value of the teaching of philosophy in the wake of the Haby reforms) as questions about the ways in which the writing and teaching of philosophy are political practices. "We" too are everywhere entangled with these questions of distance and proximity, of beginning, already deeply within the Derridean problematic and still outside it, laying out a context for it. This is one way to point toward certain problems of style, organization, and argument that press everywhere in upon the present work: "we"—reader and writer—stand neither simply inside nor simply outside the matter under discussion and can lay no claim to a naive and privileged viewpoint on it; this is both a point to be argued in and an inevitable assumption of the work.

Finally, we should remark that the Hegelian critique of Kant displays Cavell's new mode of repudiation. Insofar as it undercuts the distinction between that which is preliminary to philosophy and that which is more properly philosophical, it does not reject but recovers Kant's writings for philosophy—and does so in a way that implicitly locates the Hegelian project as simply an explicit repetition of what works only implicitly in Kant. "Repudiation" and "acknowledgment" here become very close, as close as the rupture and redoubling that are the relation between Hegel and Kant.

Hegel's basic point can be put another way. The task of the philosopher is not to build a fort the skeptic cannot storm; instead, it is not only to admit the skeptic and recognize that he too belongs to an enterprise already under way, but even to take on for itself this skepticism in its most radical form.[6] For Hegel, the abstract insistence on Nothingness betrays the same fear of truth that animates the Kantian fear of error (so that the critique of Kant here is also a critique of skepticism). If knowledge is to be nothing, it will become so only through negation in detail and not through some one-sided and blanket denial.

This is just the scepticism which only ever sees pure nothingness in its result and abstracts from the fact that this nothingness is specifically the nothingness of that *from which it results*. For it is only when it is taken as the result of that from which it emerges, that it is, in fact, the true result; in that case it is itself a *determinate* nothingness, one which has a *content*. The scepticism that ends up with the bare abstraction of nothingness or emptiness cannot get any further from there, but must wait to see whether something new comes along and what it is, in order to throw it too into the same empty abyss. But when, on the other hand, the result is conceived as it is in truth, namely as a *determinate* negation, a new form has thereby immediately arisen, and in the negation the transition is made through which the progress through the complete series of forms comes about of itself. (*PG* 79)

For Hegel, philosophy—Science—is simply there, has already appeared on the scene. Pushing this presence aside in a rush to strengthen its foundations and pushing it aside through abstract negation betray the same fear of truth and fore-close equally on the development of that Science. This development is one that arises through determinate negation, a radical skepticism in detail. It is a progress through a "series of forms" that are generated out of their critiques of themselves—so that the path of philosophy lies through the appearance of Science, with all its errors.

It can be regarded as the path of the natural consciousness which presses forward to true knowledge; or as the way of the Soul which journeys through the series of its own configurations as though they were the stations appointed for it by its own nature, so that it may purify itself for the life of the Spirit, and achieve finally, through a completed experience of itself, the awareness of what it really is in itself.

Natural consciousness will show itself to be only the Notion of knowledge, or in other words, not to be real knowledge. But since it directly takes itself to be real knowledge, this path has negative sig-nificance for it, and what is in fact the realization of the Notion counts for it rather as the loss of its own self; for it does lose its truth on this path. The road can therefore be regarded as the pathway of *doubt*, or more precisely, as the way of despair. (*PG* 77-78)

The notion of science belonging to natural consciousness is, indeed, the Notion of Science—but, at the outset, nothing more. It is the appearance of Science, but it is also the *mere* appearance of Science, not yet adequate to itself nor able to understand itself: "It is not yet science in its fully realized and propagated truth simply by virtue of making its appearance." It will become fully articulated and unfolded Science only through radical criticism of every determinate position it takes up. Because such criticism insists in each instance on the determinacy of its negation, the process of criticism itself will generate new content, new positions of consciousness. And these will themselves be subject to renewed criticism, determinate negations set up by the very criteria that each shape of consciousness proposes for itself.[7]

The overall Hegelian scheme—whether in the *Phenomenology*, the *Logic*, or the *Encyclopedia*—always has the same form: one begins from the Notion and submits it to its own immanent critique of itself, allowing this critique to unfold through its entire chain of transformations until the Notion shows itself finally to be adequate to itself and so puts an end to its configurations. The imagery of the *via dolorosa* points toward the theological underpinnings of the project, its redemptive and puritan tendencies. The *Phenomenology* is, as M. H. Abrams has quite properly pointed out, a secular theodicy in which every truth the Notion loses along the way is recovered in the final accounting.[8]

The logic of the Hegelian enterprise is ultimately governed by the tautology "the Notion is adequate to itself," but this tautology is separated from itself by the course of the *Phenomenology*. It becomes the frame of the narrative by assuming a certain delay as proper to what it wants to say—so that it might be rewritten "the Notion (is) adequate to itself."

This "delay" becomes more directly visible if we look at what it means to begin from the fact that philosophy is already on the scene. The statement entails the recognition that when one sits down to do philosophy one is taking up a place in the history of an activity; the (Cartesian) impulse to start from scratch is entirely foreign to Hegel. The impulse to philosophy is inseparable from the developed history of that impulse. The Hegelian course is predicated on the simple fact of philosophy, which is also the fact of a history of philosophy and of a succession of philosophic systems (which are therefore not simply wrong, not to be repudiated *that way*). This course is thus necessarily an interpretation of the history in which it finds itself as a part of the process through which the germinal Notion comes to be adequate to its developed Idea. As the *Encyclopedia* has it,

> the History of Philosophy gives us the same process from an historical
> and external point of view. The stages in the evolution of the Idea
> seem to follow each other by accident, and to present merely a
> number of different and unconnected principles which the several
> systems of philosophy carry out in their own way. But it is not so.
> For these thousands of years the same Architect has directed the work;
> and that Architect is the one living Mind whose nature is to think, to
> bring to self-consciousness what it is, and with its being thus set as
> object before it, to be at the same time raised above it, and so to

reach a higher stage of its own being. The different systems which the history of philosophy presents are therefore not irreconcilable with unity. We may either say that it is one philosophy at different stages of maturity; or that the particular principle which is the ground work of each system is but a branch of one and the same universe of thought.[9]

The double view Hegel takes on the history of philosophy as system and as development knits history and discipline into a single fabric, so that whatever may be said of one may be said of the other as well. It is this melding of history and discipline that gives rise to what post-Hegelian thought conceives of as "the tradition"—the body of work in which this coincidence is realized and becomes recognizable. This is, of course, a rather vague description and is so necessarily. One of the continuing concerns of this chapter and those that follow will be with this necessity and its consequences. It should be clear that this coincidence of history and discipline is visible only from one particular, privileged point; it is one of the distressingly obvious features of Hegel's view here that, since Hegel is capable of articulating this history as the adequation of the Notion to (itself as) Idea, history in fact ends with Hegel. There are, of course, various qualifications attached to this claim; the tendency among commentators on Hegel has been to grab hold of these qualifications and show that the claim doesn't mean exactly what it seems to mean. But in crucial ways it does mean exactly what it seems to mean. It is a strong and consequential claim with which one must come to grips sooner or later. It is the preliminary determinant of whatever it might mean to do "post-Hegelian philosophy" and it determines this activity as, in the first instance, impossible. It is this claim and its consequences that we will be exploring in Heidegger, Lacan, and Bataille. In this section I want only to lay out its most general form.

Truth in philosophy is traditionally defined as some form of *adequatio intellectui ad rem*—an adequation of thought to its object. A true statement is one that "matches" the thing it is about. In Hegel the initial push for the dialectic arises from an untruth, the inadequacy of the Notion to itself, to its Idea. The end of history is the concrete realization of truth and the adequation of the Idea to itself. This all works within the traditional mold. But it also conceals within itself a radically historicized notion of truth, a sense that is dependent on time and system. Because history itself is now scaffolded by the propositional form, it is possible to say that such-and-such an event is true—"The Roman Empire is true"; "Napoleon—the world spirit on horseback—is true" (or, as one might later be tempted to say within a more Heideggerean frame, "The National Socialist state is a mittence of Being"). The propositional form of truth has not been dropped, but it has been displaced into the whole of the historical and systematic process: history as process and proposition is true and so, equally, are its parts. Epistemology and theodicy crisscross in a narrative of philosophical redemption; the Absolute Idea extends its grace to all life and thought:

> In the course of its process the Idea creates that illusion, by setting an antithesis to confront it; and its action consists in getting rid of the illusion which it has created. Only out of this error does the truth arise. In this fact lies the reconciliation with error and with finitude. Error or other-being, when superseded, is still a necessary dynamic element of truth; for truth can only be where it makes itself its own result. (*EL* 212 *Zusatz*)

In such a passage one sees how far the concrete operations of the Hegelian dialectic are from the traditional picture of truth. The *adequatio* remains minimally, but necessarily, present in the relation of the Idea to itself (a relation that is of course refracted within every shape of consciousness and serves as the ground for that shape's dialectical overcoming of itself), but "truth" now lies essentially in the dialectical moments of surpassing and "error" in those of opposition and alterity. The whole of this process is also "true"—so that error ends by belonging to truth as, so to speak, its condition of visibility.

The sense of truth at work here, emerging within Hegel's writing, is one that pulls away from propositional adequacy and inclines to ground itself instead in the objectivity of the enterprise itself. "Objectivity" here is obviously somewhat special, disciplinary rather than scientific or epistemological, closer perhaps to Aristotle than to Descartes. Within the encircling propositional frame, Hegel seems to be working with a meaning of truth that might be described as the Notion in its articulation—what is true is what belongs to this articulation, and as such is not something that can be partitioned wholly off from error, since error is also a part of what belongs to this articulation, this sort of objectivity.[10] This sense of truth as the Notion-in-articulation ultimately undermines the propositional frame itself. I pointed to this in my suggestion that the fundamental tautology might be rewritten as "the Notion (is) adequate to itself."

> What has been really made explicit is the oneness of subject and predicate, as the notion itself, filling up the empty 'is' of the copula. While its constituent elements are, at the same time, distinguished as subject and predicate, the notion is put as their unity, as the connection which serves to intermediate them: in short: as the Syllogism. (*EL* 180)

With this the proposition is caught up in a radically reflexive scansion of itself; the logical syllogism is no longer a simple chaining of subjects and predicates, but a complex system through which subjects and predicates are distributed and positioned with respect to one another. The whole of the dialectical movement of the *Encyclopedia* is the Absolute Syllogism:

Nature, the totality immediately before us, unfolds itself into the two extremes of the Logical Idea and Mind. But Mind is only Mind when mediated through Nature. Then, in the second place, Mind, which we know as the principle of individuality, or as the actualizing principle, is the mean; and Nature and the Logical Idea are the extremes. It is mind which cognises the Logical Idea in Nature and thus raises Nature to its essence. In the third place, again, the Logical Idea itself becomes the mean; it is the absolute substance both of Mind and of Nature, the universal and all pervading principle. These are the members of the Absolute Syllogism. (*EL* 187 *Zusatz*)

I have claimed that Hegel's philosophy is built around a problematic of positionality; at this level his claim is, in effect, that all positions in their possible relations to one another can be fully mapped out. The resultant whole is transparent despite the opacities found at any particular position. We can know this because the whole has been laid out. Metaphysics has ended in Hegel.

Philosophy has realized itself and is no longer merely possible; philosophy has realized itself and as such is now impossible. "Post-Hegelian philosophy" can only be an oxymoron (unless, of course, one finds Hegel simply irrelevant—a gorgeous excess of speculation of no philosophic consequence. But then one will not find "post-Hegelian" an interesting or sensible description of a philosophic position at all). If there should nonetheless emerge something that must be described through this phrase, its mere existence will force—or testify to—a radical shearing within the tight structure of history, truth, and discipline that welds Hegel's philosophy to itself. "Post-Hegelian philosophy," simply by naming itself, lays waste the propositional frame on which the Hegelian whole depends, and can find itself only by carrying the problematic of positionality— first set in place as a question about the philosopher by Kant, and then radicalized as a question about the relation of philosophy to itself in Hegel—deeper into the central core of philosophy, perhaps into its very notion of truth (as in Heidegger) and perhaps beyond that into the merest fact of its textual embodiment (as in Derrida).

After Hegel (I): The Disposition of Philosophy

The general shape of the Hegelian legacy is clear enough in advance. The post-Hegelian prosecution of philosophy will be committed to assuming its errors as a condition of its pursuit of truth and will have to do so apart from any promise of redemption of those errors in the closed totality of history and system. It will, that is, be increasingly inclined to pose itself not in terms of a claim to knowledge, but in terms of a certain art of display, a bringing of the world to light—and that light will be understood to imply a necessary and concomitant shadow or system of shadows, unable to attain either to a state of pure and sourceless light or to the security of a system of self-canceling and self-fulfilling crosslightings. It will be committed to seeing this display as crucially bound to time and to the stuff of history, but it will not see history as any kind of guarantee—of sense, of philosophy, of human being—and indeed will increasingly come to see in history and its claims over sense a certain suppression of what is necessary to philosophy. History more and more will seem the arena in which philosophy is removed from itself and from which it must be recovered.

Hegel is the philosopher of the philosophic tradition; in his writing that tradition is closed and fulfilled, consummated. But this very act is also constitutive of that tradition, making it visible as such and so open to what will necessarily appear as its "outside." Hegel creates what will be named the "metaphysical enclosure" (Heidegger) and the "logocentric closure" (Derrida)—to philosophize after Hegel is to do so from somewhere else, somewhere from which that enclosure is in view.

This picture—of philosophy as engaged, against itself and its tradition, in rediscovering a deeper and more deeply temporal play of truth and error, light and shadow—can serve as a first shape of Heidegger's philosophy. But it is important to see that this more or less properly philosophic project is not the whole of Hegel's legacy. The movement that pushes history to its limits also pushes philosophy as an objective discipline to its limits; and what would be post-Hegelian finds those limits, that discipline, already violated. Hegel's legacy will not be realized simply within the terms of philosophy, however radical and revisionary. In the following pages we will be as interested in Hegel's "extra-philosophical" legacy in the psychoanalysis of Jacques Lacan and the exuberant indiscipline of Georges Bataille's writings as in Heidegger's philosophic appropriation of Hegel.

There is a further difficulty for us that needs airing here as we try to trace the shape of a Hegelian legacy. It is above all Hegel who shows what it means to take history as a vehicle of sense and a means of understanding. Hegel's writings invent and justify a vision of intellectual history that is vastly persuasive—a history in which thoughts engage one another, often in extraordinarily complex ways, and so offer up problems and solutions and developments tightly integrated into a single, forward-looking, and moving narrative. We cannot avoid assuming some such picture here—even as the figures we will be exploring are all set more or less radically against it. One way of putting this would be to suggest that Hegel's *Phenomenology* can legitimately and powerfully serve as a context for Derrida only to the extent that it does so precisely as a text and not, finally, as a movement of Spirit or being or history. The shape of the field in which we move now obliges us to believe in the effectiveness of texts *as texts*—not as philosophies or worldviews or systems of thought. The historical situating of Derrida becomes almost a species of textual commentary; we will see just how close deconstruction is willing to push these two things when we turn to Derrida's attempt to address the question of a "Freudian legacy" in the next chapter.

In the following pages we are going to be interested in a very few passages from the *Phenomenology* insofar as they are the sites within which certain aspects of (Heidegger's and Bataille's and Lacan's) post-Hegelianism might be said to be inscribed—passages from the preface, introduction, and the chapter called "Independence and Dependence of Self-Consciousness: Lordship and Bondage," which is a crucial early step in the production of the *Phenomenology*'s subject-object as a consciousness and a self-consciousness. We will, in effect, be tracing the "shear structure" of Hegel's crystal, looking to see on what faces it cleaves when struck with the fact of time and the prefix "post-".

A few words may be in order here about the mere facts of the matter. Hegel had no early and enduring impact in France, and indeed his work remained largely untranslated until the middle of this century. Raymond Queneau, in an article on Bataille's lifelong intrigue with Hegel, picks out an emblematic cluster of events around 1930:

> Jean Wahl published *La Conscience malheureuse dans la philosophie de Hegel* [The unhappy consciousness in Hegel's philosophy] (1929); Gurvitch, *Les Tendances actuelles de la philosophie allemande* [Current tendencies of German philosophy] (1930); Levinas, *La Théorie de l'intuition dans la phénoménologie de Husserl* [The theory of intuition in Husserl's phenomenology] (1930). Heidegger appeared in *Bifur* in 1931, and Husserl's *Cartesian Meditations* were published in French the same year—which was also the centenary of Hegel's death.[11]

Two years later, Alexandre Kojève arrived in Paris and began a series of seminars on Hegel that lasted for most of the decade. The twenty years from 1930 to 1950—that is, roughly the years between Lacan's dissertation and his groundbreaking "Discours de Rome," (Discourse of Rome) or between Bataille's first draft of an economic theory, "La Notion de dépense" (The notion of expenditure), and its most developed statement, *La Part maudite* (The condemned portion), or between Kojève's arrival and the emergence of Jean Hyppolite's magisterial commentary on Hegel, *Genesis and Structure of the Phenomenology of Spirit*—are a period of intense absorption in Hegel. This is an absorption at once burdened and enabled by the entanglement of Hegel's phenomenology with Husserl's, and of Husserl's phenomenology with Heidegger's existential thought. Much of what is most deeply compelling and problematic in contemporary French thought is rooted in the work and ferment of this period.

It is perhaps of special interest that Hegel and Heidegger should have appeared in France so tightly bound together, because Heidegger's thought is overwhelmingly oriented to Kant. Heidegger's two translated works on Hegel share a certain tentativeness and a sense of a distance in need of bridging quite alien to his work on Kant. ("The Ontotheological Constitution of Metaphysics" offers itself as "an attempt to begin a conversation with *Hegel*," while *Hegel's Concept of Experience* is explicitly written as a dialogue between Heidegger and Hegel's introduction to the *Phenomenology* with the apparent object of understanding nothing more than the book's title.[12] It is not accidental that Heidegger selects precisely that text in which Hegel is most concerned with establishing his distance from and relation to Kant.)

I have suggested that the Hegelian tautology "the Notion is adequate to itself" ought to be read as if the copula were set in parentheses, as an emptiness to be filled with the unity of the Notion, and I have suggested that the bare thought of a "post-Hegelian philosophy" is enough to lay waste this frame. From the bare post-Hegelian position, everything that is packed into the tautology, into the Notion, can appear as a forgetting or suppression of the "is" at its heart. The tradition, one might say, can come to itself, articulate itself, only through a certain forgetting of what it is for something to *be*, to ("actively," as it were) *is*. From here the tradition can and must be thought as essentially the "forgetting of Being" and even (in a phrase reminiscent of Heidegger that reverses the volitional rhetoric of the Hegelian Notion) "the self-forgottenness of Being."

In some ways, Heidegger's response to and repudiation of Hegel seems simple enough. It amounts to the assertion that Hegel fastened on to the wrong object—"the actual knowledge of what truly is"—and that Heidegger has now gotten hold of the right one—the "is-ing" of what is, the question of Being. But this is, of course, continuous with Hegel's repudiation of Kant: it repeats the claim that the precursor has gotten himself into trouble by letting epistemological worries take precedence over the truer and (in some sense) more obvious business of thinking. The work of philosophy—the philosophic work—has ended by displacing, losing, or forgetting the experience on which it is—must be—founded. Heidegger's small book *Hegel's Concept of Experience* holds itself precisely in the ambivalent play between conceptuality and experience, offering itself finally as a meditation on the appearance and eventual disappearance of the word "experience" in Hegel's titles and subtitles for the work. The general program behind this "dialogue" with Hegel's thought and experience is laid down in Heidegger's first major work, *Being and Time*:

> Tradition takes what has come down to us and delivers it over to self-evidence: it blocks our access to those primordial "sources" from which the categories and concepts handed down to us have been in part quite genuinely drawn. . . .

If the question of Being is to have its own history made transparent, then this hardened tradition must be loosened up, and the concealment which it has brought about must be dissolved. We understand this task as one in which by taking *the question of Being as our clue*, we are to destroy the traditional content of ancient ontology until we arrive at those primordial experiences in which we achieved our first ways of determining the nature of Being—the ways which have guided us ever since.[13]

Even as Heidegger repeats the Hegelian repudiation of Kant and even as he repeats and radicalizes in his central figures the rhetoric of that repudiation, making the proximity of Being even more deeply internal and intimate than Hegel's Absolute laughing at the lime-twig lure and doubling Hegel's road to the Absolute with his own woodland trails, half-covered over, leading nowhere and so not walked in view of any goal[14]—even as, then, Heidegger's work repeats and is worked in response to Hegel's, it can do so only by returning to Kant and renewing in Kant the question of the conditions of possibility of any experience whatsoever. But for Heidegger these conditions will be, in the end, ontological—terms of our relation to Being—and not epistemological. Heidegger takes as the charter for his engagement with Kant the first *Critique*'s "Highest Principle of All Synthetic Judgments":

We then assert that the conditions of the *possibility of experience* in general are likewise conditions of the *possibility of the objects of experience*, and that for this reason they have objective validity in a synthetic a priori judgment.[15]

Being and Time begins, in effect, by offering a rewriting of Kant's principle of reason as a fundamental statement about the ontological implications of human existence:

Understanding of Being is itself a definite characteristic of Dasein's Being. Dasein is ontically distinctive in that it *is* ontological. (*BT*, p. 32)

Dasein—"existence, life, being" according to the dictionary and built from *da*, "here" or "there," and *sein*, "to be"—is Heidegger's word for human being. Human being is unique among beings because it exists, essentially, in relation to Being. *Da-sein* shows in its very construction the internality of that relation, and so has that relation as an essential question put in and through— finally *as*—the structure of its experience.

The very fact that we already live in an understanding of Being and that the meaning of Being is still veiled in darkness proves that it is necessary in principle to raise this question again. (*BT*, p. 23)

Kant's text is an exemplary instance of a life lived within an understanding of Being and in which that understanding is nonetheless veiled. Heidegger, moving through the sclerotic articulations of Kant's text toward their primordial source in the (ontological) experience of Kant, locates himself in an implicitly romantic—post-Kantian and pre-Hegelian—position and takes up again the search for some sort of *tertium quid*. And when this search has run its course, it will have to face Hegel's critique of philosophic romanticism:

> Dealing with something from the perspective of the Absolute (for which we may now read "Being") consists merely in declaring that, although one has been speaking of it just now as something definite, yet in the Absolute, the A = A, there is nothing of the kind, for there all is one. To pit this single insight, that in the Absolute everything is the same, against the full body of articulated cognition, which at least seeks and demands such fulfillment, is to palm off its Absolute as the night in which, as the saying goes, all cows are black—this is cognition naively reduced to vacuity. The formalism which recent philosophy denounces and despises, only to see it reappear in its midst, will not vanish from Science, however much its inadequacy may be recognized and felt, till the cognizing of absolute actuality has become entirely clear as to its own nature. (*PG* 16)

This then will be our itinerary, leading from an examination of Heidegger's attempt to recover the experience of the conditions of possibility of experience from Kant's analysis thereof to a confrontation with the complex condition of Hegel's legacy of sheared identity and tautology.

The knowing subject of the first *Critique* appears dual. On one side it is open through sensory intuition to the things of the (more or less) external world; on the other side it appropriates these sensory intuitions to a network of categories of the understanding. A manifold of appearances thus impinges on a passive sensibility and is appropriated under the unity of the self and its categories of understanding. It is these two poles of sensory multiplicity and imposed unity of understanding that post-Kantian thought finds to be too deeply sundered from one another, whether as phenomenon and noumenon (so that Kant was felt to reinflict rather than overcome a radical skepticism) or as sensory intuition and categorial understanding. The early attempts to reestablish the unity of experience across its apparent dismemberment had—"naturally"—inclined to find that unity in the structure of self and understanding, since these clearly represented the unifying pole within the system. The sought-after Absolute tended to take the form of a Transcendental Ego. Heidegger's cross-grained emphasis on the priority of Being gives the lead to the passivity of the intuition and so discovers a new site for the problem.

In Kant, it is the faculty of the imagination that mediates between sensible intuition and the categories of the understanding (as it is the imagination that mediates everywhere in Kant, among the critiques as well as within them). Heidegger's investigation of the ontological ground of the analysis of the first *Critique* is an investigation into the nature of an imagination capable of performing such mediation. Sensibility and understanding are opposed as temporal to atemporal, passive to active, and manifold to unitary; and it is the imagination that offers the possibility of passing from each of these terms to the other.

But pure concepts of the understanding being quite heterogeneous from empirical intuitions, and indeed from all sensible intuitions, can never be met with in any intuition. For no one will say that a category such as that of causality can be intuited through sense and is itself contained in appearance. How, then, is the *subsumption* of intuitions under pure concepts, the *application* of a category to appearances possible? . . .

Obviously, there must be some third thing, which is homogeneous on the one hand with the category, and on the other hand with the appearance, and which thus makes the application of the former to the latter possible. This mediating representation must be pure, that is, void of all empirical content, and yet at the same time, while it must in one respect be *intellectual*, it must be in another sensible. Such a representation is a transcendental schema.[16]

This "transcendental schema" is not a concept and yet is something more than an image; it is something like a method for producing images in accordance with a concept, a rule-generating function.

At its simplest level, the schematism is that whereby we are able to recognize this particular mass of inert and rumbling fur as belonging under the concept "cat," this instance of an apple as belonging under the concept "apple" or the concept "fruit," or these five apples as subsumable under the concept "five." But in the layering of Kantian analysis, this function accomplishes larger work. The transcendental synthesis of the imagination is the most abstract repetition of the operation of the schematism, appropriating the formal manifold of sensibility in general to the understanding in general. It binds the pure form of intuition—time—to the atemporal unity of the self and so establishes what Kant describes as the transcendental and synthetic unity of apperception, the place in general in which experience can occur, the mutual presence of subject and world. A Heideggerean might speak of this as the "worlding of the world"—the coming to be of that horizon within and against which anything that is appears.

What is the imagination that it can accomplish such world-creating mediation? It is, in the first instance, a temporalization of the categories of the understanding; indeed, at the most abstract level this is the only meaning we can give the notion. The schematizing imagination works as a "determination of time."[17] For Kant the imagination, beyond this, is "an art concealed in the depths of the human soul, whose real modes of activity nature is hardly likely ever to allow us to discover, and to have open to our gaze.'' Further Kantian description of the imagination involves nothing more than reference to and adaptation of the table of categories in terms of temporal determinations.

But for Heidegger, the real question has only just been broached. The crucial task is to push on through this notion of the schematism to what it both reveals and conceals: the objectivity of the object ("the worlding of the world") and the subjectivity of the subject ("the depths of the human soul").

If the imagination is able to generate determinations of time, if it is able to mediate between the flow of outer events and appearances and the inner stasis of the understanding, then (this is Heidegger's thought) it must be temporal in a sense more radical than is presented by the apparent alternatives; it must be a "time forming" from which both sensibility and understanding can be grasped as derivative. Heidegger urges a conceptual Gestalt shift, so that the single term of the imagination comes into the foreground as a figure against the divided background of its polarization into a sensibility and an understanding. Instead of thinking of the imagination as something added to the Kantian analysis to bridge a gap within it (a *tertium quid*), Heidegger asks us to think of the emergence of the gap as itself an act of the imagination—which is always already a bridging of it. One is, I think, in the end forced to feel, to imagine, one's way into this new picture—to sense how it exerts a certain pressure on one's grammar—"always already," for example, is a recurrent Heideggerean phrase that is (or attempts to be) directly responsive to the notion of temporality involved here. This is a notion that inclines one to speak of expression and recognition rather than knowledge; the shape of time is such that we find ourselves always already within it—"thrown" or "protended" by it. Time is not the simple and empty frame within which we are, as it were, free to understand; our understanding itself derives from a time in which we are (always, already)—it is penetrated with temporality, and its business with the world can begin only in acknowledgment of this.

Temporality, Heidegger argues, is the horizon of Being. Time—deep, originary time—is that by which beings unfold in their Being, the means of their presence. It is that by which we are worked, and it is as we let ourselves be so worked that we can begin to come to grips with the understanding of Being within which we live.

This "retrieve" of Kant, this attempt to show that beneath Kant's text there are visible the outlines of a deeper problem and presence of Being and its necessarily temporal horizon, is implicitly responsive to pressures imposed by Hegel. Hegel had, in effect, presented the apparently linear flow of historical time as ultimately closed on itself, come full circle in the adequation of the Idea to its Notion. Heidegger, as a philosopher, finds himself already thrown out of this charmed circle. And if he can so find himself, the circle must be other than simply closed against him—it must be cut or broken. The working of time is the working of this circle that cannot close itself, that can only turn through itself, bringing into light and casting into shadow, leading the world into articulation that falls always and necessarily short of totality.

This "temporality" is the way in which Being shows itself, revealing and concealing at once; it is according to the rhythm of this temporality that the *Critique of Pure Reason* belongs to the history of ontology and is subject to both an act of destruction and an act of retrieve. The *Critique* is, on this view, not a set of right or wrong statements about the world or even "the worlding of the world," but a site of and for the recognition of Being.

Implicit and inevitable in this picture is a tendency for temporality and language to press toward one another, becoming the joint medium through which Being is concealed and revealed. Together they spell out the structure of *Dasein* as the being that is ontically distinctive in being ontological, so that its (ontical) existence is everywhere caught up in the larger movement of Being as it gives itself through time and language. A number of Heidegger's more evocative (or cryptic) phrases cluster around the confluence of these various notions: time is "the horizon of Being"; man is "the shepherd of Being"; language is "the house of Being"; and so on. These phrases together point toward the essentially hermeneutic structure of human understanding—an understanding that is fundamentally determined as interpretive rather than knowing and is so determined by *Dasein*'s implication in a circuit that belongs, in the first instance, to Being and not to itself—"the there of Being." Proximity to Being will be registered by a submission to the "speaking of Being"—to the way in which Being gives itself to language and to *Dasein*. It is finally the language of poetry that alone is capable of being fully responsive to Being, of bringing it to light. The phrases cited above come to a point in the title (itself a citation from Hölderlin) of a late (1951) essay " . . . Poetically Man Dwells . . . "[18] The activity of philosophy, beside this primordial poetizing, is secondary, derivative, and conservative at best; it is the moment at which the revelation of Being becomes open to the "tradition" of *Being and Time*, liable to "hardening" or forgetting.

In *Being and Time*, Heidegger claimed to recover from or supplement Kant with "an ontological analytic of the subjectivity of the subject" (*BT*, p. 45). But this recovery of the subjectivity of the subject is accomplished precisely through a submission of the subject to the conditions of objectivity. The "subjectivity of the subject" is found to lie outside of or prior to the subject. Every subject must be said to emerge into an already constituted, already structured world. The fundamental structure of this world is given through the workings of the retrieved Kantian imagination, originary temporality. This temporality is a continual movement beyond and out of itself, a system of determinate possibilities emerging from the past and coming toward the present as the future. The past then is not a line of dead facts of fixed and ordered significance, but a continuing determination both of and from the present on the basis of the possibilities emerging from it through the future. There is no irruption of a subject into an empty space of time, which the subject would then proceed to fill, to act in and on. There is in Heidegger's work no "space" of time at all; his thought can be described as an attempt to think as cleanly as possible the sheer temporality of time—that which makes it something other than our spatializations of it allow.

"Facticity"—the fact of prior structuration, of the way in which the subject must find itself through a certain "always already" that betrays the eccentricity of the subjectivity of the subject—names a certain belatedness as fundamental to human being. It names also the belated position of the philosopher (elaborating the problematic of positionality handed down from Kant) with respect to both the activity of the poet and the philosophic tradition. It generates Heidegger's double project of destruction and retrieve that both is and is not a project of "demystification."

And here, of course, I am claiming Heidegger as a modernist philosopher—one for whom the relation of the present practice of an enterprise and the history of that enterprise has become problematic, one whose "own practice and ambition can," in Cavell's phrase, "be identified only against the continuous experience of the past."

A part of what this means is that there can always be a certain discomfort in calling Heidegger a philosopher at all. One will perhaps feel justified so long as it is clear that the history with which Heidegger is (problematically) engaged is the history we all understand to be "of philosophy." But this engagement is predicated on the notion that this history is precisely the forgetting of itself: the history of philosophy is the mask of thinking, other than the thought of Being. The question of Being is what is unthought "in" philosophy. Heidegger's development consists in a continual sharpening of the opposition between the thought of Being and the work of metaphysics, and so also in an ever more radical, and ever more generous, critique of the tradition—a critique, in particular, of what Heidegger comes to call the "onto-theo-logical constitution of metaphysics"—and it is under this title that Heidegger engages in his "attempt to begin a conversation with *Hegel*."

"The Onto-theo-logical Constitution of Metaphysics" is one of a pair of lectures given in 1957 and published under the joint title *Identity and Difference*. Its companion piece, "The Principle of Identity," is a meditation on the inner complexity of the assertion A = A. As often in Heidegger's later work, the primary reference for this text is pre-Socratic (in particular, Heidegger worries at the sense of *to auton*, "the Same," in Parmenides' "For thinking and Being are the same")—but it should be clear in advance that the two pieces are profoundly linked to one another as attempts to think within and without the tradition. The attempt to engage in conversation with Hegel about the constitution of metaphysics cannot but entail a meditation on the obscurity and lucidity of identity.

This attempt at conversation with Hegel has for its first topic the necessity of thinking about philosophy as conversation:

Hegel rigorously thinks about the matter of his thinking in the context of a conversation with the previous history of thinking. Hegel is the first thinker who can and must think in this way. Hegel's relation to the history of philosophy is the speculative, and only as such a historical, relation. (*ID*, p. 43)

This recognition of a problematic relation to the past common to both bodies of thought opens naturally enough into an attempt to make out the difference between the Hegelian and Heideggerean modes of conversation, and thus invites a summary description of the kind of relationship at work in, for example, Heidegger's reading of Kant:

For us, the criterion for the conversation with the historical tradition is the same [as it is for Hegel], insofar as it is a question of entering into the force of earlier thinking. We, however, do not seek that force in what has already been thought: we seek it in something that has not been thought, and from which what has been thought receives its essential space. . . . The criterion of what has not been thought does not lead to the inclusion of previous thought into a still higher development and systematization that surpass it. Rather, the criterion demands that traditional thinking be set free into its essential past which is still preserved. This essential past prevails throughout the tradition in an originary way, is always in being in advance of it, and yet is never expressly thought in its own right and as the Originary. (*ID*, pp. 48-49)

This formulation means to distinguish the Heideggerean stance from the totalizing onward roll of Hegelian dialectic—but its very statement—"set free . . . still preserved . . . "—brushes inevitably up against Hegel's language, and so Heidegger is led to further attempts to distinguish his movement—"the step back"—from Hegel's *Aufhebung* (and we will see Derrida try to undo this distinction, or to show it undoing itself, by pressing on the inevitable entwinement of negation and step within the French word *pas*).

The Hegelian sublation urges the recognition of an identity; the Heideggerean step back intends the recognition of a difference. Hegelian dialectic is the detailed display of beings in their multiplicity and as they sum themselves up into a whole, so that for Heidegger the logic of identity finally undergirding the Hegelian project serves to display, if we but step back and look, metaphysics as a problematic flattening out onto the level of mere beings of the deep question of Being. Metaphysics shows itself as onto-logy insofar as it is concerned with beings in their common multiplicity, and as theo-logy insofar as it is concerned with beings as a whole and in relation to a highest being, an Absolute.

The onto-theo-logical constitution of metaphysics is then, for all its compelling unity and totalizing power, a divided constitution, concealing and revealing a deeper difference and a deeper unity (as the imagination opens a deeper abyss within and so offers a deeper unity to the Kantian project):

> Because the thinking of metaphysics remains involved in the difference which as such is unthought, metaphysics is both ontology and theology in a unified way, by virtue of the unifying unity of perdurance.
>
> The onto-theological constitution of metaphysics stems from the prevalence of that difference which keeps Being as the ground, and beings as that which is grounded and what gives account, apart from and related to each other; and by this keeping, perdurance is achieved. (*ID*, p. 71)

The difference between onto-logy and theo-logy is a derivation of the prior unity of the ontological difference, and the apparent unity of the two in the constitution of metaphysics is the forgetting of that difference.

The pressure all of this imposes on Heidegger's language should be clear enough. It is a small step to his suspicion that "our Western languages are languages of metaphysical thinking, each in its own way" (*ID*, p. 73), and so to the accompanying fear that this language and its inherent complicity with metaphysics is always on the way to reappropriating or undoing the work achieved by the step back: "Everything that results by way of the step back may merely be exploited and absorbed by metaphysics in its own way, as the result of representational thinking" (*ID*, pp. 72-73). This fear is adequately, if partially, glossed as a fear that the integrity of the step back cannot be guaranteed in the face of the Hegelian *Aufhebung*. Heidegger can resist Hegel only so long as he can insist on the priority of difference over its schematization into the terms of a progressive dialectic, and much of his most difficult writing can be said to mean primarily by virtue of its resistance:

> While we are facing the difference, though by the step back we are already releasing it into that which gives thought, we can say: the Being of beings means Being which is beings. The "is" here speaks transitively, in transition. Being here becomes present in the manner of a transition to beings. But Being does not leave its own place and go over to beings, as though beings were first without Being and could be approached by Being subsequently. Being transits (that), comes unconcealingly over (that) which arrives as something of itself unconcealed only by that coming-over. Arrival means to keep concealed in unconcealedness—to abide present in this keeping—to be a being. . . .

Being in the sense of unconcealing overwhelming, and beings as such in the sense of arrival that keeps itself concealed, are present, and thus differentiated, by virtue of the Same, the differentiation. That differentiation alone grants and holds apart the "between," in which the overwhelming and the arrival are held toward one another, are borne away from and toward each other. . . .

In our attempt to think the difference as such, we do not make it disappear; rather, we follow it to its essential origin. (*ID*, pp. 64-65)

"Difference as such": this is what needs to be thought in the face of Hegel. To think difference as such is to recall philosophy—metaphysics—to its properly abyssal ground in the thinking of Being, in experience, in that place where our articulations find their origin.

But it is of course far from clear what it might be to think "difference as such." For Heidegger much of the obscurity of this task lies concealed in our inability to think identity as such. This is something we all tend to think we can do: A = A. But this, for Heidegger as for Hegel, fails to state what it claims to represent:

The formula A = A speaks of equality (between two things). It doesn't define A as the same. The common formulation of the principle of identity conceals precisely what the principle is trying to say: A is A, that is, every A is itself the same. (*ID*, p. 24)

Even this formulation doesn't satisfy Heidegger, and, pushing on it, he pushes once again on the limits of our language:

Does the principle of identity really say anything about the nature of identity? No, at least not directly. Rather, the principle already pre-supposes what identity means and where it belongs. How do we get any information about this presupposition? The principle of identity itself gives it to us, if we listen carefully to its key note, if we think about that key note instead of just thoughtlessly mouthing the formula "A is A." For the proposition really says: "A *is* A." What do we hear? With this "is," the principle tells us how every being is, namely: it itself is the same with itself. The principle of identity speaks of the Being of beings. As a law of thought, the principle is valid only insofar as it is a principle of Being that reads: To every being as such there belongs identity, the unity with itself. (*ID*, pp. 25-26)

Heidegger's reading of the principle of identity is a repetition in a minor key of his reading—destruction and retrieve—of Kant; Heidegger presses here through the "is" as he presses through the notion of the imagination in the first *Critique*. His reading also exemplifies the step back as opposed to the Hegelian

Aufhebung. Whereas Hegel in effect embraces and radicalizes the propositional frame in order that the speculative whole of the world may be subsumed within its own tautological totality, Heidegger refuses its apparent settlement of the question of identity in order to reach a prior moment in which a thing appropriates itself to itself and so becomes capable of figuring (and being forgotten) in such dry formulae as A = A. This step back would capture the radical fact of mediation and synthesis within identity itself prior to its schematization by the simultaneously onto- and theo-logical structure of metaphysics. This move seems at once pre- and post-Hegelian, attempting to register the fact of mediation in its Hegelian centrality, but attempting to do so by plunging precisely into the night of identity within which, for Hegel, "all cows are black."

"The Same" becomes in Heidegger the name for that difference by virtue of which identity comes to prevail within our language and our metaphysics. The recollection of the Same is then at war with the terms with which we would embody it; our task is accordingly always to move back toward the origin of those terms, toward their essential inward sense, the living kernel within the husk of tradition and received formulation, the seed:

> Our facing the difficulty that stems from language should keep us from hastily recasting the language of the thinking here attempted into the coin of terminology, and from speaking right away about perdurance instead of devoting all our efforts to thinking through what has been said. For what was said, was said in a seminar. A seminar, as the word implies, is a place and an opportunity to sow a seed here and there, a seed of thinking which some time or other may bloom in its own way and bring forth fruit. (*ID*, pp. 73-74)

I have quoted at length from *Identity and Difference*, because an awareness of Heidegger's language is at least as important to our purposes as an awareness of his "argument." On the one hand, we can recognize in Heidegger's stance toward the tradition the ground plan of the position Derrida will later take up— Derrida assumes, like Heidegger, a certain closure of the tradition in the wake of Hegel and finds his primary task—deconstruction—as a revision and perhaps radicalization of the operation Heidegger called variously "destruction," "retrieve," "appropriation," "a step back." But at the same time, Heidegger seems to offer the paradigmatic instance of the object of Derrida's critique—the thing called "phonocentrism," or "logocentrism," or "phallocentrism," and so on. The terms Heidegger deploys in his attempt to find a site for philosophy after Hegel are precisely the terms on which Derrida's critique fastens most powerfully and compulsively: "the Originary," "unconcealment," "arrival," "abiding," "presence," "the Same," "saying," "hearing," "appropriation," and even "seminar." At the same time, Derrida will valorize many of the terms of Heideggerean disparagement—"formulae," "coin of terminology"—and radically reconstrue still others in ways that outrace their apparent place in Heidegger's argument—recognizing a notion of metaphor at complex work in the assertion that "Being transits (that), comes unconcealing over (that) which arrives as something of itself unconcealed only by that coming-over," or insisting newly on the complexity of "that differentiation (that) alone grants and holds apart the 'between' " (*ID*, pp. 64, 65).

Derrida stands to Heidegger very much as Hegel stood to Fichte and Schelling, in a relation at once of rupture and repetition, continuity and critique. To be able to pose this relation as such—as Derrida implicitly does in his wary reference to "something . . . that could be called an 'event' " and his explicit awareness of the provisional and strategic nature of his deconstructive operations—is to advance into a thought of history that is not open to Heidegger. For Heidegger, history, no longer the unifying frame through which meaning and being are unfolded but simply a derived, sclerotic block to those things, is condemned to be merely that series of disguises beyond which—epochally, Heidegger says—Being episodically shows itself. No particular law of continuity or discontinuity links any one such "mittence" or "advent" of Being to any other. The field divides in two, becoming either wholly redeemed by its openness to Being or wholly empty through its suppression of Being; either a random set of disguises or a game that has been played out, its possibilities of movement are in any case exhausted. In the end, what is rational in history is empty; what counts is irrational: and the two aspects can only slide against one another without touching. It is this pure, contactless sliding that makes Heidegger finally, and radically, an irrationalist. We will see Derrida recognizing and reacting against this Heideggerean motif in Lacan as well.

It is in his fundamental inability to think history as such that Heidegger ends as something other than "post-Hegelian" (however responsive his work may be to Hegelian motifs). In a sense, Heidegger spells out what it is to philosophize after Hegel but remains unable to find that oblique slice through his precursor that would make visible a new site for philosophy. Even as he points to the closure of metaphysics in Hegel, he is continually led to drag out the last act of metaphysics, distinguishing (or attempting to distinguish) its closure in Hegel from its consummation in Nietzsche and both of these from the turn (*Kehre*) to come in his own thought—so many distinctions that simultaneously slur and suppress what ought to be problematic. This final inability to think the tradition as a problem leaves him unable to do more than reassert the ("deeper") autonomy of the philosophic enterprise, taming the very difference his thought discovers in order to hold it within the propriety of the Same, the mutual co-appurtenance of, for example, thinking and Being, saying and hearing, the intimacy of a conversation.

Living up to the Heideggerean demand to think "difference as such" will necessitate breaking with the assumed hegemony of the Same and with the

Heideggerean-Parmenidean belonging together of thinking and Being in originary and poetic speech. In the long run, a thought that would be of "difference as such" will have to break both with the claim to some sort of deep philosophic propriety and autonomy and with the oppositional drama that supports it—in this sense deconstruction both depends on a recognition of and works to acknowledge fully the ways in which Hegel's legacy is not—cannot be—confined to any seminar but is and must be more widely broadcast (this points toward the interest the text of Derrida's seminar on the Freudian legacy and its narration will have for us later on).

Derrida's project can be said to begin from Heidegger's. But we can also say that Derrida's experience of Heidegger is of a continuing and radical failure of the closure of metaphysics, so that Derrida begins in explicit contestation with that project and its insistence upon—rather than questioning of—the autonomy and identity of philosophy itself. As Derrida argues the necessity of a certain impropriety and impurity for philosophy, so the experience that forms and informs his practice of deconstruction is itself not solely philosophic. Of particular interest to us here, because of their explicit and central reference to things Hegelian, are the psychoanalysis of Jacques Lacan and the hyperbolically generalized theory of excess elaborated by Georges Bataille, and it is to them that we now turn.

After Hegel (II): Philosophy Beside Itself

We will appear here to be crossing a border, and a dialectically charged one at that, passing from some properly philosophical "inside" to an improper "outside" on the way to assembling them into some final Idea of Deconstruction adequate to the germinal Notion of the Hegelian Legacy. This appearance is inevitable and in that sense not simply false—it is the deep risk internal to deconstruction as well as to its presentation here. As we will see, deconstruction intends, in effect, a simulacrum of dialectic, disrupted at every point of its itinerary—it repeats and contests the risks of Heidegger's step back.

Deconstruction's (broken) dialectic can be said either to begin from a peculiarly problematic object or to found itself in no simply definable tradition. If we follow out the first statement we will find ourselves describing or justifying our work not in terms of adequacy to some given notion or Idea, but in terms of strategies, ways of getting at the thing in question. If we take up the second statement, we will find ourselves repudiating any attempt to fix the definition of "the tradition" or "the enclosure." The enclosure as such is visible only from the privileged position of a Hegel—a position infinitely extended in Heidegger's realism of the (forgottenness of Being everywhere beneath the) tradition. Derrida begins where, however necessary it may be to speak of a metaphysical enclosure as if one could somehow stand outside, we have no choice but to recognize our own belonging to that tradition and enclosure:

> The expression "long metaphysical sequence" well indicates that for me it was not a question of taking "metaphysics" as the homogeneous unity of an ensemble. I have never believed in the existence or consistency of something like metaphysics *itself*. . . . Keeping in account such and such a demonstrative sentence or such a contextual constraint, if I happened to say "metaphysics" or "the" closure of "metaphysics" . . . very often elsewhere . . . I have put forward the proposition according to which there would never be "metaphysics," "closure" not being here a circular limit bordering a homogeneous field but a more twisted structure which today, according to another figure, I would be tempted to call: "invaginated." Representation of a linear and circular closure surrounding a homogeneous space is, precisely, the theme of my greatest emphasis, an auto-representation of philosophy in its onto-encyclopedic logic.[19]

This figure of "double invagination" can serve to describe the relation between the two apparent sides of our broken dialectic—sides that are only "inner" and "outer" on, as it were, a local basis, for a certain duration and purpose, strategically.

Psychoanalysis figures repeatedly and variously in our accounts of the modern. It has been taken to represent the demystifying onslaught of modern science, a last outburst of poetry in a rationalized age, a way out from under the modern burdens of history and guilt, or the normalizing tool of contemporary capitalism; and all of these representations have opened out into a series of claims for or critiques of Freud's work to the point that one may well feel it both necessary and difficult to return psychoanalysis to itself, to Freud's text.

Jacques Lacan's writings, for all their obscurity, have for their announced goal simply this return to Freud, the restoration of psychoanalysis to its specific practice and discipline. In many ways this is an enterprise that could have arisen only in France: Sherry Turkle has done much to trace the way in which the long French resistance to psychotherapy in general and psychoanalysis in particular led to an explosive and highly theoretical interest in Freud at a time when the rest of the world assumed it had already understood and absorbed the psychoanalytic impulse. A central element in the French reception of Freud is its coincidence with the reception of Hegel. The coupling of Hegel and Freud in Lacan's writing is something new in the history of psychoanalysis (more orthodox philosophic references are to Kant or to Nietzsche) and is responsible for much of what seems most powerful in Lacan's attempt to restore psychoanalysis to visibility. It is responsible too for the overwhelming interest Derrida takes in psychoanalysis as, in Lacan's hands, it works the complex boundaries between philosophy and psychology.

For Lacan, the objectivity of psychoanalysis resides in its disciplined adherence to its object, the Unconscious revealed in the Freudian text. The impulse here is close to Hegel's in that it too turns away from preliminary and directly epistemological considerations in favor of an adherence to what already exists and is under way. Psychoanalysis so conceived can become something like a "science of the experience of the Unconscious" complementary to the Hegelian science of the experience of consciousness, and this suggests that it can, in significant ways, gain an understanding of itself through a certain appeal to the *Phenomenology of Spirit*. This appeal will of course also open up the differences between Freud and Hegel, authorizing an implicit psychoanalytic critique of Hegel. This double movement of appeal and critique will provide our entry into Lacan's work. It should hardly need stressing that this approach is partial and interested, a very particular version of Lacan.

Lacan's path intersects the course of the *Phenomenology* most obviously when it comes to matters of desire and mutual recognition:

> The very desire of man is constituted, Hegel tells us, beneath the sign of mediation; it is a desire to have its desire recognized. Its object is a desire, that of the other, in the sense that man has no object constituted for his desire without some mediation, which is evident even in his most primitive wants—in, for example, the fact that even his food must be prepared—and which one rediscovers throughout the development of satisfaction from the conflict of master and slave through the entire dialectic of work.[20]

Before turning to an elaboration of the Hegelian reference in this passage, some preliminary observations may be in order. The general location of desire "beneath the sign of mediation" refuses, from the outset, any biological reading of psychoanalysis and is thus of a piece with Lacan's rejection of the translation of Freud's *Trieb* by the English "instinct." This radical distinction between the psychoanalytic and the biological was enabled, for Lacan, by Lévi-Strauss's early work, *The Elementary Structures of Kinship*; its presentation of culture as a simultaneously linguistic and social order through which man lays claim to himself as something other than natural is the basic form of Lacan's "Symbolic Order." It is the Symbolic that is able to articulate Lacan's early work on narcissism and the "mirror stage" with the central Oedipal motif of classical psychoanalysis. The "sign of mediation" is equally the "mediation of the sign."

When Lacan insists that desire constitutes itself beneath the sign of mediation, he is arguing that desire is an achievement and not a natural given—thus is something that answers neither to a biology of (instinctual) need nor to any simply conceived anthropological "lack" that could be somehow made up or filled in. Situating this "achievement" entails abstracting from Lacan's writings a theory of child development that these writings are in large measure designed to resist for reasons that will become apparent later. If we do abstract such a theory, we get a story along the following lines:

Of an infant virtually nothing can be said except that it exists—in some sense—in state of free-floating indifferentiation that is strictly ineffable and unknowable. Some myths may help to understand the child's later development out of and on the basis of this state. We may say (as Lacan sometimes does) that man, as distinct from other animals, is born too soon, is out of step with himself, is (as) an anticipation of what is not yet there (his own integral totality). Or we may say, more mythically, that it is as if the Aristophanic myth of the primordial androgynes were true, that human being is the sundering of a totality that once existed in another place and is thus a search for the "other half" that once made it whole. Or we may say, most simply, that human being is the sort of being that can come to construe itself as "lacking," and that the vicissitudes of such construals are the vicissitudes of (what in man are not) the instincts. It is, in any case, because the infant is somehow less or other than whole that it can come to have its self and its desire as a problem (and this can seem to echo Heidegger's *Dasein*, that being whose Being is a problem for it).

It is, Lacan argues, through an other that the child first comes to its self. The paradigm for this difficult and alienated assumption of self is given in the "mirror state," the period during which the infant learns to recognize its reflected image (and one of the points here is of course that this "recognition" cannot be read as re-cognition; the knowledge of self is founded on this [mis]recognition, and not vice versa). The infant of the mirror stage inscribes itself

> in a primordial ambivalence which appears to us, as I have indicated, as that of a mirror in that the subject identifies itself in its sentiment of Self with the image of the other and the image of the other comes to captivate that feeling in him. . . .
>
> Thus, the essential point, the first effect which appears from the *imago* in the human being is one of the alienation of the subject. It is in the other the subject identifies itself and even experiences itself first of all.[21]

The infant comes to itself in alienation, in slippage against itself and as other than whole. In Aristophanes' account, after their division the androgynes are marked on their surfaces by the seams where the cut faces have been sewn up by Hephaestus. For Lacan such a system of seams may be taken as a metaphor for the libido, which would then be described as an irreal organ coincident with the surface of the body; each seam may likewise be said to mark an erogenous zone, a site for totalization or completion. The erotic impulse is thus fundamentally tied to the search for an integral self and so is ultimately reflexive:

> Since we refer to the infant and the breast, and since suckling is sucking, let us say that the oral drive is getting sucked, it is the vampire.[22]

This oral drive is fundamentally autoerotic, but its autoeroticism is necessarily mediated by an object "around" which it turns on itself, calling forth a distinction between the "aim" (the breast) and the "goal" (the self). This emergence of erotic appetite as a means to the grounding of the self brings us to the opening moments of the *Phenomenology's* dialectic of desire:

> 174. The simple 'I' is this genus or the simple universal, for which the differences are *not* differences only by its being the *negative essence* of the shaped independent moments; and self-consciousness is thus certain of itself only by superseding this other that presents itself to self-consciousness as an independent life; self-consciousness is Desire. Certain of the nothingness of this other, it explictly affirms that this nothingness is for it the truth of the other; it destroys the independent object and thereby gives itself the certainty of itself as a *true* certainty, a certainty which has become explicit for self-consciousness itself *in an objective manner*.
> 175. In this satisfaction, however, experience makes it aware that the object has its own independence. . . . Thus self-consciousness, by its negative relation to the object, is unable to supersede it; it is really because of that relation that it produces the object again, and the desire as well. (*PG* 174-75)

Our parallel can be maintained however, only so long as we isolate the erotic object from its implication in another subject. For Hegel this encounter of the independent consciousness with the object is prior to the encounter of that consciousness with another consciousness, whereas for Lacan the whole developmental sequence occurs within the overarching context of the preexistent sociolinguistic order, the Symbolic. It is this difference and its consequences that we want ultimately to explore, but we can get at its full scope only by looking at the moment in which Lacan and Hegel coincide completely—in the analysis of the struggle for recognition. The dialectical transition to this moment is given in the continuation of the passage we have just cited:

> It is in fact something other than self-consciousness that is the essence of Desire; and through this experience self-consciousness has itself realized this truth. But at the same time it is no less absolutely *for itself*, and it is so only by superseding the object; and it must experience its satisfaction, for it is the truth. On account of the indepen-

dence of the object, therefore, it can achieve satisfaction only when the object itself effects the negation within itself, for it is *in itself* the negative, and must be *for* the other what it *is*. Since the object is in its own self negation, and being so is at the same time independent, it is consciousness. In the sphere of Life, which is the object of Desire, *negation* is present either *in an other*, viz. in Desire, or as a *determinateness* opposed to another independent form, or as the inorganic universal nature of life. But this universal independent nature in which negation is present as absolute negation, is the genus as such, or the genus as *self-consciousness. Self-consciousness achieves its satisfaction only in another self-consciousness.* (*PG* 175)

The upshot of all this is at once simple and complex:

179. Self-consciousness is faced by another self-consciousness; it has come *out of itself.* This has a twofold significance: first, it has lost itself, for it finds itself as another being; secondly, in doing so it has superseded the other, for it does not see the other as an essential being, but in the other sees its own self.

180. It must supersede this otherness of itself. This is the supersession of the first ambiguity, and is therefore itself a second ambiguity. First, it must proceed to supersede the *other* independent being in order thereby to become certain of itself as the essential being; secondly, in so doing it proceeds to supersede its *own* self, for this other is itself. (*PG* 179-80)

The complexities of this problematic discovery of self as other and other as self are for Lacan the central teaching of Hegel. The Hegelian dialectic of Desire as sketched out here marks out the region proper to psychoanalysis as the science of (necessarily human) Desire insofar as it is unable to confine itself to the level of mere appetite (capable of attaining to some form of satisfaction) but must push beyond the object in order to pose itself for itself and in an other. What a given self-consciousness demands of that other consciousness through which it finds itself is a recognition of itself as autonomous and independent. It implicitly demands that the other consciousness negate its own independence in such a way as to let the given self-consciousness secure itself within itself. (My independence means that I do not need you.) But because it is only through the other consciousness that the given consciousness can attain such security, the negation of that other consciousness is finally a loss of security for the given consciousness. (My independence is assured only through my not needing *you*; and if you are not there, my independence from you can no longer be assured.)

The immediate consequence of this struggle for recognition in which two self-consciousnesses face one another and demand each other's negation in favor of their own autonomies is the dialectic of master and slave, the result of which is the submission of one self-consciousness to another and then a reversal of that submission, all of which works to set up a moment of mutual recognition and forgiveness. This recognition comes, much later in the *Phenomenology*, as the transition to the religious shape of consciousness, itself the threshold of Absolute Knowledge.

It is just here that psychoanalysis breaks with Hegelian *Phenomenology*, insisting that the Imaginary dialectics of mother and child find no solution except through the disruptive intervention of a third—paternal—person who announces the necessary submission of both mother and child to a Symbolic law that precludes any totalization. Hegel's image of the family, in *The Philosophy of Right*, is one in which parent and child simply alternate positions through the mediation of a process of "education" that is the domestic repetition of the education of consciousness to philosophy in the *Phenomenology*. Oedipus is not a figure for Hegel (and, indeed, it is in *Antigone* and not *Oedipus Rex* that Hegel finds his tragic paradigm). From the standpoint of a psychoanalysis that draws upon the *Phenomenology* in order to understand itself, Hegel finally appears to claim to find an integral and autonomous individuality at the level of the Imaginary, and this can determine the questions with which we will be concerned throughout the remainder of this section:

—Our fundamental interest lies in determining the relation of a psychoanalytic logic that feeds on the structure of the *Phenomenology,* even as it is unable to endorse its resolution, to the language and logic of that text. The claim that psychoanalysis is a paradigmatically modernist discipline is to be filled out in terms of its participation in and dependence on a certain failure of the Absolute. We want to tease out of the *Phenomenology* itself the structure of this "failure"—to see along what faces the crystal shears, and to see the consequences of this shearing at work within the theoretical structure of psychoanalysis. All of which is to say that we want to see Lacan's psychoanalysis as specifically and consequentially "post-Hegelian."

—Our task must be to work in Hegel at the structure of reading Hegel. It is only the reading of Hegel that can strongly ground something that can with justice be called the post-Hegelian. We will see that our object is, in the end, the interplay between the reader's claim to read and the text's claim to mastery over that reading. We want to get at the way in which to read the *Phenomenology* is already to find oneself as, somehow, post-Hegelian even as the text would claim to close off that possibility.

—This means that we have to make some attempt to come to grips with the difficult notion of the Absolute and its quasi-eschatological aspects. As remarked earlier, whatever we may want to say about the "real meaning" of Hegel's claims to have attained the end of history and the fulfillment of philosophy, we must begin by recognizing that these claims are made, are radical, and are prior to any modifications, however "obvious," we might want to make.

If we cannot say with any real satisfaction what the Absolute *is*, we can certainly say something of what it *does*: it closes the *Phenomenology*, proclaiming the final resolution of its conflicts and displaying the adequacy of knowledge to itself. The consciousness whose course we have followed through some five hundred pages of dialectical cunning and reversal is now fully a philosophical consciousness, ready to enter into—to read or to write—the system of the *Logic*. —But there is something funny here: we had thought to bypass the necessity for a preliminary, more or less Kantian, movement and now we find ourselves simply to have completed it.

Hegel's preface, written after the completion of the *Phenomenology* itself, functions as a kind of retrospect on the processes of the *Phenomenology* and as a prospect toward the larger and more properly philosophic system of the *Logic*. It is thus as much a postface to the Absolute as it is a preface to the text, located logically somewhere that is at once prior and posterior to the *Phenomenology of Spirit*. It has for its implicit task the reabsorption of the *Phenomenology* into the larger system, breaking down the appearance of the text as "merely preliminary." It has, in a certain sense, to make the *Phenomenology* disappear (so that we can say that although the *Phenomenology* is absolutely necessary to the Hegelian project, it is [or ought to be] absolutely unnecessary to the system—a ladder to be thrown away after it is climbed: the preface is the gesture that would throw it away).

We might say: the *Phenomenology ought not* be a self-standing text; it ought to efface itself before its achievement of the standpoint of Absolute Knowledge; it intends its own radical transparency before the final self-showing of the Absolute. Or, we might also say: it intends to educate its reader to that standpoint, to transform that reader into the fully philosophic consciousness of the *Logic*, a consciousness capable of recognizing itself in the Absolute. The persistence of a reader exterior to the Absolute, the insistence of some lingering textual presence in the face of the Absolute—these are the coupled moments that the preface would finally render impossible.

The preface, I am suggesting, is that place where the *Phenomenology* would ensure its absorption of itself and of its reader. It would attempt to guarantee the movement of *Phenomenology* beyond any lingering, merely textual presence. Such a movement beyond textuality is the simplest—perhaps the only— sense one can grant Hegel's claim to the self-showing of the Absolute. That the project is incoherent means nothing here; what we are trying to give an account of is why it doesn't quite make sense and what the consequences of that are.

The preface would then be prior to the *Phenomenology*, giving the "rules" for its successful reading; at the same time, it is necessarily posterior to the whole of the *Phenomenology*, since it is only from the standpoint of Absolute Knowledge that one can grasp the necessity for the sort of reading the preface would establish. Finally, the preface is itself a part of the *Phenomenology*—the part that has for its essential object the *Phenomenology* (including itself). Its job is to make—somehow—all this mass of interlocking language "vanish." This is very different from saying that the purpose of the preface is to give us "Hegel's theory of language"—that theory belongs to the *Phenomenology* itself. The task of the preface is to work a transformation that is capable of embracing the language in which any Hegelian theory of language is itself couched. The preface is called upon to produce a rule for reading that does away with the act of reading and makes of the text a pure showing.

This view points to a gap between language known as an object within the history of experience and the language by which that history is known and communicated. The two cannot be subject to the same constraints, and the preface must bridge the gap between them. Putting the issue this way lets us see the way the preface is left, after the *Phenomenology* has run its course, to grapple with the issues the introduction had claimed to bypass. The initial avoidance of Kant comes home here. The moment of preliminary critique turns out to have been only displaced by the movement of the text from its initial Kantian context into the specifically logico-linguistic region within which the preface works. The *Phenomenology* must still end by showing itself to be something other than preliminary.

The initial, introductory evasion of the epistemological question depends, as we have seen, on the givenness of the philosophic Notion, the idea of philosophy. The same insistence of the Notion will, in the preface, hold together the logical and prosodic aspects of what Hegel calls the "speculative judgment" (or "proposition")—and it is on the actuality of the speculative proposition that the Hegelian project depends. Finally, the Notion organizes as well a certain denial of the reader and of reading as a subject and an activity exterior to the *Phenomenology*.

The Notion is the principled object of philosophy through which it defines its disciplinary propriety. We are claiming for it here a triple function in Hegel's text:

(1) The denial or surpassing of epistemology and preliminary critique in the introduction.

(2) The guarantee of the logical force of the Absolute Proposition and so also of the speculative judgment in the preface.

(3) The denial of the reader and reading in the preface.

This triple function defines the structure through which the *Phenomenology* can claim to control its own reading. Our claim (the reader's claim) is simply that the persistent "readability" of the text has consequences that it is radically unable to control—consequences that subvert the claims of the text and vouchsafe to the reader the space in which post-Hegelian thought unfolds. The mere act of reading is sufficient to undermine Hegel's attempt to circumscribe rigorously the limits of the discipline of philosophy.

Hegel's discussion of the speculative proposition emerges through a critique of the traditional logical sentence. This critique attempts to establish within and as if beneath that sentence a deeper movement that is to be thought of as proper to the Notion. The exposition develops through two stages:

(1) Traditional logic is held to be in opposition to the Notion. The Notion struggles against the confinement of logical form and asserts itself as a "counterthrust" within that form.

(2) The sentence—formerly logical and now recognized as containing a counterthrust and movement against itself—takes on a prosodic form that is a direct reflection of the working of the Notion in language.

This overcoming of the opposition between Notion and logic by language forces Hegelian science to understand itself in the last analysis rhetorically.[23] It entails also a shift in the primary locus of meaning. The sentence now appears as "dead" but for its implication in a larger, more embracing system of sentences—a text.[24] And this migration of meaning demands in its turn a transformation of the criteria of truth, now detached from any image of logical adequacy and insisting instead in the coherence and systematicity of the text:

—This conflict between the general form of a proposition and the unity of the Notion which destroys it is similar to the conflict that occurs in rhythm between metre and accent. Rhythm results from the floating centre and the unification of the two. [*Der Rhythmus resultiert aus der schwebenden Mitte und Vereinigung beider.*] So, too, in the philosophical proposition the identification of Subject and Predicate is not meant to destroy the difference between them, which the form of the proposition expresses; their unity, rather, is meant to emerge as a harmony. (*PG* 61)

The stake is the status of the logical subject, the autonomous A of which B is predicated: It is this subject that is undermined by the system of sentences— the text that continually displaces its apparent autonomy and priority into other sentences, rendering the world finally thinkable, in an Hegelian phrase, as both subject and substance. The subject is thus recuperated at the level of the text-as-totality-of-language. The "erasure" of the *Phenomenology* in order that it become a self-showing of the Absolute is accomplished through a "linguefaction" of the world—the self-showing of the Absolute is a showing forth of language. The ladder is not so much thrown away as shown to be that to which it appeared to lead. The Notion is at once that which guarantees the largest logical form of the *Phenomenology* (its ultimate adequation to itself) and that which releases it from the sway of epistemological critique. The Absolute is the Notion's rhythmic scansion of itself.

Which is to say that the Absolute is the product or result of no reading exterior to itself. The "rhythm that results from the floating centre and the unification of the two" is a wholly internal product of the interplay of "metre" and "accent," and not the consequence of a reading, a scansion that would be the result of an exchange between reader and text. It is indeed this relation of exchange that Hegel everywhere rejects; the Notion, as the givenness of philosophy, is the denial of (rhetorical) exchange.

> 1. It is customary to preface a work with an explanation of the author's aim, why he wrote the book, and the relationship in which he believes it to stand to other earlier or contemporary treatises on the same subject. In the case of a philosophical work, however, such an explanation seems not only superfluous but, in view of the nature of the subject-matter, even inappropriate and misleading. For whatever might appropriately be said about philosophy in a preface— . . . none of this can be accepted as the way in which to expound philosophical truth. (*PG* 1)

The opening paragraphs of the *Phenomenology* are engaged in a radical denial of the rhetoric of prefacing along with all that such a rhetoric (or any rhetoric) implies about the relation of text to reader in the name of the nature and notion of philosophy. This is characteristic of Hegel's prefaces and introductions, except in those instances (the lectures on fine art for example) in which the topic is a subdivision of philosophy and so can be treated in an anatomy. The totalization of the subject as and in language depends on a preliminary rejection of any autonomous and exterior reading subject.

I want then to say that there is a certain tension that cannot accurately be said to be *in* the *Phenomenology* but that certainly must be said to belong *to* it: a tension between, on the one hand, its totalizing claim over its proper scansion and the concomitant recovery and valorization of the absolute subject, and, on the other hand, the fact of its necessary submission to a reader—or, a tension between its necessary appeal to a certain rhetoricity in understanding its own operations, and its refusal of any field in which such a rhetoric could be understood. Within this tension it is the reader who comes to know himself as that by means of which the Notion's scansion of itself is realized.

The reader finds himself as the one who is unable to acknowledge his relation to the text within the terms the text would impose on him and thus discovers himself as a particular exclusion on which the *Phenomenology* depends. The reader may even discover himself as *herself*—as at once engendered and denied by the experience of Hegel. The subject of psychoanalysis would then emerge in the same moment as its object. For this reader, excluded from the text, the Notion's scansion of itself can be no more than metaphorical, belonging to the order of signification and not that of totality or being. The reader is inevitably that phenomenological nonsense whose suppression is the condition of phenomenological sense—a sense which is thus no longer total.

This "reader," thought abstractly and for itself, appears now as a systematic unconscious proper to the *Phenomenology*—linguistically structured by its field and yet nonsignificant from the standpoint of the adventure of consciousness enacted in the text. And because Hegel aims to show the world as subject and substance at once, the reader's self-discovery is complex, double—a discovery of what it is to be a self and of what it is to be a discipline. This Unconscious has emerged from a systematic interlacing of language with the disciplinary claims of philosophy—the articulation of its autonomy and objectivity—in such a way that philosophy demands henceforth to be thought of as the kind of thing that operates this kind of exclusion—the kind of thing that has this kind of unconscious. Drifting into more explicitly Lacanian terms, we can say that a contestation of its claims to Imaginary autonomy and identity with itself is inscribed within philosophy itself as a moment of radical self-criticism, a call for acknowledgment. The Heideggerean project of destruction/retrieve responds to this call; so also Derrida's "deconstruction"—and Derrida's response is explicitly informed by psychoanalytic considerations. The mutual entanglement of psychoanalysis and philosophy we thus arrive at opens out both into a psycho-analytically informed notion or critique of philosophy and into a philosophic contestation with the claims of psychoanalysis. Derrida's deconstruction can, for example, appear as a psychoanalysis of the history of philosophy—but it can appear equally as a continuing and radical critique of psychoanalysis. These various relations between the two disciplines will form the substance of our presentation of Derrida in the next chapter. For the moment it is enough to have seen something of the way in which psychoanalysis can lay claim to the Hegelian legacy and of the escape it appears to offer from the totalizing progress of Hegelian dialectic.

After Hegel (III): The Philosopher's Death

Georges Bataille's lifelong argument with Hegel began as simple opposition to the closed totality that seems the end of Hegel's dialectic. As Raymond Queneau puts it, describing Bataille's early writings, "the enemy is . . . the pan-logicism of Hegel and the determination to oppose himself like a brute to any system had itself no system." But as Bataille became more familiar with Hegel, largely under Kojève's tutelage, this easy irrationalism became more complex. In Queneau's words, Bataille gradually came to Hegel "to define himself not through opposition, but, in a sense, through fraternization." Although Bataille's problem with Hegel can be said to have remained always within the terms of system and antisystem in which it was initially posed, it became, within those terms, ever more nuanced and ever more aware of itself as necessarily unable to escape them, bound in and to them. Queneau concludes his essay on Bataille and Hegel as follows:

> For nearly twenty years he compared himself against Hegel, or rather against the different Hegels discovered one after another by the French philosophic public. Ending by perceiving the *true*, he knew himself—knew himself as radically non-Hegelian, but with an awareness also that this self-knowledge could not have come about except after knowledge of a doctrine to which he said nothing else was comparable—thus rediscovering himself, mediated but not reduced.[25]

The sense of this mediated self-discovery through Hegel is perhaps best reflected in a passage from Bataille's *L'Expérience intérieure*:

> Small comic recapitulation: Hegel, I imagine, touched the extreme. He was young still and feared going mad. I imagine even that he elaborated the system to escape (every form of conquest is no doubt the act of a man fleeing a menace). *Supplication is dead in him.* Even seeking safety, passage beyond, one continues to live; one can never be sure; one must continue to entreat. Hegel, living, won safety, killed supplication, *mutilated himself.* There remained of him nothing but an artificial arm, a modern man. But before mutilating himself, he doubtless touched the extreme, knew the entreaty: its memory draws him back to the glimpsed abyss, to annul it! The system is the annulment.[26]

The closed ring of the system appears here as the papering over of an abyss that cannot or will not be faced any longer, and Bataille's clear suggestion is that the *Phenomenology* is to be read toward the experience it would conceal or evade. The psychoanalytic and Heideggerean resonances of this should be obvious.

"The rational is actual; the actual is rational"—thus Hegel in the preface to the *Philosophy of Right*. The sentence is as succinct a summary of Hegel's system as anything he ever wrote. Bataille would have us see in it, in its very concision, symmetry, and simplicity, the annulling of an abyss—and would have us see Hegel, writing it, being led back to the very edge of that abyss. In the Hegelian text the statement does indeed lead us to a moment unique in the philosopher's works. It is tempting to describe this moment as Hegel's own brief, posthumous, post-Hegelian instant—a moment in which he brings himself to the very brink of a recognition that he has left the dark of his post-Kantian predecessors' absolute night only to leave himself marooned in the grey on grey of dusk, the night still, or again, ahead. Bataille, a sun worshipper of sorts, might be said to begin from this statement and to move ever more deeply and more willingly, back or ahead, into the night no longer called "cognition reduced to vacuity" (*PG* 16) but "la nuit de non-savoir" (*Oeuvres*, V: 40)— perhaps, cognition sophisticatedly reduced to vacuity.

If the rational is actual and the actual is rational, it would seem to follow that what is possible is in fact actual and what is not actual is in fact impossible: that is, the space one wants to call that of the possible has no proper existence, dividing immediately into the actual or the impossible. Possibility—or impossibility—would be a name of the abyss. This seems one of the things Hegel is pointing to in his image of the grey on grey: actuality as it is given through Hegel's philosophy stands as figure against no ground of possibility deeper and richer than itself. This is clearly one way of getting at the sense of the post-Hegelian anxiety so visible in the young Marx or in Kierkegaard or wherever the Hegelian system appears as capable of absorbing in advance any philosophic position that would present itself as novel, as posterior to or other than the system. It is an easy and obvious move from this anxiety to taking up the cause of the brute and irrational against an omnipresent hyperrationalism—the position from which Bataille's writing career begins.

It is rather more difficult to see a way from this closure of possibility, of philosophy and of human being, to some more positive statement of legacy. It is far from clear that or how one might take up the task of philosophy again. But, at the same time, the very insistence on such difficulties marks the necessity for and, in some measure, the actuality of post-Hegelian thought. Something of the logic entailed here was mapped out in the previous section; we are now facing again the problems on which that section closed. It might seem that the solution to all these problems about being post-Hegelian is to dismiss Hegel (in any number of ways—as wrong, as misguided, as basically right but in need of correction . . .). Such dismissals are, however, more than dismissals of certain texts; they are (would have to be) dismissals of a position whose power has been felt and which cannot be so simply denied. Jackson Pollock does not present a crisis to everyone—only to those for whom painting matters in a certain way, and, for them, to sidestep the issues posed in Pollock's painting would be to sidestep their selves.

All of which is to say that it is precisely in the measure that one buys Hegel (that one finds his claims about philosophy and about human reality compelling), that one will find oneself faced with the problem of the post-Hegelian—and this means that the first condition any ''solution'' to the problem must meet is that it do justice to this sensed power. The post-Hegelian emerges out of one's sense of the truth in Hegel, and not from a determination of falsity.

In terms of Bataille's privileged *topos* of the possible and the impossible this means that the issues must be posed finally not through the valorization of a new (irrationalist) truth against the old (rationalistic) falsehood of System, or through the championing of a radical openness of human being against the closure of the Notion. Rather, they must be posed out of rationality, out of closure; so that one ends by wanting to know what it is to say that human possibility as such lies in the impossible. This work draws the consequences of Hegel's power. It is to choose a region that is necessarily defined as post-Hegelian and that is structured everywhere by its complex reference to Hegel, and it is to acknowledge one's self as already located in such a space. The progression from the Hegelian to the post-Hegelian is organized neither by the emergence of Truth nor by any new knowledge, but as a movement of acknowledgment.

For Bataille, the problem is to understand how human possibility is given as the impossible. His job is to elaborate a logic of the (im)possible. This logic is worked through in Bataille's writing in a number of forms—as a theory of religion and mystical experience, as a poetics, as a theory of and literary practice of eroticism, as an economic theory . . . The project is encyclopedic, but also post-Encyclopedic—richly interconnected, but deprived of any final unity or closure. Bataille's early "Dossier 'hétérologie'"—a parody of the Hegelian *Encyclopedia* with its numbered sections and *Zusatzen*—is an emblem for the whole of his work.

Here we can focus on one relatively circumscribed area of Bataille's thought. Our primary reference will be to the 1955 essay, "Hegel, la mort et le sacrifice" (Hegel, death and sacrifice) and it will lead us to the economic theories advanced in "La notion de dépense" and *La Part maudite*.

"Hegel, la mort et le sacrifice" is probably Bataille's most developed statement on Hegel. It is announced as an "extract from a study of the fundamentally Hegelian thought of Alexandre Kojève."[27] The terms in which Bataille pays his tribute to Kojève may serve as an indirect measure of the pressure Bataille felt from Hegel:

> The originality and, it must be said, the courage of Alexandre Kojève is to have seen the impossibility of going further, and, in consequence, the necessity of renouncing the creation of an original philosophy and with it the interminable recommencement that is witness to the vanity of thought. ("Hegel," p. 21)

The article begins from a concern with Hegel's panlogicism and theoreticism, especially as it tacitly determines the course of the *Phenomenology* in the preface. Bataille looks in particular at the following passage:

> Death, if that is what we want to call this non-actuality, is of all things the most dreadful, and to hold fast to what is dead requires the greatest strength. Lacking strength, Beauty hates the Understanding for asking of her what it cannot do. But the life of the Spirit is not the life that shrinks from death and keeps itself from devastation, but rather the life that endures it and maintains itself in it. It wins its truth only when, in utter dismemberment [Hyppolite has "le déchirement absolu"], it finds itself. It is this power, not as something positive, which closes its eyes to the negative, as when we say of something

that it is nothing or is false, and then, having done with it, turn away and pass on to something else; on the contrary, Spirit is this power only by looking the negative in the face and tarrying with it. This tarrying with the negative is the magical power that converts it into being. (*PG* 32) (in "Hegel," pp. 26-27)

Bataille ends his citation here, but we may as well finish off the paragraph:

This power is identical with what we earlier called the Subject, which by giving determinateness an existence in its own element supersedes abstract immediacy, i.e., the immediacy which barely is, and thus is authentic substance: that being or immediacy whose mediation is not outside of it but which is this immediacy itself. (*PG* 32)

Bataille's concern with this passage is to show how it is—in the terms of the "small comic recapitulation"—an annulment of a perceived abyss and so the founding of a system. The passage is, of course, about the power of the Hegelian Negative. It is a part of Hegel's effort to take the skeptic more seriously than the skeptic takes himself, and so to move beyond mere nothingness to determinate negation, thus opening the way for the dialectic. A different reversal of the skeptical position, one that hypostasizes "mere nothingness" into a Nothingness (which presumably then *is*, in some strong if vague sense), leads to a position usually considered mystical. It is a variation on the "night in which all cows are black" that Hegel is so concerned to avoid; it is also "the dark night of unknowing" to which Bataille is always so attracted. It is not surprising to see Bataille venturing a footnoted correction of Kojève's reading of this passage in order both to reassert the possibility of this mystic position and to undo that possibility:

Here my interpretation differs somewhat from Kojève's. Kojève says simply that "impotent beauty is incapable of fitting itself to the exigencies of the Understanding. The aesthete, the romantic, the mystic—all flee the idea of death and speak of Nothingness as if of something that *is*." This defines the mystic in particular admirably. But the same ambiguity is found also in the philosopher (in Hegel, in Heidegger) at least in the end. Indeed, Kojève seems to me to fail in not envisioning, beyond classical mysticism, a "conscious mysticism," knowing itself to make a Being of Nothingness and even defining that impasse as belonging to a Negativity which will, at the end of history, no longer have a field of action.

This atheist mysticism, *conscious of itself*, conscious of having to die and disappear, would live, as Hegel says, *evidently speaking of himself*, "in utter dismemberment"; but for him, this is only a moment: unlike Hegel, the atheist mystic would not pass beyond it— "looking the negative in the face," but unable to transpose it into

Being, refusing to do so and maintaining himself in ambiguity. ("Hegel," pp. 29-30)

This not only locates with some precision the enterprise of Bataille's mystical writing, *La Somme athéologique*, and its centerpiece, *L'Expérience intérieure*, but displays as well the way in which Bataille tends to read Hegel. The statement that the life of the Spirit maintains itself in utter dismemberment must be (among other things) a statement Hegel makes about himself and his philosophizing. (In the text proper Bataille writes, "In the passage cited from the Preface, Hegel on the contrary affirms and describes a personal moment of violence" ["Hegel," pp. 28-29].) The problem for Bataille is that Hegel fails to see in this a demand for nonclosure, for something other than the security and satisfaction of a completed philosophy: "It is not an unchained violence" ("Hegel," p. 29). The difference between Hegel's "utter dismemberment" ("déchirement absolu," "absoluten Zerrissenheit") and Bataille's "déchirure originelle" is the difference given in the statement that "the system is the annulment." But if the very affirmation of an experience of this sort tends already to a betrayal of that experience, Bataille's own writing is subject to the same threat to which he claims Hegel has succumbed; it may itself become the annulment of what it intends to communicate. This is the most obvious way in which language itself finally becomes problematic for Bataille—an issue to which we will return shortly. The relation between Hegel and Bataille that has been sketched in this paragraph is neatly captured by a simple juxtaposition: "Hegel, I imagine, touched the extreme. He was young still and feared going mad. I imagine even that he elaborated the system to escape"—"What obliges me to write, I imagine, is the fear of becoming mad."[28]

Bataille's concern with the Hegelian paragraph before us is only secondarily with this opening toward a problem of ineffability. His main interest in the essay lies in thinking through "the activity of dissolution . . . the power and work of the *Understanding*" (*PG* 32) that Hegel is presenting here, and the domestication of that activity to philosophic ends. This activity is conceived by Hegel under the two aspects of work and death, as the labor of the negative. These two terms are closely coupled in the dialectic of master and slave marking that dialectic as a particular repetition of the one with which we are concerned at present. This central linkage of work and death is for Bataille one of the great strengths and distinguishing marks of Hegelian philosophy. With one eye clearly on the master and slave (and clearly under the influence of Kojève), Bataille points to

the continual connection of an abyssal aspect and a tough, earthbound aspect in this philosophy, the only one with a pretension to completeness. The divergent possibilities of opposed human figures confront and unite with one another there: the dying figure and the proud man

who turns from death, the figure of the master and that of the man
bound to his labor, the figure of the revolutionary and that of the
skeptic whose desire is limited by egoistic interest. This philosophy is
not only a philosophy of death. It is one also of class struggle and of
labor. ("Hegel," p. 30)

It is one moment in this dialectic of work and death that Bataille would
explore by pointing up the presence of a certain sacrifice in the passage we have
cited: the emergence of the Spirit from Nature is—Bataille is following Kojève
here—a sacrifice of its (animal) nature. "In a sense, Man has revealed and
founded human truth in sacrificing: in sacrifice, he destroys the animal within
himself, letting remain only, of himself and of the animal, the incorporeal truth
Hegel describes" ("Hegel," p. 31). It is sacrifice, Bataille suggests, that answers
most precisely to Hegel's description of the Spirit that finds itself in utter
dismemberment.

The attempt to think about sacrifice and Hegelian Negativity together quickly
points to a problem. Both Hegel and the practitioner of sacrifice insist that death
is somehow to serve as the bearer or revealer of the deeper truth of Negativity
and Totality. But, as Bataille remarks, "In reality death reveals
nothing. . . . Once the animal being which supports it is dead, the human
being itself has ceased to be" (p. 32). There is—from this point of view—a trick
being played in or by Hegel such that his subject manages to live through
("survive," but also "come to life") its death. "In other words, death itself
becomes conscious (of itself) at the very moment at which it annihilates the
conscious being" (p. 32). But this is precisely the trick upon which the practice
of sacrifice turns.

In the sacrifice, the sacrificer identifies himself with the animal killed.
Thus he dies in seeing himself die, and even, in some sense, does this
by his own will, willingly, with the arm of sacrifice. ("Hegel," p. 33)

Hubert and Mauss, whom Bataille is certainly following here, refer to the
way in which the sacrificer "prudently" sets himself aside;[29] Bataille is somewhat blunter: "But this is a comedy!"

But if this is indeed the way in which the Spirit emerges from Nature, it is
at least a consequential comedy—one that shows man as a creature rooted still
and always in nature, fooling himself into a passage beyond, willfully imagining
for himself an impossible autonomy (and doing all of this in some measure
"successfully"). This can appear as a condemnation of sorts, or as a liberation—

Man does not live by bread alone but also by comedies in which he
willingly mistakes himself. In Man, it is the animal, the natural being,
that eats. But Man attends to cult and to spectacle. Or, again, he can
read: then literature prolongs in him, in the measure that is authentic

or sovereign, the obsessive magic of the tragic or comic spectacle. ("Hegel," p. 34)

By bringing sacrifice to bear upon the Hegelian passage, Bataille can advance several claims.

First, he can claim to have placed Hegel's text as a certain kind of unacknowledged spectacle, a staging of the passage from Nature to Spirit behind its own back—papering over the abyss it nonetheless betrays. This is tantamount to attributing a literary existence to the text; in this it approaches the terms of criticism developed in our previous section.

Second, the reduction of this passage to spectacle operates an implicit denial of the Hegelian assertion that "accident as such . . . should attain an existence of its own and a separate freedom . . . the tremendous power of the negative . . . the energy of thought, of the pure 'I' " (*PG* 32). By so doing Bataille refuses the systematically powerful conjunction of thought, negation, and self that organizes the *Phenomology of Spirit* and refuses as well the envisaging of death as an event able to emerge wholly from the contingency of nature. There are severe limits on Bataille's willingness to describe human reality in terms of such markedly Hegelian notions as Heidegger's "being-toward-death." This is perhaps best thought of as a part of Bataille's "realism," his attempt to remain true to Hegel's "continual connection of an abyssal aspect and a tough, earthbound aspect."

Finally, if death and negation are not themselves unified, are not reliable bearers of meaning, the entire progress of the dialectic in the *Phenomenology* becomes open to possible disruption at every point along its course. This dialectic remains nonetheless that through which human being is to be grasped—even as its passage is now opened to the impossible. The apparent consequences of the Hegelian slogan—"the actual is rational; the rational is actual"—have been reversed. The impossible now defines, guarantees, and disrupts the sense of every moment of the *Phenomenology*.

For example, the life-and-death struggle for recognition that results in the emergence of the master and slave in the opening moments of "Self-consciousness" now appears as a comedy that both depends on and is subverted by the simple fact that neither "master" nor "slave" is really risking anything. The figures that do risk death are phenomenologically invisible; they drop out and leave behind only their survivors. But it is these figures, as if hovering about the fringes of the *Phenomenology*, that attain the (imaginary, impossible) position of irreversible sovereignty at issue in the dialectic—the position from which we might be said to recognize the mastery of the master (however inadequate *that* mastery proves in the dialectical event). That "we" can so recognize the master is important here; the point from which "we" accomplish this is constitutive of our reality—even though it cannot be articulated by the

Phenomenology. What has to be caught here could be caught by no *Phenomenology*—except in this willfully perverse fashion. If the actual is rational and the rational is actual (and it is), then what remains ("merely") possible is impossible (and it is): and the difficulty is to find a way to say yes to both these sides at once—to affirm the real and continuing (im)possibility of our human being.

Bataille's economic theories are probably best thought of as attempts to marshall evidence for or to display the concrete workings of the (im)possible. *La Somme athéologique* would then be Bataille's attempt to convey the experience of the (im)possible, to locate those places where the (im)possible might be touched, glimpsed, affirmed.

The economic writings include the early essay "La Notion de dépense" and the later *La Part maudite*. Bataille intended to use the latter title eventually to cover three volumes (much the way *La Somme athéologique* brings together under its single head a number of theretofore independent texts)—the first was to be a revision of *La Part maudite* under the new title *La Consumation* (Consumption), the second was to be called *La Souveraineté* (Sovereignty), and the third (later published separately) was to have been *L'Erotisme* (Eroticism). Only the first volume—*La Part maudite* or *La Consumation*—and the early essay are properly considered economic writings—and even here the term is applied loosely at best.

For instance, Bataille's economics begin from the sun. If, he suggests, we conceive of the earth as a single, global economic system, we find that all its wealth comes ultimately from outside of itself as energy received continually from the sun. The fundamental economic-energetic situation of life is not one of scarcity but of surplus; and the fundamental problem is accordingly not one of making good a shortage but of managing an excess: "*It is not necessity but its opposite, luxury, which poses to living matter and to man their fundamental problems*" (*Oeuvres*, VII: 21).

It is from this point of view—the standpoint of "general economy"—that Bataille states his "elementary fact":

> the living organism, in the situation determined by the play of energy on the surface of the globe, receives in principle more energy than is necessary for the maintenance of life: the extra energy (or wealth) can be utilized for the growth of the system (the organism, for example); if the system can grow no more, or if the excess cannot be entirely absorbed into growth, then it must necessarily be lost without profit, spent, willingly or not, gloriously or else catastrophically. (*Oeuvres*, VII: 29)

Those specific economies organized around growth and the conservation of economic or energetic wealth are called by Bataille "restricted economies." Such systems are necessarily inscribed in and dependent on the larger general economy—whether they acknowledge that dependence or not. But at the same time, there is no sense in which one can speak of a "general economy" apart from its effects on or refractions through the projects of growth and conservation given within the restricted economy—just as the notion of "sovereignty" is bound wholly to the "restricted" dialectic of master and slave whose disruption and (im)possibility it is. If we recall here once again Bataille's "small comic recapitulation," we can see that what it claims Hegel to have seen and fled, to have (visibly) annulled with his system, is the fact that the progress of Spirit depends on the necessity of pure and irrecoverable loss. This is why some part of Bataille's critique can be put in terms of Hegel's settling for or succumbing to satisfaction or in terms of an act of self-mutilation that is the killing of supplication in himself. Bataille's "atheist mysticism" is visible in the background here.

In this view, the difference between the Hegelian and the practitioner of sacrifice lies in their understandings of their local economic situations: the Hegelian is committed to a faith in the autonomy of the restricted economy and is therefore submitted to the catastrophic expenditures demanded by the priority of excess (expenditures he cannot acknowledge); the practitioner of sacrifice lives in a society of consumption, organized by its awareness of the necessity for glorious celebrations of pure loss—potlatch, sacrifice.

The Aztecs are Bataille's privileged example of such a consuming society. (Their mythology also intersects repeatedly with Bataille's own.) What struck Bataille about the Aztecs was above all their belief in the sun as itself a sacrifice, a god who has thrown himself into (his own) fire. All Aztec life and achievement took their sense from this sacrifice and from the need for its continuation, for the sun to be fed. The Aztec practice of human sacrifice was modeled on and pressed toward the limit of solar sacrifice as pure and gratuitous loss. The solar sacrifice lies on the far side of the prudence remarked by Henri Hubert and Marcel Mauss; the sacrifices that imitate and maintain it would themselves touch at that far side, break the restricted terms of everyday life and labor, in order to realize a world of sovereignty and intimacy.

> From the moment a world of things is posited, man becomes himself one of the things of that world, at least for the time he works. It is from that diminution that man at all times struggles to escape. In his bizarre myths and cruel rites man is from the beginning *in search of lost intimacy*. (*Oeuvres*, VII: 62)[30]

This peculiar blend of Marx and Durkheim is typical of Bataille.[31] It should be apparent that this formulation of sacrifice and related practices returns us to the passages we have discussed in Hegel, in the preface and in the dialectic of master and slave, through the opposing figure of work. Sacrifice recovers human being and possibility from its submission to the restrictions of "project" and utility—or would: it continues to be the case that sacrifice works only for those who generously renounce their right to be sacrificed. Bataille concludes:

This understandable absence of rigor nonetheless changes nothing in the sense of the rite. All that matters is an excess which surpasses the limits and the consumption of which seems worthy of the gods. Men escape at this cost their diminution; they lift at this price the heaviness introduced in them by avarice and the cold calculus of the real. (*Oeuvres*, VII: 165)

The cost of such intimacy, radically, is death; but for Bataille this changes nothing in the sense of things. An imaginary goal can have real consequences, and if "intimacy" is strictly not possible, its possibility is nonetheless real—intimacy is (im)possible: what counts for Bataille is to maintain it as such, to remain capable of acknowledging this (im)possibility within an order of language and society that would more simply deny it.[32]

But this brings finally to a head the implicit problem with which Bataille has been faced all along; *La Part maudite* puts it this way:

My researches have aimed at the acquisition of a knowledge. They have demanded coldness, calculus. But the knowledge acquired is of an error implied in the coldness inherent to all calculation. In other words, my work has tended first of all to *increase* the sum of human resources, but its results have taught me that accumulation is nothing more than a delay, a recoil before the inevitable due date when accumulated wealth has value only in the instant. Writing the book in which I have said that energy cannot in the end but be squandered, I have myself employed my energy and my time for work: my researches have responded in a fundamental way to the desire to increase the sum of goods acquired by humanity. Will I say that in these conditions I cannot but respond to the truth of my book and that I cannot continue to write? (*Oeuvres*, VII: 20-21)

This is a problem of positionality with a vengeance, the central problem of communication in Bataille. Bataille lacks any guiding disciplinary matrix through which to pose this issue. Instead, his writings tend to fall into either the "science" of *La Part maudite* or the "mysticism" of *La Somme athéologique*, and the problem of communication likewise falls into two complementary forms. Either communication, in the everyday sense, is a betrayal of what must be communicated; or real communication, "intimacy," can arise only through a destruction of the terms of everyday language and understanding. Bataille fights the former betrayal by trying to make such propositions as "the sexual act is in time what the tiger is in space" (*Oeuvres*, VII: 21) figure within the economic "science" of *La Part maudite*; he elaborates the latter possibility theoretically as a problem of ineffability in *L'Expérience intérieure* and practically by an insistence on the materiality of language.

It is language, in the end, that marks the (im)possibility of sovereignty:

> Sacrifice is then a means to sovereignty and *autonomy* only to the extent that *signifying* discourse does not inform it. To the extent that signifying discourse does inform it, that which is *sovereign* is given in terms of *servitude*. ("Hegel," p. 40)

The *Phenomenology's* exclusion of anything not informed by discourse (see *PG* 95, which implicitly establishes a grasp of language as the *terminus a quo* for anything that would count as "an experience of consciousness") is emblematic and can return us to Bataille's problem with Hegel's vision of redeeming Negativity:

> Thus the simple manifestation of the link between Man and destruction, the pure revelation of Man to himself (at the moment at which death fixes his attention) passes from sovereignty to the primacy of servile ends. . . . A slippage cannot fail to be produced, to the profit of servitude. ("Hegel," pp. 40, 41)

This "slippage" points back toward the possibility of sovereignty, at the same time announces the limits of any movement toward a recovery of such sovereignty, and so determines the shape of Bataille's "correction" of Hegel:

> If he fails, one cannot say that this is the result of an error. The sense of the failure itself differs from that of the error that causes it: only the error is perhaps fortuitous. It is more generally that one must speak of the "failure" of Hegel, as of an authentic movement, heavy with sense.
>
> In fact, man is always in pursuit of an authentic sovereignty. It seems that in one sense he has this sovereignty initially, but there is no doubt that this cannot then be in a conscious manner, so that in another sense he does not have it, it escapes him. We will see that he pursues in a variety of ways that which always steals away from him. The essential thing is that one cannot reach for it consciously, cannot search for it, because research distances it. But I believe that nothing is ever given to us except in such an equivocal fashion. ("Hegel," pp. 42-43)

The central pursuit of our sovereignty can only lead to ever more extreme affirmations of what escapes from our discourse, from our projects and our calculations. For Bataille these are affirmations that embrace shit and sacrifice and, above all, laughter—not only as it escapes its submission to discourse and project, but also as it affirms the comic (im)possibility of our sovereignty, intimacy, and communication.

With this last "the idea of seriousness itself"[33] is indeed threatened—in, as it were, its own name. This threat can only become more visible as Bataille's affirmations are turned back on themselves, no longer simply affirming what escapes our discourse, but affirming as well what escapes in and as our discourse, its inessential accidents—for example, its materiality; the sheer contingency of writing, for example; the inevitable fact that a *Phenomenology of Spirit* is only as it is given over to print, publication, and even copyright.

Chapter 3
Psychoanalysis and Deconstruction

Questions of Tradition and Method

Psychoanalysis of Philosophy: The Status of "Freudian Concepts"; Philosophy and Psychologism; Freud and Hegel

It can be tempting to describe Jacques Derrida's work as in large measure an extension of psychoanalysis into the history of philosophy. Despite Derrida's insistence to the contrary (in the section called "The Exorbitant Question of Method"), the reading of Rousseau offered in *Of Grammatology*—probably the work best known to Derrida's English-speaking audience—looks like a particularly sophisticated variety of psychobiographical analysis, showing the inevitable inscription of the word "supplement"—the word with which Rousseau would name writing, his own writing in relation to speech, and culture in relation to nature—in a larger psychosexual economy (in which it names also masturbation in relation to normal sexuality). If one finds *Of Grammatology* powerful, one is likely to feel that the careful tracing of the consequences of this double inscription ends by showing a new and more coherent version of Rousseau—and a version that depends on the discovery of the psychoanalytic key to Rousseau.

If one fights past this appearance—reads the *Grammatology* carefully—there is still the temptation to think of Derrida as replacing Heidegger's "forgottenness of Being" with his own "repression of writing," so that the new project is a logical, if critical, development out of a central line of philosophic speculation, finding its new truth—writing—essentially in the same place and way (that is, as the secret and real center of an enterprise that does not know itself) as the older truth of Being. This picture has, for us, the pleasant consequence of encouraging a rapprochement between Derrida and Cavell or Wittgenstein on the ground of their parallel therapeutic ambitions for philosophy (and the way to this rapprochement has already been prepared by Cavell's insistence on a parallelism between Heidegger and Wittgenstein). Derrida would, of course, be a latecomer in this philosophic clinic: he sees the world's ills in terms of forces and hegemonies rather than the presumably easier terms of ontological absent-mindedness and is thus prone to confuse politics and therapy, to confound kill and cure.

Whatever the value of such a picture—and its value is certainly greater than this parodic presentation of it admits—Derrida's writings on Freud begin precisely as an attempt to break it down. Derrida's earliest essay on psychoanalysis presents itself as having been preceded (in its oral version) by an introduction concerned to address two points in particular:

(1) Despite appearances, the deconstruction of logocentrism is not a psychoanalysis of philosophy. . . .
(2) An attempt to justify a theoretical reticence to utilize Freudian concepts, otherwise than in quotation marks; all these concepts, without exception, belong to the history of metaphysics, that is, to the system of logocentric repression which was organized to exclude or to lower (to put aside or below) the body of the written trace as a didactic and technical metaphor, as servile matter or excrement.[1]

In this chapter we will move through these two points repeatedly and from a variety of angles. As we shall see, "appearances" here are persistent and, in the end, constitutive; they cannot be simply or finally put aside, and psychoanalysis has become one of the most insistent references in Derrida's writing. The interest deconstruction takes in psychoanalysis is permanent and complex: its continuing rediscovery of this interest is of a piece with its continuing rediscovery of itself and its project of radical self-criticism. Deconstruction finds itself ever more deeply in its controversy with psychoanalysis—a controversy whose central terms have already been given in the remarks we have cited. We will see, for example, that Derrida's recent interest in the psychoanalytic work of Nicolas Abraham and Maria Torok is in large measure still caught up in "an attempt to justify a theoretical reticence to utilize Freudian concepts, otherwise than in quotation marks," with the difference that the enterprise has become more radical, no longer poses itself as a concern about the "application" of Freudian concepts outside of psychoanalysis but reaches instead into the very heart of psychoanalysis, suggesting that there is no arena (including that of psychoanalysis itself) in which Freudian concepts can be used without quotation marks.

Modern philosophy in both its Anglo-American and Continental variants is, to a great extent, definable through its resistance to psychologism—perhaps more cogently by its obligation to acknowledge some form of psychologism, transcendental or empirical, as its constitutive temptation. "Psychologism"— like "theatricality"—is a risk both ever changing and omnipresent, figuring increasingly now as precisely that which was to protect us from it, as "epistemology." If we define psychologism as the tendency to think that all can be made clear for and by a consciousness fully transparent to itself, the threat of psychologism is or can come to be as fully embodied in Hegel's *Phenomenology of Spirit* as in some more obvious psychology of consciousness. In such a field, psychoanalysis, with its insistence on a necessary and systematic Unconscious, can appear as a means beyond any such simple psychologism. Lacan, for example, can make Hegel look merely psychological; this is one way of restating the force of our earlier remark that "Hegel finally appears to claim to find an integral and autonomous individuality at the level of the Imaginary." But nothing can guarantee the radical exemption of psychoanalysis from psychologism, and the threat inevitably reappears in this new region in an altered form. Lacan in particular appears to enter a tacit claim for the adequacy of a science of mind to the task and place of philosophy. The claim of psychoanalysis to scienticity comes to carry the claims to integrity, transparency, and self-adequacy previously borne by the consciousness at the center of a simpler psychology or phenomenology.

A late footnote to *The Interpretation of Dreams* can open this field for us from a slightly different angle:

> The proposition laid down in these peremptory terms—"whatever interrupts the progress of analytic work is a resistance"—is easily open to misunderstanding. It is of course only to be taken as a technical rule, as a warning to analysts. It cannot be disputed that in the course of an analysis various events may occur the responsibility for which cannot be laid upon the patient's intentions. His father may die without his having murdered him; or a war may break out which brings the analysis to an end. But behind its obvious exaggeration the proposition is asserting something both true and new. Even if the interrupting event is a real one and independent of the patient, it often depends on him how great an interruption it causes; and resistance shows itself unmistakably in the readiness with which he accepts an occurrence of this kind or the exaggerated use which he makes of it.[2]

This passage seems to me typical of much of what is most powerful and most maddening in Freud: interrupting his own text, Freud seems to engage in an excessive excursus upon an obviously exaggerated proposition about the exaggerated use the analytic patient may make of interruptions in the analysis; whatever may have initially been obvious about the technical rule ends by being utterly lost—but significance, inevitable significance, is secured in the face of the most radical of contingencies—death, war. Freud's gesture here—even in its hesitancy, its attempt to recall itself to the limits of a "technical rule"—is fully as sweeping as anything in Hegel. Like the Hegelian dialectic, this rule of resistance admits of nothing irrecuperable or radically accidental. Even what is "real" and "independent of the patient" ends up inside the analysis (as indeed the register R ends up defined and enclosed by the Imaginary and the Symbolic in Lacan's various schemata).

This problem—this tendency toward a certain psychologism, a certain imperialism of sense—persists throughout Freud's work, becoming most explicit and dramatic in *Beyond the Pleasure Principle*. In that text the search for something beyond the pleasure principle finds its evidential ground in those

> cases where the subject appears to have a *passive* experience, over which he has no influence, but in which he meets with a repetition of the same fatality. There is the case, for instance, of the woman who married three successive husbands each of whom fell ill soon afterwards and had to be nursed by her on their death beds. . . .
>
> If we take into account observations such as these . . . we shall find courage to assume that there really does exist in the mind a compulsion to repeat which overrides the pleasure principle.[3]

That Freud's example here is radically and inevitably unconvincing (and not helped any by a second example drawn from Tasso and invoking a "strange magic forest")—that the entire progress of Freud's argument to this point in the text has been a progress of failed examples—these things need not concern us here, except insofar as they help make visible the way in which this meditation repeats even in its hesitations the simpler gesture of the footnote on resistance. In each case, the gesture is one that would subsume all of reality under the logic of psychoanalysis. This is, as we will see, structurally of a piece for Derrida with that representation through which voice would understand itself as pure self-affection and so subsume all meaning under itself, condemning writing as a mere secondary representation (of a representation), meaningless and wholly exposed to contingency. What Derrida now calls "phallogocentrism" is the ultimate outgrowth of what began as "phonocentrism," the illegitimate and incoherent privileging of speech over writing in the philosophic text.

Our aim in the following pages is to explore this complex field: to see the ways in which psychoanalysis is at once an enabling force and an object of criticism for Derrida; to follow some of the turnings through which the critique deepens and widens its scope; and to understand this permanent controversy as it is caught up in—articulates and is articulated by—the problems of philosophic discipline and history. At the heart of this field is Derrida's quarrel with Lacan. It is through this controversy that we will pose the question of "deconstructive criticism,'' and the problematic relations between psychoanalysis, criticism, and deconstruction will be of continuing importance throughout the remainder of the book.

Odds and Evens: The Argument with Lacan

However, we will begin at some remove from these larger issues; we will, in fact, begin from a consideration of randomness and coin tossing. The material on which we will be drawing here can be found in the "Introduction" and "Parenthèse de parenthèses" (Parenthesis on parentheses) appended to Lacan's "Seminar on 'The Purloined Letter'" and in the second volume of Lacan's collected seminars, *Le Moi dans la théorie de Freud et dans la technique de la psychanalyse* (The ego in Freudian theory and in psychoanalytic technique) – the seminar in which the reading of Poe was first developed.[4]

In these pages we are going to stay close to the original seminar—that is, we are going to be concerned with the logical problems raised in and illustrated by the seminar on "The Purloined Letter" rather than with the literary critical problems perhaps raised by it. For Lacan, these problems cast light on the structure and limits of the intersubjective logic invoked by the mirror stage and its Imaginary interimplication of self and other. In particular, they show something of how the workings of the Imaginary assume and are limited by a prior order— the Symbolic—which is itself not submitted (which cannot be submitted) to the mastery of any subject or any simple dialectic of self and other. What is at stake for Lacan here is the way in which human reality is always and already submitted to language and signification.

Lacan's meditation begins from a child's game (which Poe's Dupin offers as an analogue to his own activity in finding the stolen letter) in which I am to guess whether you are holding an odd or even number of fingers behind your back. Is there a long-run winning strategy for such a game? There would seem to be two ways for me to play, at least in principle. The first, almost unimaginably naive, would be for me to guess whatever struck me as right to guess (for the moment we can call this random guessing). The second would be for me to ''identify'' with my opponent, realizing that I am an object of knowledge for him or her, that he or she is capable of putting himself or herself in my place and anticipating my guess. A third strategy—in which I undertake to make myself unanticipatable by guessing deliberately ''at random''—collapses back into the first. But in so doing it renders the second apparent strategy nugatory: it reveals the game as always at once too random and too reflexive. There is no winning strategy at odds-and-evens, despite the fact that one can know the laws of randomness and despite what one may feel as an almost palpable secret order only just out of reach.

Lacan shows that a random sequence can in fact conceal a surprising amount of order. If, for example, we take a random sequence of odds-and-evens, heads

and tails, pluses and minuses− + + − − − − − + − − + − + − + + − + − − − + −
+ + . . . − and go on to mark that chain off into overlapping groups of three −
abc, bcd, cde− (+[+/−) (−][−//−) (+][−//−) (+][−//+) (−][+//+)
(−][+// . . . −which can be disentangled into− (+ + −) [+ − −] /− − − /
(− − −) [− − +] /− + − / (+ − −) [− − +] /− − − / (+ − −) [− + −] /+ − + /
. . . −we can (reasonably) easily see that the rules governing this new sequence are in fact highly orderly. There are three possible types of groups
involved: two symmetrical groups−one constant (that is, either + + + or
− − −) and the other alternating (+ − + or − + −)−and a set of asymmetrical
groups (+ − −, − + +, + + −, and − − +). If we have produced three pluses
(call this a group of type [1]), our next move will create a new group that will
be either another three pluses (+ + +/+) or two pluses and a minus (+ + +/−).
From group (1) we can either advance to one of the asymmetrical formations
(group [2]) or remain in place:

If we have produced the minus and so find ourselves now in the second position, we can expect that our next move will give rise either to another asymmetrical group (+ + −/−) or to a symmetrical and alternating group (3):

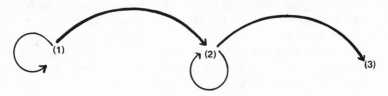

A little reflection will suffice to show that there is a significant difference
between two subgroups of (2), which we will distinguish as (2a) and (2b). This
distinction is purely positional (that is, what composes subgroup [2a] depends
upon whether the group [1] from which one starts is − − − or + + +, and that
will change as the system chugs along):

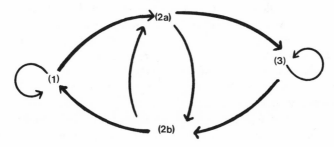

Some of the rules of this system are that there is no passage from (1) to (3) except through the mediation of (2), and that the passage from (1) to (3) is significantly different from the passage from (3) to (1).

If we go on to take the transformations themselves as our terms, we can construct a still more complex network:

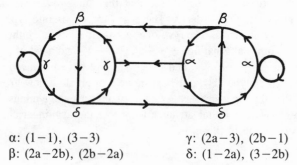

α: (1−1), (3−3)   γ: (2a−3), (2b−1)
β: (2a−2b), (2b−2a)   δ: (1−2a), (3−2b)

Where—or how—does all this elegant order exist? Not, certainly, in the brute fact of random pluses and minuses—that is sheerly contingent, purely statistical. If it were not, then all of this would help us to a winning strategy at odds-and-evens—which it simply cannot do: odds-and-evens is a game one can manage at best not to lose. But—one wants to say—these laws are close enough to that order that it is possible to believe that they can be made to count for the game: their presence, their possibility, seems to hover about the game, promising an impossible victory. What you and I both know when I attempt to outthink your outthinking of me at odds-and-evens is that the game is not without order; what neither of us can admit (or can admit only with great difficulty because it will cost us the game) is that there is nothing in that order which we can touch or make count for the game. We face each other as in a mirror and through a glass, but the real logic of our relationship, the structure of our intersubjectivity, is at work elsewhere.

Where then does all this elegant order reside? One reasonable answer would be to locate it in the apparatus of parentheses and brackets with which we have encumbered the simple sequence of pluses and minuses, but the deeper answer demands our seeing that these brackets are just a simple reflection—a remarking—of what is already present in the bare presentation of the pluses and minuses. The structures we have laid out were generated by our mere ability to remark randomness—the same ability that makes us think we can win at odds-and-evens. "Randomness" cannot appear for us except as a *random order*, marked already with significance.

In *The Psychopathology of Everyday Life* Freud goes to some lengths to show the impossibility of choosing a random number.[5] His argument could be cast into the terms of our game by our saying that if I play against you and I am an analyst, I will win in the long run—because in that long run your choices will not be random, will become visible for me as they are conditioned by your Unconscious and its conflicts. Lacan uses the game of odds-and-evens to advance a claim that is more radical and more palpable—not that a human being cannot pick a random number, but that for a "speaking subject" (one of Lacan's favorite designations for the subject of psychoanalysis) there is no such thing as a random number. What we have stipulated here as a random sequence, what we can generate artificially as such, what we think we can know as the brute finality of randomness—all of this is always and already given to us as *random order*, appropriated to the Symbolic. (If Dupin can find the purloined letter it is because of the way both he and the letter are inscribed within such an order, and not because of Dupin's supposed superiority at the unwinnable game of odds-and-evens.)

Someone goes into analysis. This person thinks that he or she lives in a world composed of forces and counterforces, actions and agents, accidents, failures, happy surprises, and disasters, and that he or she has, let us say, certain problems understanding or controlling his or her self, his or her relation with other people or things. This person, we can say, comes into analysis seeking a winning strategy at odds-and-evens, the special knowledge the psychoanalyst is supposed to have.[6] All Lacan can give is the hard knowledge that it is not like that, there is no way to that kind of victory, because, in the end, there is no simple random world to be guessed at from within the strategies of reflexivity. The appearance of such a world and such a strategy is itself an effect of the priority of the Symbolic order of signification over both self and world. This Symbolic is not something one can come to have or master or be—it is the logic behind the veil, the real machine that moves the characters who claim intention and agency only through an inevitable misunderstanding of themselves and of their real position in the world (Dupin's strategy in recovering the letter is not what he thinks it is because Dupin is neither who nor where he thinks he is).

If we try to push the three Lacanian registers still closer to the game of odds-and-evens, we are going to say:

(1) The Imaginary is the way we live the gap between the real contingency of the world and its recuperation into the law of the Symbolic that we can never quite touch.

(2) The Real is at once the measure of the gap between the Imaginary structures of our desire and the Symbolic law that sets the limit to that desire, and the ground, source, and content of that law.

(3) The Symbolic is the truth of what the Imaginary can perceive only as the Real.[7]

That is, the three registers are so imbricated on and enfolded in one another as to allow no outside to the system they compose—no surface on which something other than itself—other than a destiny—might impinge. In particular, everything one wants to call the real (everything one has every reason to call the real) turns up on the inside of the system as "the Real." There are no accidents.

And yet this has to be nonsense: a real chain of accidents has been somehow elided, forgotten, or suppressed; and it is only on the basis of this chain that the system could have been thought at all. (But this should sound like what we sketched as the implicit Lacanian critique of Hegel—and should show as well how Lacan's psychoanalysis seems to end by taking up once again the Hegelian task of redeeming experience, no longer just for consciousness but for the Unconscious as well. The philosophical trick here will be to balance this permanent human interest in redemption against its own conditions of possibility, to hold to the hard and obvious lessons that so repeatedly drove Bataille to impossible and self-defeating theories: our relation to the world is untouchable, ineffable, and irredeemable; we discover it only as we break our speech and thoughts on it.)

We can put this another way: everything comes to pass in Lacan's psychoanalysis as if what one wants to call reality had been divided in two—into a merely accidental, contingent, and wholly excludable reality that remains forever outside the circle of psychoanalytic sense (to the point of being unable even to impinge on that circle from the outside: the radical claim is that there is no relation at all between inside and outside), and a Real that lies at the very heart of psychoanalysis and is wholly understood by it. And yet these two are the same; the division is impossible and is unable to recognize itself as such. One obvious temptation is to offer a psychoanalytic diagnosis of this—to speak of a repression of accident and a resulting structure of *méconnaissance*. If the issue is posed in this way, it will always appear possible for psychoanalytic theory to overmaster the intended critique since it need only reassert itself as the science of repression, of *méconnaissance*, of the divided subject. And yet every time it performs its gesture of mastery, it repeats its repression of the contingent and leaves itself open once again to the same critique. It is to this delicate line, to this oscillatory and finally permanent controversy that Derrida clings in the repeated assertions that "despite appearances, the deconstruction of logocentrism is not a psychoanalysis of philosophy" and that "logocentric repression is not comprehensible on the basis of the Freudian concept of repression."[8]

Psychoanalysis emerges for Derrida at the limit between "logocentrism" and the "critique of logocentrism":

Our aim is limited: to locate in Freud's text several points of reference, and to isolate, on the threshold of a systematic examination, those elements of psychologocentric closure, as this closure limits not only the history of philosophy but also the "human sciences," notably of a certain linguistics. If the Freudian breakthrough has an historical originality, this originality is not due to its peaceful coexistence or theoretical complicity with this linguistics, at least in its congenital phonologism.[9]

We will be exploring the controversy of deconstruction with psychoanalysis as it unfolds across Derrida's various articles and across the various topics of the structure of the person, the objectivity of science, and the logic of legacy and tradition. In so doing we will stumble again and again across the structure of mutual enfoldedness that we have developed out of Lacan's play with random sequences and the Derridean critique of it. The confrontation is perhaps most succinctly posed in the juxtaposition of the "lesson" Lacan draws from "The Purloined Letter"—"A letter always reaches its destination"—with Derrida's counter to it—"that a letter can always not arrive at its destination"—

> Its "materiality" and its "topology" result from its divisibility, its ever-possible partition. It can always be broken up irrevocably and this is what the system of the symbolic, of castration, of the signifier, of truth, of the contract, and so forth, try to shield it from. . . . Not that the letter never arrives at its destination, but part of its structure is that it is always capable of not arriving there.[10]

But here—as Derrida remarks throughout "The Purveyor of Truth"—we are getting ahead of ourselves.

Psychoanalysis and Philosophy: Critical Realism;
De-idealization; Mise-en-abîme

What, after all, is our interest in all of this? We have seen that psychoanalysis seems able to take up once more the task of philosophy and seems able to pose the problem of tradition—the project of a destruction and a retrieve—for philosophy in a new way. But it is also in psychoanalysis that there is the greatest risk that this "taking up again" could turn out to be another form of *Aufhebung*, returning into rather than pushing beyond the limits of the tradition, relieving it as one guard relieves another, rather than offering us relief from it (*prendre la relève de* . . . [changing the guard] is a Derridean rendering of Hegel's *Aufhebung*). Neither philosophy ("by itself") nor psychoanalysis ("by itself") can prove adequate to the challenge of being post-Hegelian; the challenge demands that the two be put to work, as it were, within one another—demands a thought of heterogeneity rather than purification. The elaboration of such a system of mutual self-criticism is a project that depends on a strong and explicit sense of its disciplinary moorings—even as these moorings guarantee nothing and give themselves over only to suspicion and contestation.

Deconstruction faces the history of philosophy without any access to some deeper truth of that history (a truth like, for example, Heidegger's Being in its revealing and concealing), and so also without access to terms in which to ground a criticism of that history or even—more radically—in which to ground a recognition of it as "the tradition." Derrida is explicitly unable to offer any "realistic" description of the "logocentric closure" parallel to Heidegger's descriptions of the "metaphysical enclosure." For Derrida this enclosure itself is describable as an artifact of the strategies employed to criticize it—with the further provision that the existence of some such artifact is (now) a condition of any philosophic writing whatsoever. I want to say here that if Heidegger can be described as the last "epistemological realist" in a tradition complicated beyond endurance after its achievement in Hegel, Derrida would stand as a "critical realist"—and it is frequently difficult in reading Derrida to hold present for oneself the interlacing of the two terms, "criticism" and "realism": the first seems always to "reduce" the world to a "mere" text and play of signifiers, while the second seems always to boil down to a long-winded insistence on the obvious—patients' fathers do die without being murdered, letters do get lost, things are more complicated than that—and even on the trivial—copyrights and footnotes and margins and shoelaces . . . [11]

The two terms work together above all wherever the idealist gestures by which philosophy leads itself beyond the world are enabled by a denigration of writing. For the person I am calling a critical realist, the most striking instances of such denigration arise precisely in those philosophic texts that refuse to recognize that they are in fact written and so subjected to all the frailties they would attribute to writing and on which they would ground their rejection of it. For example, what is one to make of the condemnation of writing in a text like Plato's *Phaedrus*?[12] What is one to make of the fact that this rejection goes hand in hand, within the text, with a valorization of an inward writing on the soul that serves as the basis of the voice and speech the dialogue would finally valorize over the debilitating duplicity of writing? How deeply does one want to say the tradition is confused here? Could this be fixed simply by recognizing the truth about writing? (What would that truth be?) These are questions about the medium of philosophy, questions designed to force recognition of that medium. They are, at bottom and belatedly, Kantian questions, and we do well to recall him here:

> Misled by such a proof of the power of reason, the demand for the extension of knowledge recognizes no limits. The light dove, cleaving the air in her free flight, and feeling its resistance, might imagine that its flight would be still easier in empty space. It was thus that Plato left the world of the senses, as setting too narrow limits to the understanding, and ventured out beyond it on the wings of the ideas, in the empty space of the pure understanding. He did not observe that with

all his efforts he made no advance—meeting no resistance that might, as it were, serve as a support upon which he could take a stand, to which he could apply his powers, and so set his understanding in motion.[13]

Heidegger took from Kant a thought about the inward essence of philosophy and so sought to find the pure kernel of thinking that lay concealed at the very heart of the tradition as what it had forgotten. Derrida, in contrast, takes from Kant a thought about resistance, support, a certain heterogeneity.[14] For him the "logocentric closure" can only be an enabling strategy for displaying the philosophic ways in which we forget our philosophic selves, escape the world in which we (would) live: it is a belated and radically self-critical de-idealization of the Heideggerean metaphysical enclosure and the Hegelian tradition. It exists where it is read; it insists where it is written.

De-idealization inevitably trails in its wake the notion of demystification, something we recognize as one of the fundamental projects of the modern spirit. Freud, with Marx and Nietzsche, is generally taken to be one of the great masters of such truth telling and the suspicion it entails. But the demystifier's truth cannot guarantee itself against its submission to idealization—even Marx's "materialism" can become one more idealist trope (and almost inevitably will once it escapes its critical function and pretends to name something directly).[15] So also the terms by which Freud names for us our embodiment—"phallus," "feces," "self," "other" . . . Things can easily become confused in the crisscrossing of de-idealization and demystification–the simple demystifying insistence on the phallus may become a vehicle of idealization, just as an apparently abstract reformulation of the phallus may be the most powerful way back to Freud's realism (or, this reformulation may escape the world as thoroughly as, at first blush, it appeared)—there are no guarantees, one has to gauge one's position and act, strategically, upon that estimate. What one takes for one's phallus may turn out to be one's fetish, or just a cigar.

The logocentric closure is not conceivable—as against both its Heideggerean and Hegelian precursors—as any simple limit, linear or circular, on the history of philosophy. It is internal to philosophy and to philosophic texts. It is, accordingly, not a limit one could somehow cross, step beyond—*il n'y a pas d'au-delà*.[16] The very condition of possibility of philosophic objectivity and discipline imposes an ultimate and radical heterogeneity on it (so that while a context for Derrida may have appeared as divisible into a properly philosophical part and an extraphilosophical supplement to that, it is in fact the case that both parts are "properly" philosophical and were so precisely insofar as they escaped from or contested the closure of philosophic discipline). In the final analysis, this closure (however qualified as metaphysical or phonocentric or logocentric or phallogocentric—or even simply as a previous history of errors and uncontrolled speculation) is itself part of a certain philosophic self-understanding, such that to contest it demands not only that we attempt to break out of it but also that we break with the idea of that closure as something to be broken out of. (But of course here psychoanalysis has much to tell us about the limits of any "final analysis.")[17]

I have suggested that the sense of Derrida's "critical realism" becomes most concretely accessible wherever the idealist gestures by which philosophy leads itself beyond the world are enabled by a certain denigration of writing. As a practical matter, this means that the deconstructionist interest in a given philosophic text will tend to settle on that moment—or chain of moments— through which the text would articulate and master itself as (other than) textual, those places where the text attempts to determine for itself a simple "outside" in which it is not implicated, to which it has no relation. This can give deconstruction the appearance of a practice or philosophy of self-reflection, the privileged moment of which would then be that of the *mise-en-abîme*. J. Hillis Miller has proposed that this term be rendered in English as "interior duplication," but the tendency has been (even in Miller's own writing) simply to take the term over as it is. The expression is originally heraldic, referring to the setting of a smaller version of a given shield at the center of that shield; its emergence as a central term in Derrida's work can be said to have been prepared by its use in Gide (*Les Faux-monnayeurs* [*The Counterfeiters*]), Leiris (*L'Age d'homme* [*Manhood*]), and Ponge (*Le Soleil mis en abîme* [*The Sun Placed in the Abyss and Other Texts*]). As should be clear from the heraldic sense, the *mise-en-abîme* implies an infinite perspective on and reduplication of the initial motif: the Morton Salt girl carries Morton Salt bearing the Morton Salt girl carrying Morton Salt bearing the Morton Salt girl carrying . . .

With this appearance of infinite self-reflection, the deconstructionist interest bears precisely on its disruption—a disruption that can be thought of either as a blocking of adequate self-reflection (the intervention within the field of reflection of something both necessary to it and radically heterogeneous with respect to it: the insistence of the general economy within the appearance of its restriction), or as that which obliges the field of self-reflection always to a further reflection, a supplement of *mise-en-abîme* that allows the process of self-reflection no rest, no moment of self-adequacy (and this movement can be described as the always belated effort of a restricted economy to expand itself far enough to master and subsume the general system within which it is inscribed). . . . All real *mise-en-abîme*s end in disruption: after three Morton Salt girls we are faced with nothing more than a few dabs of blue, yellow, and white. A *mise-en-abîme* that continues into the infinite is merely ideal, and its appearance stands in need of explanation, say deconstruction. (It is noteworthy that Miller, discussing the term, apparently does not recognize the problematic idealism that slips into the notion and, in fact, seems to fall in with it by suggesting that *mise-en-abîme* be respelled, as it now is by most Yale critics, as *mise-en-abyme*, thus making the word *"abyme* itself a *mise-en-abyme.")*[18]

Despite a strong appearance to the contrary (an appearance we can now place and acknowledge), deconstruction is a practice and philosophy of self-reflection only in order to be a practice and philosophy of its disruption—a philosophy of consciousness only in order to be able to trace out that system through which the Unconscious makes its presence felt. It is in this perspective that we can grasp the appearance of deconstruction as a certain psychoanalysis of philosophy: it is, after all, psychoanalysis that has taught us what it is to have an Unconscious for an object and that makes available the model through which we can speak of a repression of writing. But if this model becomes available only through precisely that repression of writing . . . ? Then psychoanalysis itself is possessed of an internal limit like that of the logocentric closure of philosophy—psychoanalysis can become the site for a deconstructive exploration wholly comparable to that which deconstruction brings to bear on the texts that belong more obviously to "the philosophic tradition" (an entity whose apparent unity is utterly shattered by this inclusion of psychoanalysis within it).

It is thus that philosophy—deconstructive philosophy—comes to find itself in its controversy with psychoanalysis and to claim that this controversy is one outside which neither philosophy nor psychoanalysis can be found. It remains for us to attempt to fill the gap we have left between the game of odds-and-evens and our meditation on the fate of logocentrism.

Contre-Bande: *The Opposition; the Legacy;* Anasémie; *the Exorbitant*

Derrida's writings on psychoanalysis can be sorted into three large groups—first, those on Freud and the relation of psychoanalysis to the metaphysical tradition ("Freud and the Scene of Writing," "Spéculer—sur 'Freud' " [To speculate—on "Freud"], "Du tout" [Of all]); those belonging to the controversy with Lacan ("The Purveyor of Truth," a long footnote in *Positions*, and some extended remarks in "La Double Séance" [The double session] and "La Dissemination" [Dissemination], both in *Dissemination*); and finally, the recent writings on the work of Nicolas Abraham and Maria Torok ("Fors," "Me—Psychoanalysis," and various remarks in the two interviews "Entre crochets" ["In brackets," or, perhaps, "Hooked"] and "Ja, ou le faux-bond" [Ja, or the broken word]). These groups are of course highly artificial; the various texts mentioned all contest their classification to a greater or lesser extent, communicate with and open into one another in a variety of ways, and so on. In addition, this sort of classificatory scheme takes no notice of the myriad of passing remarks to be found throughout Derrida's writings, and bypasses as well whole texts that simply refuse easy schematizing (*Glas* [Death knell] and "Envois" are certainly the most obvious examples).[19]

Here we will simply trace one possible itinerary through this body of writing, showing one version of the way in which these essays do and do not hang together—a way in which Derrida works psychoanalysis and a way in which psychoanalysis works Derrida. Our particular interest lies in moving from the general considerations on deconstruction that have engaged us this far to a more specific focus on the role of literature within the strategies of deconstruction. This is a route that will lead us from fiction to fiction. The opening fictions are those taken from Imre Hermann by his students Nicolas Abraham and Maria Torok; I cite at considerable length:

—As to that which never was—is it anything other than the poem one is? —As to that which never was, the couch remembers. . . . Myself; poetry, that re-membering animates my verses.

—My poem, here it is, you are going to hear it. It is as rigorous as mathematics and as fantastic as a fairy tale. Yes, fantastic, because its content, its support of images, surges from my fantasy, or from the fantasy of those who call themselves knowing, "savants." But also rigorous because it is postulated in all our thoughts, all our gestures, all our life. . . . For the moment let us learn to see: primitive hordes, pithecanthropes, young apes hanging on mothers, mothers hanging on branches, eyes shining with wildness, the burning stare of the leader, the forest, the forest, the good, original forest, then, suddenly, cataclysms, glacial cold, fire, infants hanging from their mothers, mother hanging from the tree, fire, fire everywhere, a fire that chills (*un feu qui "jette le froid"*), a fire that heats as well, yes, but at such a cost, at the price of becoming torch oneself, torch burning with shame, the red fires of shame, the firey lightning of the look that shames, the regard that like fire releases (*décramponne*) the infant from the mother, releases the mother from the infant, from the infant become her tree. . . . The mother and the child! Always! Their indissoluble unity! Dissolved nonetheless, dissolved too soon, that is what we are the memory of, enacted memory, acting memory: there is our most primitive human instinct, our filial instinct, always frustrated, always at work!

—Now you see that what I have just said . . . is no longer of the order of the science fiction of the past nor of the observational science of the present, but of the order of first truth (*vérité première*) or of *Vé-ri-té* itself, the without-foundation of all foundations, the fantasmatic, the mathematic; the mythological, the economic, the polemic, the political; the -ocracies, magics, techniques, arts. . . . Yes, without "the-shining-eyes-that-have-released-the-infant-from-the-mother-too-soon" we would still be within the simian poetic of the secure maternal pelt. . . .

What is it that could have forced our primordial mother to lose her long thick pelt, the passive organ of instinct? It must have been that she herself had been dropped and that she thus formed a melancholic identification with "no-hair-for-baby" (pas-de-poils-pour-bébé). Then, just as she had been let fall, so she let fall all her pelt, thus making of her now hairless skin a first notice that reality exists, that it is precisely that which is not, that which fails instinct. . . . And all of mother-culture, is it not made of just this "reality" of lack, transformed into the illusion of attachment and grip (cramponnement)?[20]

These passages resonate through much of Derrida's recent writings, especially his essays on Blanchot and the extraordinary "Envois" that opens La Carte postale (Post card). We want here to remark the way in which these passages seem to resurrect in the name of a new and more radical rigor for psychoanalysis much of the worst of Freud's own tendencies toward a biologically mythologized history. It is this overtly fictional tale of apes and hair and fire that Jacques Derrida would erect (in contre-bande, in double-bande) against Lacan's psychoanalysis and its dream of–claim to–scienticity.

Abraham and Torok offer a version of psychoanalysis that claims to find its rigor precisely in such a myth or poem rather than in the abstract schemes, formulas, and "mathemes" that have become increasingly important to Lacan. It is as if Lacan and Abraham/Torok take up two distinct and easily separable sides of the Freudian legacy: so that whereas Lacan takes up the Freud who dreamt of science and reestablishes that dream on linguistic rather than thermodynamic foundations, Hermann's students take up instead the Freud who kept disrupting his science with fantastic dreams of ontogenetic recapitulations of phylogeny. A number of contrasts between Lacan and Abraham/Torok fall out rather nicely along the lines given in this picture: Lacan's central term is desire; Abraham and Torok's is identity. Lacan expounds his vision of science in terms of the "little letters" of his quasi-algebraic "mathemes"; Abraham and Torok speak of poetry, of "capitalization" and "anasemy." Lacan sees language as always prior to human experience; Abraham and Torok see it caught up in the prior structure of cramponnement.[21]

Before we examine some of the notions advanced by Abraham–that of anasémie above all–we can profit from an inquiry into the general nature of a "legacy" that is open to this kind of division.

An examination of "the Freudian legacy" rapidly opens out into a series of interconnected issues. If, for example, we begin with the view that Lacan has returned psychoanalysis to itself, accomplished a genuine return to Freud, we have to go on to ask how this purified psychoanalysis can understand the errors and detours into which Freud's legacy fell. If a letter always reaches its destination (to take up again the terms of the Poe seminar), how did the Freudian letter go astray? How does this possibility of going astray belong to the (proper) structure of the Freudian legacy and how can it—how is it—to be thought by psychoanalysis? If, on this basis, we go on to suggest that the Freudian legacy is one that is necessarily divided (divided, among other ways, as Lacan and Abraham are divided), we can ask also what the relation is between two legatees each of whom is necessarily in the position of laying claim to psychoanalysis as such and in a way that excludes the other. (It appears here that a part of what structures the Freudian legacy is a certain system of exclusions: so that there is a logic of sorts operating behind the splits, breaks, and fissions that have characterized the psychoanalytic movement during Freud's lifetime and after, in France above all perhaps.)[22]

These interlinked questions can point to a rereading of the Freudian text as that text whose letter not only bodies forth the truth of psychoanalysis but is the continuing charter of its movement. That is, we can begin to read Freud's writings as the place where a certain legacy is forged, where a certain will is written. This will is one that includes within itself a special testamentary condition in the event that the legator outlives—survives—his presumptive heirs, a condition that forever ties psychoanalysis to the name and person of Sigmund Freud (and so also to whatever in Freud escapes the terms of psychoanalysis, what remains beyond the terms of his self-analysis). What psychoanalysis would mean by "repression" is forever other than completely that, because it cannot mean other than personally. The laws psychoanalysis wants to attribute to, anchor in, the Father and the Symbolic are always and already abrogated by the secret complicity of grandfather and grandchild, a complicity implicit in the Oedipal confrontation of father and son and disruptive of it.[23]

These are, more or less, the terms and tendencies of Derrida's extraordinary reading of Freud's still more extraordinary *Beyond the Pleasure Principle*. The final object of "Spéculer–sur 'Freud'" is–and is not–an object separate from the text and its workings–a certain Freudian rhythm of distance and proximity, inclusion and exclusion, descent and return, *fort* and *da*, recovery and loss (of a science or a self or a certain "beyond"). This rhythm, this complex patterning of hesitation and speculation, exaggeration and obviousness, is the pulsing of that logic by which Abraham and Lacan are laced in and through one another, excluded from each other–and it is also the rhythm each claims to have mastered as "psychoanalysis" (and it is finally the rhythm through which psychoanalysis is destined to [escape] itself). This rhythm is one that pulses in a different way through Heidegger's writings, and this second, transformed rhythm ripples through the Freud essay, appearing, above all, as the place marked out for an essay yet to appear, "Donner–le temps" ("Giving–time").

"Spéculer–sur 'Freud' " advances no master theory of psychoanalysis beyond the texts in question. Derrida insists that the theory given in the text is precisely that text—he insists, that is, on the literality of *Beyond the Pleasure Principle*, on the "a-thetic" writing that does and undoes the thesis it appears to offer (just as the "beyond" of the pleasure principle appears only as what continually, ceaselessly, does and undoes that principle, without thereby supplanting it or emerging as a principle in its own right). Derrida's interest lies in how psychoanalysis gets (always) beyond itself: the inevitable meaning of its literality and the inevitable literality of its meaning.

What then is psychoanalysis? How is one to speak of it outside its texts and their a-thetic logic? How is one to speak of its writing?

These terms that attempt the impossible—to grasp through language the very source from which language arises and which enables it insofar as they signify nothing other than that very return to the source of its significance—we have called these terms *anasémies*. A psychoanalytic theory recognizes itself as such precisely insofar as it operates with *anasémies*.[24]

Abraham advances his notion of *anasémie* within a very particular logic here: *anasémies* do not, in themselves, define psychoanalysis; they are the means to or occasion for a certain self-recognition. It is, it seems, entirely possible for a "psychoanalytic theory" to fail to recognize its dependence on or use of *anasémies*—but it would then fail to recognize itself as a psychoanalytic theory: it would mistake itself. Such mistakes are always possible—this possibility is itself part of what or how *anasémies* mean.

This notion of *anasémie* is given its fullest and most systematic development in Abraham's review of *The Language of Psychoanalysis*.[25] In his essay "The Shell and the Kernel" Abraham insists on the novelty and specificity of psychoanalysis ("if a conceptual organization of psychoanalysis must indeed exist, it cannot surrender its unity within the bounds of traditional thinking and its apprehension requires a new dimension yet to be found"), and he insists above all on "the radical semantic change that psychoanalysis has introduced into language."[26] This radical change is visible throughout Freud's writings. It is, for example, at work in Freud's statement that "in psychoanalysis the concept of what is sexual comprises far more; it goes lower and also higher than its popular sense."[27] What is this concept—Sex—that is other than sex? How are we suppose to think with or about it? to grasp it?

One way to think this new concept of sex would be to think it as (something like) the whole system of meanings and feelings with which the biological facts of sexuality are essentially imbrued for us, by which they are transformed and through which they come to count for psychoanalysis. Clearly, this attempt moves in the right direction, gets closer to what the psychoanalyst means by Sex (it may even be what the psychoanalyst thinks he means by Sex): what it wants to say is that Sex is the kernel of whatever our ordinary usage of sex wants to say, what that usage has to have grasped in order to say what it does. It is the living kernel beneath the hardened shell of popular usage.[28] But these formulations are almost paradigmatically phonocentric, opposing the vital inward presence of (good) sex to the dead husk that passes as the popular currency of (debased) sex. The definition we are looking for cannot pretend to separate the wheat from the chaff in this way. If our semantic model is to be that of the shell and the kernel, we are going to have to insist not only on the recession of the kernel from its linguistic embodiment but also on the way that embodiment is *its*, belongs essentially to what it is to be "enkerneled." Sex in this sense is the secret of sex (and of psychoanalysis) only as Psychoanalysis is (anasemically) its own secret; we have to replace the infinite inwardness of ever-receding kernels with the logic of an enkerneling that calls forth always a supplementary kernel.

Beyond the Pleasure Principle turns on the difficulties of a pleasure principle in a system that permits of "a pleasure that cannot be felt as such" (and that can even be felt as pain). What Abraham would have us recognize is the anasemic functioning of pleasure within psychoanalysis:

> What then is the principle of coherence of a discourse where Pleasure no longer means what one feels, where Discharge refers to something other than what one sees? In this tangle, some would be tempted to appeal to a phenomenological description of the meanings at issue. [This is roughly the way we first attempted to handle the example of Sex above; Sex is the sexuality of sex, how it counts for us—Abraham would write this as "sex."] . . . Now, strangely enough, metapsychological capitals steadfastly reject the quotation marks of the phenomenologist. The concept of Pleasure cannot be bracketed. . . . Our graphic ploy is suggestive enough to attract attention to the following: the effect of capitalization invokes a mystery, the very mystery of the unthought that burdens reflexive philosophy with a congenital naiveté. It reveals the opaque gratuity of the *distance* that separates the reflecting subject from himself, a distance endangering even patent notions founded on an illusory proximity to self. . . . To state this is already to designate, if not to resolve, the problem which faces us: how to include in a discourse—in any one whatever—the very thing which in essence, by dint of being the precondition of discourse, escapes it? If non-presence, the kernel and ultimate ground of all discourse, is made to speak, can it, must it, make itself heard in and through presence to self? Such is the form in which the paradoxical situation inherent to the psychoanalytic problematics appears.[29]

It is the distinction between the phenomenological "pleasure" and the anasemic Pleasure that is central here; the movement claimed for the "metapsychological capitals" is not toward a deeper inner meaning of the thing—sex, pleasure, the unconscious—but toward the thing itself:

> This, then, is the role of the capitals: instead of *re-signifying* them, they strip words of their signification, they *de-signify* them, so to speak. . . . Psychoanalytic de-signification *precedes* the very possibility of the collision of meanings. The capitals carry out de-signification in a very particular and precise mode, capable of defeating signification and, at the same time, of laying bare the very foundation of the signifying process. Their rigor resides in the always singular way in which they oppose semantic actualization—that Pleasure should mean *pleasure*—all the while referring precisely to the non-presence from which "pleasure" emerges and which, in "pleasure," manages to be represented. In order to make such a capitalized discourse into something other than a mystical or religious illusion, the second step of the exegesis should take it upon itself to define the requirements, constraints, and the universe proper to this scandalous semantics of concepts designified by the action of the psychoanalytic context and revealed as such through the ploy of capitalization.[30] [This last recommendation may be taken to describe Derrida's reading of *Beyond the Pleasure Principle*—and it should be clear that the terms of that reading are thus fundamentally critical rather than theoretical.]

We will pause over these two long citations only long enough for a few fugitive remarks. The designifying movement toward the thing itself, this desperate clinging to the singed hairs of the world, names the workings of reference for Abraham; it is the fact of *décramponnement* that makes our meaning a work of mourning.[31] We should note as well that the project of including in a discourse that which "by dint of being the precondition of discourse, escapes it" is a Bataillean project, and its risk of sliding into "mystical or religious illusion" a Bataillean risk; such a project (and such risk) is called forth by our recognition of the ways in which Lacanian analysis ends up repeating Hegel and the consequent recognition of the way in which the Hegelian legacy demands a thought of heterogeneity. We can on this basis see how exactly Abraham's notion of anasemic designification answers to Lacan's insistence on the remarkability of any random sequence—how this notion works to recover *la chose même*, the thing itself, from its theoretical oblivion.

Capitalization is of course far from being the only ploy of designification. We have already seen Abraham employ two other such devices—the reduction of a phrase to a string of words or the reduction of a word to a string of syllables (*pas-de-poils-pour-bébé, Vé-ri-té*), and the use of *sans* to force a sort of eccentric and critical enkerneling (as in *le sans-fondement de tous fondements* [the without-foundation-of-all-foundations] or, more simply, *le fondement-sans-*

fondement [foundation-without-foundation]).[32] Derrida uses all three of these devices with some frequency in his recent writings.

For Derrida, Abraham is a man who speaks above all about translation,

> even from one language into itself (with the "same" words suddenly changing their sense, overflowing with sense or exceeding it altogether, and nevertheless impassive, imperturbable, identical to themselves, allowing you still to read in the new code of this anasemic translation what belonged to the other word, the same one, before psychoanalysis, that other language, makes use of the same words but imposes on them a "radical semantic change").[33]

A psychoanalytic text is, in this light, its own absolute homonym, exceeding its own apparent simplicity and integrity at every point. Abraham's formulation of *anasémie* allows Derrida to understand the disciplinary economy of psychoanalysis, its adherence to its proper object—its purity[34]—as already transgressive, "general" (in Bataille's sense), and other than "merely" disciplinary: psychoanalysis, we will say, is necessarily and variously excessive, peculiar, exorbitant, and everywhere open to criticism and reading. Its difference inheres everywhere within its absolute homonymy: *différance*.

It is of course just this to which we were pointing in our discussion of the Freudian legacy and its implications in and for a movement (that does not step) beyond the pleasure principle. Derrida's reading of Freud's text is a critical elaboration of the anasemic structure of the Pleasure Principle, showing how the divisions and oppositions that characterize the institution of psychoanalysis (its founding, the means of its continuation) are inscribed within the absolute homonymy of the text—just as a simple chain of pluses and minuses ends up as its own absolute homonym and runs the risk of losing itself or of becoming sundered from itself within that apparent identity. So also "Freudianism" ends as its own homonym, a complex *anasémie* through which the founder inscribes himself—permanently, necessarily—within the structure of what would be more simply a science: so also a certain experience of consciousness insists in and recedes from the Hegelian Experience of Consciousness, stands at once as condition and subverter of its proper science, is both readable and unreadable, written and unwritten, thought and unthought, within it.

The exorbitant economy of anasemic homonymy reorganizes and redistributes the relations between fiction, theory, and history in and around psychoanalysis in such a way that it is no longer possible to exclude from the corpus of psychoanalytic seriousness its textual moments of madness, absurdity, or (less romantically) ridiculousness—the primal horde, the hairless ape, or the influence of the lunar period on the mucus membranes—or to exclude from the canon of psychoanalytic science its overtly speculative moments. We can say that this economy demands our acknowledgment of the inevitability of a fictional supplement to psychoanalysis or, equally, that it demands our acknowledgment of the way psychoanalytic theory is responsive to something other than truth (perhaps, truth-without-truth).[35] We could also say that recognition of the anasemic structure of psychoanalysis has the effect of freeing fiction and theory to one another, or of placing both these terms as secondary to and enabling of a more fundamental critical and self-critical undertaking.

What I have just referred to as the "freeing of fiction and theory to one another" will be explored more fully in the ensuing chapters, but it is important to see here that this setting aside of truth as a central organizing and distinguishing term cannot but undercut certain notions of history—a subversion on which I have presumed already in speaking of the anasemies of the *Phenomenology* above. "The radical semantic change that psychoanalysis has introduced into language" existed in language prior to psychoanalysis, but could not be recognized as such. The psychoanalytic recognition of anasemy and absolute homonymy has consequences that rebound, through a logic psychoanalysis recognizes as that of Deferred Action, upon the whole of the history in which one would presume to locate the simple "event" of *anasémie*. We can be content here neither with the picture of a certain radical change introduced into a preexistent and simpler language at a certain time, nor with the idea that this apparent change is simply the recognition of what had really always been the case: the "event" we are trying to grasp here is complex—insists on time, takes time, works in time.

We can say that through the lens of *anasémie* "the tradition" becomes visible as its own homonym, and the historical field becomes the privileged playground in which theory and fiction interlace with one another, permitting such mad hypotheses as a historical "repression of writing" (in which—we can say now—"repression" must be read anasemically, as Repression, within and without psychoanalysis at once). Perhaps more madly still, we might write about the influence of Hitchcock on Freud or of Plato on Socrates. We can feel what this would be about, its subject and critical legitimacy can easily seem clear enough; the madness of theory counts as it enables reading, and reading counts as it counts or fails to count. The power we find in Lacan's reading of Freud is clear and familiar enough; the power Derrida attributes to Abraham is less familiar—critical, ungrounded, strategic. Derrida could be wrong here—but he would then simply have been wrong: a legitimate and paradigmatic critical failure.

Derrida's epistolary text "Envois" works in and out of his discovery of and fascination with a medieval woodcut that portrays—mistakenly? accidentally? with the cunning of history?—a certain "plato" dictating to his apparent scribe "Socrates." To a greater extent than any other Derridean text (including *Glas*), "Envois" operates within an explicit interlacing of fiction and theory, history and its subversion, autobiography and philosophy, holding itself at the very limit of (de)signification and (un)readability. The rules for its reading are perhaps given in some remarks Derrida made elsewhere, on Blanchot:

The double invagination of this narrative body in deconstruction [for which we might simply read, "the logic of anasemy"] overruns and exceeds not merely the opposition of values that make the rules and form the law in all the schools of reading, ancient and modern, before and after Freud; it overruns a delimitation of the fantasy, a delimitation in the name of which some would here abandon, for example, the mad hypothesis to "my" fantasy-projection, or to that of one who says "I" here, the narrator, the narrators, or me, who am telling you all this here. This unreadability will have taken place where it remains: that's the proof. From here on it's up to you to think what will have taken place, to work out both the conditions for its possibility and its consequences.[36]

As "rules" these statements are open to the same logical criticisms as the simpler slogans "All reading is misreading" or "All reading is rereading." The ground on which they can claim to stand is one that is anasemically structured (and so no ground at all): "This text then must be deciphered with the help of the code it proposes and which belongs to its own writing."[37] It is around this notion of *anasémie* that we can pose questions about Derrida's language—the ways in which it means, the ways in which it is invariably excessive, always inadequate—or about his idiom, the ways in which he clings to it, the ways in which he is pinned on it, the ways in which it ends as other than mere idiolect: questions of style.

[Questions of Style]

[Such questions of style emerge in the interstices and pauses of our reading of the relation between Derrida and psychoanalysis. At the same time, Derrida's style is everywhere explicitly answerable to the terms of this reading and relation—the logic of the a-thetic uncovered in *Beyond the Pleasure Principle*, the enkerneling recession of metapsychological anasemies, the uncanny multiplication of doubles beyond and in subversion of any possibility of adequation. "Style" is also a moment for Derrida's own work of reading and deconstruction—in *Eperons* (Spurs) it is Nietzsche's "style(s)" that organize the text, and in the polemic with Lacan, it is Lacan's "style" that is said to have concealed, for a time, the shortcomings of "The Seminar on 'The Purloined Letter.'"]

In pausing here, in creating this parenthesis within the present essay, we involve ourselves, briefly, fleetingly, with another body of Derridean texts: essays on Heidegger and the fictions of Maurice Blanchot, or the poetry of Francis Ponge. At one limit of this field we touch on everything Derrida has had to say and continues to say about the signature, its uniqueness and its divisibility, as well as on the contexts and polemics that have become proper to this problematic (Austin, Searle). This new field is more nearly philosophical than the one in which we have been working so far. Even when Derrida writes on Blanchot or Ponge, it is easy to see through to the hidden agenda: Heidegger and Blanchot, Heidegger and Ponge. The transition into this parenthesis is thus a crossing into philosophy—given what we know of the boundary between psychoanalysis and philosophy, given that we now, from this side, call this relation one of "chiasmatic invagination of borders."[38]

Here, now, in philosophy and in parentheses, between psychoanalysis,[39] within the space of its homonymity, we play in and upon a question of style, clinging to the Derridean idiom until we are burned away from it.

Questions of style are here, already, questions of location—of what we have called "positionality." They are, that is, questions of how we stand in relation to philosophy—belatedly, in time or not in time—and of how we read the texts of philosophy—repetitiously, rhythmically, hesitantly.

(Under what conditions will these paragraphs have made sense? And what in these paragraphs dictates that this question be posed through the gratuitous complexity of what is called the "future perfect"?)

Here we are, no doubt, too far ahead of ourselves. What might it mean for a theory, psychoanalytic or not, to recognize itself through its anasemies? What does such a theory recognize about itself? I think we have to say here that it recognizes itself as possessed—over and above a certain context, perhaps even regardless of that context, a-thetically—of or by something like a style—*d'une style*. This style, we want also to say, is precisely that which eludes our grasp as content and recedes from us (coinciding, within a certain traditional strain of philosophy and criticism, with *la chose même*).

Let us begin by saying that for Derrida the history of metaphysics is founded on a repression of writing and is therefore organized, for the analytic eye, by the effects of that repression and so is readable against its own grain, open to the "correction" of deconstruction. Insofar as this version of the Derridean project has for its implicit goal a movement beyond repression, a step outside its history and the enclosure of metaphysics, it is faced immediately with the central difficulty that all its concepts and terms mean only within the very history they would contest. If, for example, "book" is everywhere caught up in a system that devalorizes writing in favor of speech because (roughly) speech is understood to be more nearly, more deeply, self-identical, closer to the thought it would body forth, possessed of greater integrity and force—if what a "book" is and how "publication" counts and how "copyright" becomes necessary are all determined by their belonging to such a system—what then is one to call that in which one would make public a certain revalorization or liberation of a positive and disseminatory writing? It is here, from this kind of complexity, that deconstruction begins:

> This (therefore) will not have been a book.

So begins *Dissemination*. The "(therefore)," we can say, is "understood."

The belated recognition reported in this sentence determines deconstruction from the outset as a paleonymic practice—intending to make new meanings show themselves, turn into the light, within the shells of their old names: "writing," "trace," "supplement," "gramme," . . . so many terms taking their turn at organizing Derrida's readings and writings and accompanied always by a new variant of the same caution: *"Différance* is neither a *word* nor a *concept."*[40]

> Let us begin again. To take some examples: why should "litera-
> ture" still designate that which already breaks away from literature—
> away from what has always been conceived and signified under that
> name—or that which, not merely escaping literature, implacably
> destroys it? (Posed in these terms, the question would already be
> caught in the assurance of a certain foreknowledge: can "what has
> always been conceived and signified under that name" be considered
> fundamentally homogeneous, univocal, or non-conflictual?) To take
> other examples: what historical and strategic function should hence-
> forth be assigned to the quotation marks, whether visible or invisible,
> which transform this into a "book," or which still make the decon-
> struction of philosophy into a "philosophical discourse"?[41]

The necessity for a paleonymic practice of deconstruction is viewed here as a response to a theoretical difficulty within a naive and fundamentally idealist project of escape from history. In practice this paleonymy comes to sponsor reciprocal invasions of style by content (so that nothing appears neutral, "merely rhetorical," trivial, or frivolous) and of content by style (so that every-thing appears frivolous, self-indulgent, empty). This double movement is one that becomes increasingly able to name itself as a liberation of writing—a freeing of writing to itself. If we began by describing this practice of paleonymy as a way of turning new meanings into the light within their old shells, we find now that this practice becomes a way of turning itself as it were through itself—old meanings into new shells: paleonymy into *anasémie*, negation into affirmation, double bind to *double-bande*. It becomes a practice that would everywhere demarcate the remarkability of our language, its identity with and difference from itself.

As paleonymy turns through itself to find its anasemic affirmation of itself, as the practice of deconstruction finds its way ever more surely to "writing," it becomes ever more able to recognize itself and its ground (*sans*-ground, *Abgrund*, abyss). It is thus in part himself that Derrida appears to be correcting when he writes that

> dissemination . . . does not play, as one might too easily believe, with the plural, the dispersed, the scattered, nor between multiplicity and unity, but between the unique.[42]

We have already seen something of how this insistence on "the unique" animates the argument with Lacan, and we may have glimpsed already, here and there, something of the way in which "literature" functions for Derrida as the vehicle of the unique in writing. Here—in parentheses and in philosophy—we want to see how this insistence presses Derrida back toward Heidegger. It is because this work turns always around the unique, the thing, the event, that it cannot bypass some ontological moment (even if its work is finally only to criticize).

Derrida has from the outset recognized the Heideggerean moment as "extremely important . . . a novel, irreversible advance all of whose critical resources we are far from having exploited."[43] The pressure of the Heideggerean problematic on the Derridean seems at present greater than ever, appearing most explicitly (to date) in the essay "The *Retrait* of Metaphor." The article matters to us here insofar as its critical points turn on a matter of style:

> Of more importance to me for the moment is the other of the two motifs common to Greisch and Ricoeur, namely, that the metaphoric power of the Heideggerean text is richer, more determinant than his thesis on metaphor. The metaphoricity of Heidegger's text would overflow what he says thematically, in the mode of simplificatory denunciation, of the so-called "metaphysical" concept of metaphor. . . . I would quite willingly subscribe to this assertion. What remains to be determined, however, is the meaning and necessity which link this apparently univocal, simplifying and reductive denunciation of the metaphysical concept of metaphor on the one hand, and, on the other, the apparently metaphorical power of a text whose author no longer wishes that what happens in that text and what claims to get along without metaphor there be understood precisely as "metaphoric," nor even under any concept of metalinguistics or rhetoric.[44]

Derrida's interest in the gap between the metaphoric power of the Heideggerean text—its style—and its theses on metaphor is, as this passage makes clear, an interest in the unity and simplicity of the metaphysical tradition and so also in the "reality" of that object whose absence, repression, or forgetting is the unity of that tradition. For Heidegger, the denunciation of the distinction between literal and metaphorical as "metaphysical" would free his language into a deeper propriety—tying, for example, such statements as "language is the house of Being" to the deeper ground of a-lethia and freeing it from any merely metaphysical reading as either literal or merely metaphorical, simply true or simply poetic or evocative. (It is, in effect, as if it is Being that is to ground, to fill out our reading of "house"—rather than "house" opening the way to a particular sight of Being.) The sense Heidegger wants to attribute to (what appear as) metaphors in his text is the sort of sense we have seen Abraham attribute to the phenomenological understanding of sex as "sex"—caught up in an inward movement, generative of deeper sense, truth, and presence.

Derrida's critical and deconstructive task is then to show that Heidegger's text cannot escape its own, "mere" metaphoricity. With this Derrida renews an argument first advanced in "The White Mythology" and does so in response to criticisms by Paul Ricoeur calling particularly for a clarification of Derrida's relation to Heidegger, a spelling out of his critical, rather than realistic, stance toward the "metaphysical enclosure."[45] The argument for the radical insistence of metaphor in language is simple enough—all that needs to be shown is that the condition for any metaphor whatsoever is a plurality of metaphors, and that this must mean a plurality that can neither be reduced to the literal nor be subsumed under some larger and more embracing meta-metaphorics. The argument insists on the heterogeneity of language, the incoherence of any dreams of any ideal homogeneity or simplicity of meaning.

Heidegger appears to be entering a claim for just such a dream prior to or deeper than the distinction of metaphorical and literal. Derrida's deconstructive reading sets out to demonstrate that this recessive movement beneath the separation of literal and metaphorical, poetic and philosophical, itself depends on a heterogeneity which repeats that of the literal and the metaphoric and which it cannot think—and which thus sets in motion the gap that is so apparent in Heidegger's writing between its theses on metaphor and its superabundant metaphorical power. At issue here is the way in which a certain withdrawal or retreat of Being behind and before the metaphysical tradition and its distinctions can and cannot organize a plenum of sense, can and cannot make itself (philo-sophically) present to us—how far, finally, we can lay claims to a metaphysical tradition and an escape from it—how far we can step beyond or back from our condition. Derrida's reading shows that the organizing withdrawal of Being, its retreat, is unable to organize and master its own sense, is submitted to *anasémie*:

> When trait or *retrait* is said in a context where truth is in question, "trait" is no longer a metaphor of what we usually believe we recog-nize by this word. It does not, however, suffice to invert the propo-sition and say that the withdrawal (*re-trait*) of truth as non-truth is the proper or the literal by way of which current language will be in a position of divergence, of abuse, of tropical detour in any form. Withdrawal is no more proper or literal than figurative. . . . *Retraits* thus writes itself in the plural, it is singularly plural in itself, divides

itself and reassembles in the withdrawal of withdrawal [that is, this
Heideggerean "mystery," "the self-concealing of Being," and so on,
appears as the guarantee of an inwardness of sense, papering over the
way in which each of its terms is in itself already plural, divided,
borne away from itself]. It is what I have elsewhere tried to name *pas*.
It is a question here of the path again, of what passes there, or not.[46]

These last words can be taken to figure for us a part of Derrida's argument
with Lacan and with what remains Heideggerean in Lacan; we would want then
to say that neither Heidegger nor Lacan can think the possibility (and so the
necessity) of a detour, of something other than the path. In the terms of a contrast employed earlier Derrida is claiming that behind the apparent richness of
the image, the road that lies behind Heidegger's ontological "forest paths" is
no less direct than Hegel's road to the Absolute (and also, of course, no less tortured), no less prone to pass beyond the terms of the world.

But for us now the difference between Derrida and Heidegger can be most
simply marked in a point of style: Heidegger casts his final terms centripetally
and phenomenologically (the Being of beings, the neighborliness of neigh-
boring, and so on), whereas Derrida casts his centrifugally and anasemically
(and so as other than final)—truth without truth, foundation without foundation.[47]

If I write for example: the water without water, what happens? Or
again, a response without a response? The same word and the same
thing seem withdrawn from themselves, delivered from their reference
and their identity, even as they continue to let themselves pass, in their
old bodies, toward something entirely other hidden in them.[48]

The closing lines of this passage elude translation and approach a limit of
Derridean writing, becoming very close to something like the pure rhythm of
designification: "Mais pas plus que dans 'pas,' cette operation ne consiste a
simplement priver ou nier, il s'en faut." (But no more than in "pas," this operation does not consist simply in privation or denial—necessarily it falls short.)
Elle forme la trace ou le pas du tout autre qui s'y agit, le re-trait du pas, et du
pas sans pas. It forms the trace or footprint/negation of the wholly other at work
there, the retreat/reinscription of the step/negation, and of the step/negation
without step/negation.

The closing sentence is nothing other than its scansion of itself, of the inner
periodicities through which it means, meaning without meaning, *voulant dire
sans vouloir dire, sens-sans-sens*. In the flickerings of Derrida's *pas* (or *Pas*) we
can feel resumed—recapitulated, deconstructed, *read*—not only Hegel's logic of
trace and negation but also Heidegger's dialogical revision of it into the step
back, a moment of retreat. Such sentences are—I want to say—"speculative
propositions," holding themselves within rather than claiming to overcome the

tension between prosody and logic. These are propositions that participate in the logic of the Hegelian *Phenomenology* even as they subvert—are acknowledgments of—it, rewriting the notion of *Aufhebung* in another place, forcing its *anasemie*:

> In order that "I find myself truly in the beyond, if the beyond is that which admits of no beyond," it must be the case that the step (*pas*) which carries me there overcome itself [*se franchisse lui-même*—for more on *franchir*, see *Signsponge*], annulling while preserving the beyond; and at the same time the structure of the step (*pas*) precludes that the double effect of *pas* (annullingffipreserving the beyond) be a negation of the negation returning to include, interiorize, or idealize that step (*pas*). This is the strange process of which the negation of the negation (in its powerful system) is but a determined effect, *du pas, un pas.*[49]

These "speculations" rhyme absolutely as well with those of Freud in *Beyond the Pleasure Principle*:

> What we have retained of *Beyond* . . . , is it anything other than a rhythm, the rhythm of a negation (*pas*) that always *returns* (*revient*), that returns from leaving (revient de partir)? That has always just left again [*Qui vient toujours de repartir*—we might also say then, "that has always just replicated itself" and with only a slight change of accent (Hegel: "the conflict that occurs in rhythm between metre and accent"), "has always just distributed, divided, itself"]? And if there is a theme in the interpretation of this piece—a theme rather than a thesis, it is perhaps *rhythmos*, and the rhythm of the theme no less than the theme of rhythm.
>
> If speculation remains necessarily irresolute because it plays on two tableaux, *bande contre bande*, failing to win and winning to lose, why be astonished that it progresses badly (*que ça marche mal*)? But it must progress badly to progress at all; if it lacks, if it must move, it must move badly. It staggers well, doesn't it? (*S'il faut, s'il faut que ça marche, ça doit mal marcher. Ça boite bien, n'est-ce pas?*)[50]

This staggering, perhaps drunken, march along what we might call the pathway of despair or a forest trail or a royal road we can now also call a *boite postale* or a *boîte postale*—box or limp, the way we get our mail in any case, the way our sense is delivered, to us, from us.

As this hesitant and limping dialectic passes over into music, the space in which we can claim to pose a "question of style" closes down for us, returns us from our detour. (Another opens elsewhere in which we would be called upon to dance in another style: *ce séminaire aura joué le fort:da de Nietzsche.*) But we must now pass back to Freud, literature, fiction.]

Open Questions

One way of summing up this whole matter of style would be to say that Derridean philosophy aspires to the condition of literature, and that the achievement of that condition would be at once the fulfillment of the Hegelian legacy within which such an aspiration arises, and the undoing of (or passing beyond) the philosophic interests that animate this desire. (It would be like trying to live within an economic order that refused itself any restriction whatsoever, refused itself any accumulation in the name of a radical *dépense* [expenditure] that was no longer even recognizable as such—a step beyond the problematics of transgression into a simpler annihilation of limits.) There are senses in which one would want to call this achievement the "forgetting of philosophy"—this is increasingly the name by which we tend to recognize the success of philosophy (a success which, if it is not impossible, is certainly invisible, having come to pass only where philosophy is not [is no longer? never was?] done).

The problems posed for philosophy by the terms in which it is given to think its own success cut to the very heart of its modern condition. We need perhaps only cite Cavell here:

> The figure of Socrates now haunts contemporary philosophical practice and conscience more poignantly than ever—the pure figure motivated to philosophy only by the assertions of others, himself making none; the philosopher who did not need to write. . . . If silence is always a threat in philosophy, it is also its highest promise.[51]

Derrida's critical practice of deconstruction appears or can appear as a belated and desperate Socratism, the work of a philosopher who can only write, and whose writing is always threatened with a passage over into the radical irrecuperability—*restance*—of literature. It is in seeing this that we can see also that literature is what the philosophical practice of deconstruction cannot face directly, cannot have as an object of its criticism: literature can figure for deconstruction only indirectly, as means to its radical self-criticism (or as its end, in which case it is too late).

This is not to say that deconstruction does not, like stained color on canvas, "bleed" literary theory, or that it does not cast light, even essential light, on a variety of literary works: it does, of course, all of this and is everywhere inextricably tangled up with literature and with criticism. To this point I have been concerned simply to recall the sources and motives of that entangling from their still deeper entanglement in a morass of critical assumptions about the relevance or irrelevance, necessity or gratuitousness, value or perniciousness, of deconstruction for literary and critical theory.

It is time now to attempt to rearticulate the consequences of deconstruction for such theory. In this undertaking we are going to be concerned above all with what has so far proved to be the most compelling account of how Derrida's work counts for criticism, Paul de Man's *Blindness and Insight: Essays in the Rhetoric of Contemporary Criticism*, and with the practical criticism that has followed from it. In the end we will want to know how it is that this work could give rise to an essay—a brilliant and compelling essay—which finds itself unable to know "whether Lacan and Derrida are really saying the same thing or only enacting their own differences from themselves."[52] Such "ignorance" seems too close to the forgetting with which Derrida charged Lacan in the first place, a failure of reading where such a failure ought not arise and a more sophisticated error than de Man's theory of criticism intends or can understand.

Chapter 4
Paul de Man: The Time of Criticism

The burden of the argument to this point has been that philosophy, in response to needs generated within its "own" history, has come to be at necessary odds with its self, its history, and the proprietary self-presence implicit in such notions of self and history. In these straits, philosophy has turned increasingly to criticism for an understanding of its activity, and so has risked also its possible disappearance into literature. Literary criticism and theory thus find themselves in an odd position: a discipline that has a long-established habit of looking elsewhere—primarily to science or philosophy—for models of its activity and guarantees of its sense and validity suddenly finds itself in the position of the model appealed to, and it is far from clear what consequences such an appeal should have for criticism or for theory. It seems, in general, that such an appeal should have no consequences: if I have a coat and it so impresses you that you get one for yourself (in, of course, your size), it would be odd of me to now go out in my turn and buy a coat cut to your size. It would seem the most I am called upon to do is take renewed pride in my coat—perhaps even wear it places for which I had initially thought it too shabby, and so on.[1]

The example is too easy of course. But it remains true that we do not, for the most part, expect physics (for example) to have to or even want to change itself in the light of some appeal to it from criticism or even philosophy. There is a real question about whether and—more important—how one is to think about the transition from Derrida's project to the practice of literary criticism and theory.

That transition has been accomplished for the overwhelming majority of theoretically oriented critics and scholars in and by the work of the late Paul de Man, in and by his collection *Blindness and Insight: Essays in the Rhetoric of Contemporary Criticism* above all.[2] In view of the situation I have outlined, it ought not be a major surprise that what has functioned as the foundation of the enterprise we commonly call "deconstructive criticism" takes in that book the form of a critique of Jacques Derrida's work on Rousseau. This is nonetheless a peculiar mode of foundation—as, indeed, "deconstructive criticism" may seem a peculiar and peculiarly redundant enterprise to have founded.

It is within this complex field that I want to examine the achievement of Paul de Man in *Blindness and Insight*. This is in part the achievement of a transition, and we do well to note in advance both that "transition" is a term with profound Hegelian echoes and that the question of the possibility or impossibility of transition and mediation is central to all of de Man's work. That work is in fact the transition from deconstruction to its critical acknowledgment—but it is a transition accomplished through an insistent rejection of the possibility of such mediation and transition.

These difficulties organize from the outset our examination of de Man's work and urge on us a difficult doubleness, a new version of the coupling of rupture and acknowledgment with which we have been working throughout this book: what will appear with increasing sharpness in these pages as a critique of de Man can be such only insofar as it begins as and is everywhere enabled by an acknowledgment of the deep and continuing power of that work. The critical path claims to move deeper into rather than away from the sense of de Man's work.

This path leads also into the most compelling work of some of de Man's students or followers, and here too critique and acknowledgment will be twined about one another. We are led this way because everything we have done so far has argued that psychoanalysis occupies a special place within our general field of disciplinary and interdisciplinary concerns. Acknowledgments or appropriations or rejections of psychoanalysis are images of knowing, of reading, and of writing—and the way or ways in which de Manian "deconstructive criticism" stands toward psychoanalysis can be unfolded into more general statements about knowledge and criticism. And here it is a curious fact, in need of our understanding, that de Man's implicit rejection of and explicit lack of interest in psychoanalysis (a lack of interest that seems to reflect a more or less "Sartrean" insistence on consciousness and "bad faith") is balanced, perhaps mirrored, by a strong interest in psychoanalysis on the part of some of his most prominent followers, notably Barbara Johnson and Shoshana Felman.

I suppose the first thing that should be said about de Man is that his career has been much longer and more consistent than has been generally thought.[3] Writing in France throughout the fifties and in this country in the sixties (primarily for the *New York Review of Books*), de Man established early and clearly the basic positions about literature and life with which he came to be associated in the wake of his writing on Derrida. De Man has never been in the position of follower or interpreter of Jacques Derrida, however much the essay in *Blindness and Insight*, read in relative isolation and as an upsurge of the new, may have fostered such an impression. Rather, what we see in "The Rhetoric of Blindness" is one fully formed and deeply held intellectual position facing another with which it shares or seems to share a great deal. This description can be applied also to de Man's essay on Blanchot in the same book and to his series of essays in the mid-fifties on Heidegger as a reader of Hölderlin. De Man's negotiation with Derrida is but one in a series of such negotiations; I will treat none of them here although I will touch briefly on their significance below. De Man's reading of Blanchot has recently been the object of a careful critique by Donald Marshall, and a full appraisal of de Man's dealings with Heidegger would require a separate forum.[4]

More surprising, no doubt, will be my willingness to pass by de Man's direct encounter with Derrida—even if it can be seen to follow from my suggestion that there is indeed no direct passage from Derrida to criticism. Rather than present a historically and conceptually misleading picture in which Derrida gives rise to a certain new literary critical and theoretical activity, I want to sketch out a literary critical position by which Derrida has been received (or, more harshly, to which he has been appropriated). We can then ask of this position how far it can count as an acknowledgment of criticism (the question of this chapter) and how far it can count as an acknowledgment of "Derrida" or at least of the Derrida at issue in the reading of psychoanalysis (the question of the next chapter). Acknowledgment is, as I have stressed throughout, a peculiar act, in a sense achieving itself only in its failure, and failing deeply only where it denies its self, its failure. There are failures and failures here, but there are not final terms of criticism and no final moments of damnation or salvation. We deal in (the criteria of critique are matters of) tact and tactics. The difficulties are difficulties above all of tone, of weight and balance. Such matters may seem fallings away from what we have learned to think of as Derridean and de Manian "rigor." Shoshana Felman's remarks on tact may be of service here:

> But tact is not just a practical, pragmatic question of "couchside manner"; it also has a theoretical importance: the reserve within the interpretative discourse has to allow for and indicate a possibility of error, a position of uncertainty with respect to the truth.[5]

We might equally cite Derrida:

> Much would depend on the tone I want understood. A tone is decisive; and who shall decide if it is, or is not part of a discourse?[6]

Such words risk "phonocentrism"—risking it, they demand that we recall why that would matter, what sense and necessity—or nonsense and contingency—are staked by it.

Derrida's work is, I have argued, a recognition of criticism—an appeal to it as if it offered a legitimate and (more or less) autonomous mode of knowledge. This is, for the most part, not how criticism in the twentieth century has thought of itself; it has, again for the most part, tended to think of itself as ungrounded, not (yet) scientific, in need of principles, objects, procedures, guarantees, and the like. It is in the resulting crisscross of aspirations—of philosophy to criticism and of criticism to science (say, *Wissenschaft*)—that the wager of a deconstructive criticism is made. The risk is that the critic may see in Derrida the latest, best, or most powerful source of grounding principles for criticism and will thus use Derrida to re-epistemologize criticism, to set it once more on deeper, sounder, or truer foundations; the promise is that the critic may come to some acknowledgment of his ungrounded condition and so make such peace as is to be made with his aspiration to "science." Our current use of the word "theory" is clearly governed by this double structure of risk and promise, and de Man's late essay "The Resistance to Theory" is one of the most interesting—if also most deeply disturbing—efforts to come to grips with the complexities now packed into this word.[7] That essay closes as follows:

> Nothing can overcome the resistance to theory since theory *is* itself this resistance. The loftier the aims and the better the methods of literary theory, the less possible it becomes. Yet literary theory is not in danger of going under; it cannot help but flourish, and the more it is resisted, the more it flourishes, since the language it speaks is the language of self-resistance. What remains impossible to decide is whether this flourishing is a triumph or a fall.[8]

One way of putting the central question I will be posing about de Man's work would be to ask whether this "self-resistance" is or is not the same as the activity I have been referring to as "self-criticism" or "radical self-criticism." If—as I will argue—they are not the same, what is the difference between them and what, especially, is the particularity of the one term's evasion of the other? These questions would lead in the end to Derridean questions about whether or not such distinctions can be made to stick, whether or not one can finally purge self-criticism of self-evasion, disentangle a theatrical "self-resistance" from a purer moment of "radical self-criticism." But the answer to these questions should be clear in advance and, indeed, establish such criteria as there are for the critique. I do not—except here and there—have an argument with de Man; I have a critique of sorts, a reading, that both does and does not escape or contest de Man's own terms of, for example, blindness and insight: it is, or would be, an act of self-criticism.

Probably the most frequently voiced critique of Paul de Man is that he "privileges" literature. Paul Bové can provide us with a representative cento:

A destructive reading of Bate, Bloom, Cleanth Brooks, and to a lesser extent Paul de Man, shows that they are all caught within essentially the same metaphysical critical tradition. To varying degrees all of these critics' works—consciously or not—nostalgically reify an aesthetically ordered, often humanist, tradition as an alternative to the radical flux, disorder, alienation, and death which characterizes the Postmodern world. . . . de Man's own simplifying blindness, that is, his claim that all poetic language is already demystified and not in need of destruction, emerges as an unexamined presupposition. . . . de Man reveals Derrida's perhaps necessary blindness, that is, to the possibility that literature itself can approach total demystification at times, but as an observer, he is himself partially deconstructed by his exchange with Derrida. In the chapter on Rousseau, de Man's commitment to the absolutely self-aware fictionality of all literature is revealed as an unexamined presupposition. . . . his theory of literature remains partially mystified.[9]

This welter of reifications, partial deconstructions, and partial demystifications is very largely nonsense. Yet it is a seductive kind of nonsense—one that has, always, a familiar tang to it: it is a fact of critical modernity that we suspect the "privileging" of literature—even though it is hard to know what a literary critic is to do if not that. And it is a fact of critical modernity that we take it that there is something to be "demystified" in literature, even though we know that none of the ways in which we normally make sense of the notions of "mystification" and "demystification" apply to fictions as such.

Bové's criticism is direct, simple, and traditional enough: de Man sees almost correctly, has only one small patch of blindness left—one more minor correction and he will have full, demystified critical vision. It should be clear that this kind of criticism is precisely what is not open to us, is what we have been concerned to fight off throughout this book. It is also a "mode of repudiation" (in Cavell's phrase) that de Man himself works to set aside from the very beginning of *Blindness and Insight*: "My remarks are meant to indicate some reasons, however, for considering the conception of literature (or literary criticism) as demystification the most dangerous myth of all, while granting that it forces us, in Mallarmé's terms, to scrutinize the act of writing *'jusqu'en l'origine'*" (*Blindness*, p. 14). We will not be engaging de Man's project unless and until we step up to the level at which he would repudiate the language of privilege and demystification—and, at this level, our critique will necessarily focus on whatever in de Man continues to invite this kind of correction, on what continues to set up literary criticism as a certain kind of knowledge of a certain kind of object (even one that defeats knowing). Our argument will be with those statements in de Man's work that invite the confusion of (certain defeats of) knowledge with the activity of criticism. Our thesis is nonetheless close to just what it would criticize in de Man; it is that criticism begins and endures just so long as we can set the question of knowledge aside.

De Man's desire to step away from the modern language of privilege and demystification is but part of a larger revision of modernism at work in *Blindness and Insight* and ultimately in service to a certain complex revalorization of romanticism that becomes most explicit in "The Rhetoric of Temporality" (henceforth cited in the text as "Rhetoric"). Although de Man came to feel that a selective interest in romanticism evidenced a bad literary critical conscience, his own career began from just such an interest, and it is in terms of a continuing effort to recover romanticism from its New Critical dereliction that one can most easily and clearly see the pressures driving his work forward. De Man's early project is surprisingly close to Harold Bloom's. De Man's 1962 essay "The Intentional Structure of the Romantic Image" is cast as "an effort to understand the present predicament of the poetic imagination" and offers as its conclusion:

> We are only beginning to understand how this oscillation in the status of the image is linked to the crisis that leaves the poetry of today under a steady threat of extinction, although, on the other hand, it remains a depositary of hopes that no other activity of the mind seems able to offer.[10]

Bloom's description of his own undertaking as the search for a way between the "paths of demystification of meaning and of recollection or the restoration of meaning" fits de Man's early work with uncanny accuracy.[11]

The literary-critical and historical situation in which de Man began writing was one in which the central claims of romantic poetry—loosely, those involved with notions of the Sublime, of presence, and of some essential coincidence of word and thing in poetry—were no longer allowed, had been debunked and demystified; in this situation it seemed urgent—not only as a critical issue, but also as a response to a crisis within poetry itself—to find a new way to assert the values of romanticism and romantic poetry (and it may be that this will sound not only like Bloom but also like Abrams—the difference between Abrams and de Man would then be a difference in their conception of how hard it is—how much it costs—to bring about this recovery).

Roughly, de Man's strategy has been to claim that if what appears as presence or a claim to presence can be shown to conceal a nothingness, that nothingness can equally be shown to be revealed in and by the poem:

> In the same manner that the poetic lyric originates in moments of tranquility, in the absence of actual emotions, and then proceeds to invent fictional emotions to create the illusion of recollection, the work

of fiction invents fictional subjects to create the illusion of the reality of others. But the fiction is not a myth, for it knows and names itself as fiction. It is not a demystification, it is demystified from the start. When modern critics think they are demystifying literature, they are in fact being demystified by it; but since this necessarily occurs in the form of a crisis, they are blind to what takes place within themselves. (*Blindness*, p. 18)[12]

The demystified recuperation of romanticism envisioned by de Man necessarily involves a reorganization of its internal history, devaluing Wordsworth in favor of later poets—Yeats for example—and declining a Miltonic ancestry in favor of a genealogy passing through Rousseau. In the long run, this internal reorganization of the romantic canon will not hold up, the impulse behind it will turn against the notion of romanticism itself—to the point that a "selective interest in Romanticism" becomes for de Man "clear evidence of a persistent commitment to the historical outlook that keeps haunting the textual analyses as their bad conscience."[13] This "historical predicament" is a direct consequence of his handling of romantic poetry; we will want to understand this predicament as a loss of modernism, for literature and for criticism—and we will want to understand this as a way of losing criticism.

If there is a single pivotal text in de Man's bibliography it is almost certainly the 1969 essay "The Rhetoric of Temporality." The chapter of *Blindness and Insight* devoted to Derrida is in this perspective a distinctly secondary effort, a defense of the central place the earlier work assigns to Rousseau as origin of and paradigm for romanticism. For de Man it is Rousseau's work above all that opens a path into romanticism which passes between the two pits that bracket all modern interpretations of it. "The Rhetoric of Temporality" states the central issues as follows:

When it comes to describing just in what way romantic nature poetry differs from earlier forms, certain difficulties arise. They center on the tendency shared by all commentators to define the romantic image as a relationship between mind and nature, between subject and object. ("Rhetoric," p. 178)

The contradiction reaches a genuine impasse. For what are we to believe? Is romanticism a subjective idealism, open to all the attacks of solipsism that, from Hazlitt to the French structuralists, a succession of de-mystifiers of the self have directed against it? Or is it instead a return to a certain form of naturalism after the forced abstraction of the Enlightenment, but a return which our urban and alienated world can conceive of only as a nostalgic and unreachable past? ("Rhetoric," p. 182)[14]

In these passages a position that will later be attacked by Abrams and others as illegitimately and perniciously demystifying begins by trying to take its distance from a choice that seems to leave romanticism too open to demystifying critique: if, on de Man's view, M. H. Abrams, Earl Wasserman, and W. K. Wimsatt are not themselves demystifiers, they are nonetheless creators of or complicitous with a picture of romanticism that can lead only to its demystification—that can end only by leaving us without significant access to the poetry. De Man's implicit argument—apart from any deconstructionist premise— becomes explicit in J. Hillis Miller's polemical review of *Natural Supernaturalism*: certain high valuations of romanticism are immediately reversible into radical devaluations and demystifications; interpretations of romanticism that do not explicitly face this difficulty can appear to us only as hopelessly idealistic or irredeemably nostalgic; we can gain meaningful access to the poetry only by reconceiving its poetics along another axis, through a redefinition of the romantic image outside any dialectic of mind and nature, subject and object.[15]

If de Man is reacting against a generalized modern and New Critical critique of romanticism, he is doing so precisely by prolonging the terms of that critique rather than by reasserting the romantic self-understanding against its critics. To show that romanticism properly understood is a movement from Rousseau to Yeats is to heal over its apparent break with the eighteenth century at one extreme, and to tie it directly to a seminal moment within the modernist tendency at the other. This extension of the modernist critique thus ends not only by opposing the romantic self-valorization and its renewal by Abrams and others but also by undercutting the very "modernism" from which it derived its initial terms: the rupture, the historical break and sudden dissociation of poetic sensibility that modernism sought to overcome, to reach back beyond, turns out to have existed only as a (critical and self-critical) mystification of a body of poetry that, as such, existed in seamless continuity with its proper history.[16] Both within and without romanticism, in both poet and critic, "romanticism" itself names only a moment in poetry's misapprehension of itself—is only its "bad conscience." We will see that the effect of this is to force the traditional stuff of literary history into the internal dynamics of the poem itself—thus, in a certain sense, justifying or placing Abrams's claim that de Man's criticism makes literary history impossible. But one can with at least equal justice see in this a recovery of the deep sense, the ground of possibility of what we too easily let pass for "literary history."

De Man's critical concern is, as we have indicated, with an understanding of the romantic image that he finds underlying an entire series of views he contests. Explicating Hölderlin in "The Intentional Structure of the Romantic Image," he writes that

it would follow, then, since the intent of the poetic word is to originate like a flower, that it strives to banish all metaphor, to become entirely literal. . . .
This type of imagery is grounded in the intrinsic ontological primacy of the natural object. Poetic language seems to originate in the desire to draw closer and closer to the ontological status of the object, and its growth and development are determined by this inclination. . . . At times Romantic thought and poetry seem to come so close to giving in completely to the nostalgia for the object that it becomes difficult to distinguish between object and image, between imagination and perception, between an expressive or constitutive and a mimetic or literal language. (pp. 68, 70)

A complete surrender to this desire would yield the symbolic self-understanding of romanticism de Man opposes:

This movement is essentially paradoxical and condemned in advance to failure. There can be flowers that "are" and poetic words that "originate," but no poetic words that "originate" as if they "were." ("Intentional Structure," p. 70).

The strong and saving reading of romanticism is one that does not fall in with this symbolic desire but emphasizes instead the ways in which the poetry must inevitably betray the impossibility of that desire:

Nineteenth century poetry reexperiences and represents the adventure of this failure in an infinite variety of forms and versions. It selects, for example, a variety of archetypal myths to serve as the dramatic pattern for the narration of this failure. ("Intentional Structure," p. 70)

Both de Man and Abrams may well find the Christian myth of Fall and Redemption secularized and at work in romantic verse: Abrams will, at least from a de Manian viewpoint, systematically take the working of this myth at face value, as if guaranteed by the real symbolic structure of the romantic image; de Man, in contrast, refuses to accept this structure and works to show how its failure—the noncoincidence within the image of essence and existence or of being and origination—makes of the poem a performance of the failure of redemption. Poetry thus read, slowly and closely, tells us the truth, both its own and that of our condition. Romanticism is not the secular recovery of religious forms for "thinking about the conditions, the milieu, the essential values, and aspirations, and the history and destiny of the individual and of mankind,"[17] but is instead the active purging of the theological patterning of the world: it is demystifying—it knows.

"The Rhetoric of Temporality" adds two features to this account. It attempts to name explicitly the real, nonsymbolic working of the romantic image—as "allegory" above all—and it takes up questions of temporality that are only implicit in de Man's earlier writings. De Man's notion of allegory is given its fullest development in *Allegories of Reading*. Our interest lies particularly in its interlocking with the problematic of temporality, treated in the concluding chapters of *Blindness and Insight*.[18]

The central statement of "The Rhetoric of Temporality" is:

> Whereas the symbol postulates the possibility of an identity or identification, allegory designates primarily a distance in relation to its own origin, and, renouncing the nostalgia and the desire to coincide, it establishes its language in the void of this temporal difference. . . . It is ironically revealing that this voice is so rarely recognized for what it really is, and that the literary movement in which it appears has repeatedly been called a primitive naturalism or a mystified solipsism. . . .
> We are led, in conclusion, to a historical scheme that differs entirely from the customary picture. The dialectical relation between subject and object is no longer the central statement of romantic thought, but this dialectic is now located entirely in the temporal relationships that exist within a system of allegorical signs. It becomes a conflict between a conception of the self seen in its authentically temporal predicament and a defensive strategy that tries to hide from this self-knowledge. On the level of language the asserted superiority of the symbol over allegory, so frequent during the nineteenth century, is one of the forms taken by this tenacious self-mystification.
> ("Rhetoric," p. 191)

This problematic makes much of the contrast between what the literary work may claim—may say for and about itself—and what it does—what it shows about itself. What gives itself as a symbolic style, in Wordsworth for example, will now be taken to represent a darkening of the allegorical lucidity of Rousseau— and will be troubled by its own continued submission to the allegoresis of language, so that it "will never be allowed to exist in serenity; since it is a veil thrown over a light one no longer wishes to perceive, it will never be able to gain an entirely good poetic conscience" ("Rhetoric," p. 191).[19]

It is then only with the high artifice and overt allegorism of, for example, the "Byzantine" Yeats that we can begin to see the real structure of the romantic image and so recover the connectedness of romantic poetry with its past. But this may lead us simply to overleap romanticism entirely—to reject its claims and its poetry together, finding a new foundation perhaps in the prelapsarian lucidity of Metaphysical verse. But here de Man's argument is, I think, that we risk losing the deep sense of allegory that is opened up precisely by the romantics. Certainly, for de Man "the example of Rousseau shows that we are dealing instead with the rediscovery of an allegorical tradition beyond the sensualistic analogism of the eighteenth century." We seem entitled to say that Rousseau is taken to show us both the discontinuity at the heart of allegory and the depth at which that heart can be concealed as against the too easy appearance of an allegorically unified sensibility in earlier literary periods. Such "analogisms" appear to be uneasy compromises between a deeper notion of allegory and its romantic simplification into the near-total mystification of the symbol. This deeper notion of allegory is rooted in language itself—is, as it were, a recognition of its own proper and inevitable fictionality:

> But this relation between signs necessarily contains a constitutive temporal element; it remains necessary, if there is to be allegory, that the allegorical sign refer to another sign that precedes it. The meaning constituted by the allegorical sign can then consist only in the *repetition* . . . of a previous sign with which it can never coincide, since it is of the essence of this previous sign that it be pure anteriority. The secularized allegory of the early Romantics thus necessarily contains the negative moment which in Rousseau is that of renunciation, in Wordsworth that of the loss of self in death or in error. ("Rhetoric," p. 190)

"Literature" is then for de Man essentially the allegorical process of language as it is menaced by its temptation to reference and to world beyond itself. It is, in its purest form, an upsurge of freedom, an irruption of nothingness, in the determined massiveness of the world—drawn always to a surrender of its freedom and its concomitant negativity in order to lose itself in, disguise itself as, the solidity of the world. Literature is the moment of truth in and for language, the place in which language acknowledges its failure and limits, its entrapment within itself, its fictionality. But "fiction" itself thus becomes nothing more than the measure of time—the pure fact of sequence: not only the failure of reference but also the submission of that failure to the flow of anteriority. Literature—fiction, allegory—disrupts and disqualifies all claims to referential and temporal presence, uncovering them as (failed) escapes from the brute facts of freedom, time, and language. Poetic meaning lies precisely in its noncoincidence with itself, its failure to simply *be*—a failure that obliges it not only to meaning, but to meaning something else, somewhere else—*allos agoreuein*. In this sense, allegory names the essential duplicity of all literature as it is condemned to meaning and as it is open—or opened—always to interpretation and to criticism. Allegory models all forms of figuration and indirectness as the essence of literature (and so may itself appear as a late repetition of New Critical irony).[20]

The impulse to so name literature seems deeply right, and its immense power has been abundantly evident both in de Man's work and in a growing body of work shaped by his example and formulations. We are in the midst of a full-scale revision and reinterpretation of a major element of our history and our modernity, and the angle of vision established in "The Rhetoric of Temporality" and other essays by de Man is central to this work. The interesting and difficult theoretical questions begin when we ask how far de Man's enabling formulations have committed us to a literary essentialism and how far we are bound to or implicated in particular histories and textual constellations.

Romanticism appears as a rediscovery and a forgetting of the essence of literature—as is the "easy analogism" of the eighteenth century and also the poetry of modernism. Indeed, the history of the reception of romanticism is determined by this; and literary history is itself structured by the push and pull of fiction and reference, time and transcendence, that is at work within literary language itself. The historical recognition of a "romanticism" is nothing more than the exterior reflection of our critical complicity with the mystification of the symbol. To demystify the inner structure of the romantic image is to undo as well the historical formation called "romanticism," letting it find its proper place in the simple flow of time, in the intertextual allegory called "literary history" (which then may well be no longer possible in its usual sense, becoming nothing more than the ceaseless reiteration of our submission to time, the ever-renewed demystification of our desire).[21]

De Man and Derrida may both be said to "privilege" literature, to allow it a peculiar status as an agent of demystification or deconstruction. For Derrida this status is a consequence of the nature of his philosophic object and enterprise and claims not to be prescribed by any particular theory of literature ("theories of literature" are generated from time to time as incidental features of the philosophic work). De Man takes literature as his direct object (an object whose essence is rhetoricity and indirectness), and its demystifying and deconstructing privilege is a direct consequence of its demystified nature (literature does not fool itself; it deconstructs itself).

When Derrida does attempt to face the literary text directly—as in his work on Francis Ponge and Maurice Blanchot, and, differently, in his work on painting—he does so in terms of a philosophic problem of la chose—the thing—which renews and recreates the opposition of literature and philosophy within the literary text itself, leaving the means of deconstruction once more in shadow, an indirect object once again. Here the contrast between Derrida and de Man becomes both concrete and interesting: the romantic symbol, which de Man sees only as a mystification of the truth of allegory, is likely to be taken much more at face value by Derrida, as marking the irruption of the thing, la chose, into the apparent closure and simple self-reference of the literary. La chose marks the difficult seam language makes with the world, the submission of language to heterogeneity; allegory insists on the radical withdrawal of language from the world and from itself. *La chose* is, in itself, an acknowledgment of the way in which the universe of the literary exists within a larger universe. It is the mark of the general economy within and against which the apparent closure of literature takes form—a closure allegory would name and control as its truth. Derrida's ultimate concern is no more with "the failure of reference" than it is with "polysemy": these two appearances belong to Derrida's writing insofar as each can be a moment within his effort to think heterogeneity, *différance*. I am suggesting here that de Man tends always to pull the problematic of deconstruction toward a demystification of reference, just as he tends to replace the Derridean "trace" with a Sartrean nothingness. If we say, in all justice to de Man, that this is just what allegory tries to name—the "difficult seam language makes with the world" above all—then we are saying that trying to name *that* is inherently and incurably theatrical.

We may well want to say that de Man uses his notion of allegory to erect literature into a species of Absolute, freed of the world, bent back upon and through itself, summing up within itself both time and its evasion—thus finally evading its own submission to time and world, refusing its own historicity. But if this literary absolute were itself the product of a history, a moment—perhaps—of rupture and redoubling within a certain past and a certain tradition, the question of the symbol, of *la chose*, could not be so easily sidestepped into the sheer heaven of allegory, nor could the structure of time itself be so easily parsed out into sequence and its transcendence. It is interesting to note that Derrida's interest in *la chose* emerges in response to a set of philosophical issues about art and literature elaborated most explicitly by Heidegger in his writings on *das Ding*, but finding their source and sense in Kant and, above all, in Kant's aesthetics; *la chose* appears as the philosophic concomitant of the *Absolu littéraire* established by German romanticism in its reaction to Kant.[22] With this we slip into the field whose complexities we have glimpsed already in recounting Greenberg's and Fried's views on the origins of modernism and the complicity it poses between autonomy and heterogeneity. De Man's concern with allegory and symbol appears as one more moment within such a limping dialectic—and as such it would depend radically, its claims to the contrary notwithstanding, on a system of particular historical moments.[23]

With this last formulation we are suggesting that what appears in de Man as a species of hypermodernism and as an extreme valorization of allegory against the appearance of romantic naturalism entails a radical forgetting, even suppression, of its own historical conditions of possibility (and so also of the complexity of its situation). De Man's rejection of the romantic symbol is of a piece with the dissolution of romanticism itself into a seamless flow of before and after standing in for any more complex history of rupture and redoubling, "event" and acknowledgment. Both of these are of a piece with de Man's further rejection of any possibility of "crisis" within the history of criticism (and with his disavowal of what appears in *Blindness and Insight* as a recounted history of modern criticism).

Although "allegory" is supposed to point precisely toward the temporality of language, the very attempt to so name the essence of literature seems to preclude any recognition of its historicity. Our argument here is that the temporality of language can be adequately acknowledged only by begging the epistemological question, by refusing to ask about the truth of literature.[24]

In *Blindness and Insight*, de Man's focus shifts from allegory to the general embeddedness in language of rhetoric and figural potential. At the same time and in the same movement, his interest shifts away from questions of canon and periodization toward the internal temporal dialectics of literature.

Blindness and Insight is a book of extraordinary complexity and is much more tightly built than its more or less occasional foundations would suggest. Six of its nine chapters are devoted to developing in rough chronological order a thesis about the relation between blindness and insight in the writings of a number of critics, primarily European. This discussion culminates, in the chapter devoted to Derrida, with the production of a notion of "literariness" that serves as the basis for the closing chapter's discussion of modernity and literary history. In an introductory chapter de Man rejects the suggestion that there is anything either systematic or historical in his presentation of critical positions—and this denial turns out to have deep roots in the notions of literariness and of literary history the book proposes. Although the late chapter's interest in modernity seems to be little more than a particular, albeit engaging, transformation of the notion of literariness developed in chapter 7, a thematic concern with modernism and its critique is evident at least as early as chapter 5, in which the work of the "little-publicized and difficult writer, Maurice Blanchot" is introduced precisely by its opposition to "the illusion of a fecund and productive modernity."

Our interest in the book lies primarily with the arguments about modernity and literary history in the closing chapters, but it is, I think, important to note the density of the relations between these two chapters and the two on Blanchot and Derrida that prepare them. It is, in the light of de Man's theses on romanticism, of some significance that the texts Blanchot and Derrida are measured against are those of Mallarmé and Rousseau respectively—and that it is Mallarmé who provides the standard for "modernity" in the closing chapters. It is of still greater interest to note the controlling background presence of Heidegger—Derrida's most immediate philosophic precursor, Blanchot's most sustained philosophic reference, and the object of a number of de Man's essays from the mid-fifties. All three of these writers share an insistence on the registration of some essential co-appurtenance of truth and error that makes them not simply exemplary of certain structures of blindness and insight but also competing theorists of it (so that in these chapters we see de Man's characteristic ambivalent attributions of intention—"perhaps consciously," "too deliberate not to be intentional," and so on). We might note also that Blanchot's is, without question, the body of work that has done most to form Derrida's notion of criticism, and, finally, that de Man's critique of Blanchot on the impossibility of self-reading is itself curiously traversed by verbal echoes of de Man's earlier work, especially his 1960 essay on Hölderlin (whose attraction for Heidegger de Man had discussed in essays written for *Critique* and *Monde nouveau* in the mid-fifties).[25] In general, de Man's insistence that he is providing neither history nor system but simply exemplary instances of general facts allows him here to bypass a complex tissue of mutual readings and writings—facts variously of influence, rivalry, filiation, and communication—in which his own text is crucially implicated. Much of the real work—the distances achieved, the positions transumed or appropriated—is done at this unacknowledged level, substantially deeper than the apparent argument about Blanchot's reading of Mallarmé or Derrida's of Rousseau. There is a great deal at stake in the full unpacking of the relations between Heidegger, Blanchot, Derrida, and de Man; such unpacking is, in effect, an alternate way to the critique engaged here.[26]

Our path, however, begins from the notion of literariness that de Man disengages from his critique of Derrida on Rousseau. De Man takes Derrida, interestingly, to be a would-be demystifier of Rousseau. The burden of his argument is then to reassert Rousseau's lucidity, his "self-deconstruction," in advance of any reader. It is thus that he comes to the statements that lay the foundations of deconstructive criticism:

> We are entitled to generalize in working our way toward a definition by giving Rousseau exemplary value and calling "literary" in the full sense of the term any text that implicitly or explicitly signifies its own rhetorical mode and prefigures its own misunderstanding as the correlative of its rhetorical nature; that is, of its "rhetoricity." It can do this by declarative statement or by poetic inference.

The statement is completed in a footnote:

> A discursive, critical, or philosophic text that does this by means of statements is not therefore more or less literary than a poetic text that would avoid direct statement. . . . The criterion of literary specificity does not depend on the greater or lesser discursiveness of the mode but on the degree of consistent "rhetoricity" of the language. (*Blindness*, pp. 136-37)

(De Man's own prose is for the most part a fine example of a solidly discursive mode that is consistently aware of its own rhetoricity and everywhere "prefigures its own misunderstanding.")

J. Hillis Miller, in a two-part article for *Georgia Review*, has given the clearest formulation of this notion of literature as that which deconstructs itself, names its own void:

> Literature, however, has always performed its own *mise en abyme*, though it has usually been misunderstood as doing the opposite. It has often been interpreted as establishing a ground in consciousness, in the poem as self-contained object, in nature, or in some metaphysical base. Literature therefore needs to be prolonged in criticism. The activity of deconstruction already performed and then hidden in the work must be performed again in criticism.[27]

These statements are clear and simple extensions of the position that de Man had been developing since the mid-fifties and that had already achieved sufficient form in "The Rhetoric of Temporality." Our concern now is to see how they feed into his handling of modernism.

De Man's considerations begin from the assertion that we cannot

> divide the twentieth century into two parts: a "creative" part that was actually modern, and a "reflective" or "critical" part that feeds on this modernity in the manner of a parasite, with active modernity replaced by theorizing about the modern. Certain forces that could legitimately be called modern and that were at work in lyric poetry, in the novel, and the theater, have also now become operative in the field of literary theory and criticism. . . . This development has by itself complicated and changed the texture of our literary modernity a great deal and brought to the fore difficulties inherent in the term itself as soon as it is used historically or reflectively. . . . One is soon forced to resort to paradoxical formulations, such as defining the modernity of a literary period as the manner in which it discovers the impossibility of being modern. (*Blindness*, pp. 144-45)

The first thing to remark here is that our own thesis repeats the central statement of this passage—that "certain forces . . . have also now become operative in the field of literary theory and criticism." To make this remark is to be thrown back into a reflection on the terms of criticism at stake here, on the way in which our concern is finally with the strength of de Man's formulations and with showing that strength to itself. The claim we will advance, that de Man gets caught up in a complex denial of modernism, might as easily appear as the more positive statement that he shows forth the modern precisely as its own impossibility. And indeed it seems inevitable that to argue the modern as its own impossibility is inevitably to leave one's self open to the charge of denying the modern. It may then be the case that showing the modern as its own impossibility is inevitably a dance that takes two, persisting only through a moment of repetition and critique, so that, for example, it will always be from de Man that one learns what it means for criticism to feel the weight of modernism, and so that one will, learning that, find always also that de Man has already forgotten just that: there is no knowledge to be conveyed here, only acknowledgments enacted and passed on. *Blindness and Insight* is about the crisscrossing of critique and repetition; to read it is then to engage its crisscrossed critique and repetition. This can seem a game of mirrors or a submersion in a bottomlessly knowing and corrosive irony. It can also and more powerfully become a work of recognition.

How, then, does *Blindness and Insight* set its structure of critique and repetition to work in and upon the question of modernism? How does it (fail to) acknowledge modernism—in the literary text, in literary history, and for itself?

The first movement we have already noted: *Blindness and Insight* insists on the complexity of modernism, refusing its sundering into two moments, creative and critical, traditional and antitraditional, or modern and postmodern. From this de Man goes on to define "the radical impulse that stands behind all genuine modernity" as "a desire to wipe out whatever came earlier, in the hope of reaching at last a point that could be called a true present, a point of origin that marks a new departure" (*Blindness*, pp. 147-48). The task becomes that of showing the inevitable temporal complications to which this impulse to pure forgetting, radical origination, being without time, is always and immediately open.

> Considered as a principle of life, modernity becomes a principle of origination and turns at once into a generative power that is itself historical. It becomes impossible to overcome history in the name of life or to forget the past in the name of modernity, because both are linked by a temporal chain that gives them a common destiny. . . .
> Only through history is history conquered; modernity now appears as the horizon of a historical process that has to remain a gamble. . . .
> Modernity and history relate to each other in a curiously contradictory way that goes beyond antithesis or opposition. If history is not to become sheer regression or paralysis, it depends on modernity for its duration and renewal; but modernity cannot assert itself without being at once swallowed up and reintegrated into a regressive historical process. . . . Modernity and history seem condemned to being linked together in a self-destroying union that threatens the survival of both. (*Blindness*, pp. 150-51)

In the assertion that "modernity becomes a principle of origination" we can see de Man in the very process of forgetting what he is—even as he is—teaching us about modernism and the complexity of its temporal predicament: he is already subsuming what he wants to call the modern under the truth of literature. His next assertion is:

> If we see in this paradoxical condition a diagnosis of our own
> modernity, then literature has always been essentially modern.
> (*Blindness*, p. 151)

This opens into a suite of assertions familiar enough that we need only follow
their track, interpolating an occasional comment or two.

> The ambivalence of writing is such that it can be considered both an
> act and an interpretive process that follows after an act with which it
> can never coincide. As such it both affirms and denies its own nature
> and specificity. (*Blindness*, p. 152)

This inversion of Sidney opens up the space for de Man's later (and
problematic) use of J. L. Austin's performative/constative distinction and
establishes the continuity between literature and criticism (and the complicity
between literary truth and literary mystification) reflected in the passage we
cited from Miller.

> The temptation of immediacy is constitutive of a literary consciousness
> and has to be included in a definition of the specificity of literature.
> (*Blindness*, p. 152)

It follows that the question of bad faith is always appropriately put to the
literary work—but also that the response will always show bad faith having overcome itself—by admitting itself. This in turn is responsible for some of the
tighter theoretical circles in which de Man from time to time turns: no sooner
does the essay on Derrida pose literature as demystified, rhetorically self-aware,
than it goes on to pose the now seemingly superfluous question of the difference
between "blinded" and "nonblinded" authors—the truth is that the moral battle
has always to be fought again.

> Baudelaire states clearly that the attraction of a writer toward his
> theme—which is also the attraction toward an action, a modernity, and
> an autonomous *meaning* that would exist outside the realm of
> language—is primarily an attraction to what is not art. (*Blindness*, p.
> 159)

Here, in *Le Peintre de la vie moderne* (The painter of modern life), we stand
at a central crossing in the history of modernism, an essential complication in
the specific histories of painting, poetry, and criticism that is perhaps something
more than "a good case in point" and that is too lightly dealt with outside the
weight and recognition of those histories.

> In other words, literature can be represented as a movement and is, in
> essence, the fictional narration of this movement. After the initial
> moment of flight away from its own specificity, a moment of return
> follows that leads literature back to what it is—but we must bear in
> mind that terms such as "after" and "follows" do not designate

actual moments in a diachrony, but are used purely as *metaphors* of duration. (*Blindness*, p. 159)

Now—*now*—the turn that subsumed "modernism" under the essence of literature is being repeated within literature as the appearance of temporality is volatilized into metaphor, consumed by the rhetoricity of language. From this passage we have once again unimpeded vision back to "The Intentional Structure of the Romantic Image" and forward to the tension between rhetoric as trope and rhetoric as persuasion (positing) that structures *Allegories of Reading*.

Modernity turns out to be indeed one of the concepts by means of which the distinctive nature of literature can be revealed in all its intricacy. (*Blindness*, p. 161)

The continuous appeal of modernity, the desire to break out of literature toward the reality of the moment, prevails and, in its turn, folding back upon itself, engenders the repetition and the continuation of literature. Thus modernity, which is fundamentally a falling away from literature and a rejection of history, also acts as the principle that gives literature duration and historical existence. (*Blindness*, p. 162)

With this, de Man has implicitly done away entirely with any real temporal structure to either history or literature. As he sees it, "we are more concerned, at this point, with the question of whether a history of an entity as self-contradictory as literature is conceivable" (*Blindness*, p. 162). In fact, there is nothing in principle to keep de Man from the conclusion that comes only in a 1979 essay on Shelley:

The Triumph of Life warns us that nothing, whether deed, word, thought, or text, ever happens in relation, positive or negative, to anything that precedes, follows, or exists elsewhere, but only as a random event whose power, like the power of death, is due to the randomness of its occurrence. It also warns us why and how these events then have to be reintegrated in a historical and aesthetic system of recuperation that repeats itself regardless of the exposure of its fallacy.[28]

Time has slipped away, dissolved into a universe of merely transcendent and mutually external moments: the event becomes—radically—absolutely—impossible.

In describing literature, from the standpoint of the concept of modernity, as the steady fluctuation of an entity away from and toward its own mode of being, we have constantly stressed that this movement does not take place as an actual sequence in time; to represent it as such is merely a metaphor making a sequence out of what occurs in fact as a synchronic juxtaposition. The sequential, diachronic structure of the process stems from the nature of literary language as an entity, not as an event. Things do not happen as if a literary text (or a literary vocation) moved for a certain period of time away from its center, then turned around, folding back upon itself at one specific moment to travel back to its genuine point of origin. (*Blindness*, p. 163)

But what we want to call time in its fullest complexity has always slipped between diachrony and synchrony in de Man's work, between his alternative of transcendence and duration. What was to count as a resistance to transcendence and an admission of the facts of time and anteriority has swallowed its own tail, evaded itself:

> With respect to its own specificity (that is, as an existing entity susceptible to historical description), literature exists at the same time in the modes of error and truth; it both betrays and obeys its own mode of being. (*Blindness*, pp. 163-64)

And this closes the circle of de Man's system: the temporal predicament of literature ends in epistemology—literature ends as that which gives itself as both mystifying and demystified. The position is perhaps Heideggerean, but not Derridean. It is a position that makes of the knowing defeat of knowledge—the conscious aporia—the truth of literature, and that demands of criticism only the reenactment of that truth, its renewal against the illusory inroads of time.

> Could we conceive of a literary history that would not truncate literature by putting us misleadingly *into* or *outside* it, that would be able to maintain the literary aporia throughout, account at the same time for the truth and the falsehood of the knowledge literature conveys about itself, distinguish rigorously between metaphorical and historical language, and account for literary modernity as well as its historicity? Clearly, such a conception would imply a revision of our notion of history and, beyond that, of the notion of time on which our idea of history is based. . . . The relationship between truth and error that prevails in literature cannot be represented genetically, since truth and error exist simultaneously, thus preventing the favoring of the one over the other. (*Blindness*, pp. 164-65)

We are with de Man in seeking a revised notion of history, of time; here, in this passage, we should be able to see and almost to feel de Man gaining and losing time, reaching out for something he still wants to call literary history and watching it slip his grasp. The conclusion, its assurance notwithstanding, is desperate—

> All the directives we have formulated as guidelines for a literary history are more or less taken for granted when we are engaged in the much more humble task of reading and understanding a literary text. To become good literary historians, we must remember that what we usually call literary history has little or nothing to do with literature

and that what we call literary interpretation—provided only that it is good interpretation—is in fact literary history. (*Blindness*, p. 165)

Am I then accusing de Man of blindness and insight? I suppose so. One way of putting de Man's achievement is to say that what one will have with him, when one has it, will not be an argument; he has shifted the ground out from under that image of criticism and theory, that image of criticism as theory or as informed by theory. There is no end to the need for that shifting and so there will always be a need for what appears as both argument and acknowledgment, critique. What I have with him is not a disagreement in theory.

It is easy to see now how M. H. Abrams might come to claim that de Man's deconstructive criticism "renders impossible anything that we would account as literary and cultural history." Certainly Abrams can no longer write of the decline of Symbolist verse and aspiration from the height of its greater romantic precursors (as he does in "Coleridge, Baudelaire, and Modernist Poetics") without the intrusion of, for example, J. Hillis Miller's deconstructive revelation of how just this decadence has always been present "as a shadow or reversed mirror image within the Western tradition"—romanticism's uncanny double and demon, marker of a structure of truth and error, knowledge and mystification—and not (not simply) of an event or an epoch at once historical and moral.

This article and its intersection with Miller's controversial review of *Natural Supernaturalism* can point to the way in which practical and theoretical issues are here intertwined: the argument between de Man and Abrams is an argument about symbol and allegory within romanticism and in modernism, about the continuity or lack of continuity between romanticism and modernism, and about the various complicities of these terms. To de Man, Abrams will appear to be typical of those who use the romantic mystification of the symbol in order to cordon romanticism off, historically and critically, from the contaminations of modernism, using history as the field in which to smooth out and order—cover over—the contradictions inherent in all literary language. Abrams's acceptance of a sharp, theologically patterned break between modernism and romanticism is in service to his desire to put all the good over *here* and all the bad over *there*. His periodization haunts his textual analyses as his bad conscience—and betrays itself accordingly. Miller's review of *Natural Supernaturalism* simply traces out the shape of this bad conscience.

For Abrams, on the other hand, it is clear enough that de Man can appear only as the willfully perverse undoer of even the most obvious features of our history, a mad contaminator of eras and a disrespecter of poets, a modernist run amok, broken free of all historical limit and sensibility, finding only himself wherever he looks.

In the end, of course, each is accusing the other of losing whatever it is that matters about, gives power to, is the truth of, the works we call romantic; each finds the other failing to protect the real import of the poetry against its demystification. Together they represent two opposed ways of having the past for a problem, neither one of which can thematize that problem in terms either of acknowledgment or of rupture and redoubling.

It is important to see here that de Man will feel as free to deconstruct modernism as anything else (free, that is, to show that modernist texts are as self-deconstructing as any others). If on the one hand he seems to level romanticism to allegory, on the other hand he undoes as well any claim to a pure modernist allegoresis somehow entirely beyond the temptation to symbol, reference, and representation. This is the argument he directs against Karlheinz Stierle's reading of Mallarmé in the closing chapter of *Blindness and Insight*—an argument that is explicitly as much with Abrams as it is with Stierle, and one that aims to destroy the statement of any genetic linkage between romanticism and Symbolism—whether conceived as Fall or achievement—in order to show both to be repetitions of the difficult truth of literature:

> All representational poetry is always also allegorical, whether it be aware of it or not, the allegorical power of the language undermines and obscures the specific literal meaning of a representation open to understanding. But all allegorical poetry must contain a representational element that invites and allows for understanding, only to discover that the understanding it reaches is necessarily in error. . . . To claim . . . that modernity is a form of obscurity is to call the oldest, most ingrained characteristics of poetry modern. To claim that the loss of representation is modern is to make us again aware of an allegorical element in the lyric that had never ceased to represent, but that is itself necessarily dependent on the existence of an earlier allegory and so is the negation of modernity. The worst mystification is to believe that one can move from representation to allegory, or vice versa, as one moves from the old to the new, from father to son, from history to modernity. . . . The less we understand a poet, the more he is compulsively misinterpreted and oversimplified and made to say the opposite of what he actually said, the better the chances are that he is truly modern: that is, different from what we—mistakenly—think we are ourselves. This would make Baudelaire into a truly modern French poet, Hölderlin into a truly modern German poet, and Wordsworth and Yeats into truly modern English poets. (*Blindness*, pp. 185-6)

So ends *Blindness and Insight*. As de Man absorbs "representation" into the play of allegoresis he overcomes a poetic opposition that had been implicit throughout his work and explicit in a 1962 essay "Symbolic Landscape in Wordsworth and Yeats," and in so doing he makes it clear that "modern" no longer has any meaning for his work (except perhaps "poetic," properly literary, rhetorically conscious, allegorical, knowing). "Modernity" looked like the climax and achievement of *Blindness and Insight: Essays in the Rhetoric of Contemporary Criticism*; it is instead the term that drops out in de Man's later work.

It should come as no surprise that all of this rebounds on the situation of criticism and turns *Blindness and Insight* back on itself, back to the opening essays in which it sets out to determine its own status.

A "truly modern" criticism, on de Man's account, will be one that is open to the truth of literature and that is capable of acknowledging its own determination by that truth. It is reading that knows itself to be misreading and speaks that knowledge. Such criticism speaks of the truth of literature as what it reveals behind the veil of literary mystification even as it discovers that this truth has always already shown itself. The necessity for criticism is inscribed within the internal structure of literature—but also inscribed therein is its inevitable failure. Literature gives itself to criticism as that which stands in need of a demystification that will end as self-mystification; literature itself escapes, as it were, untouched, secure in its prefiguration of its inevitable misunderstanding. Miller's formulations are once more exemplary:

> The critical text prolongs, extends, reveals, covers, in short, cures, the literary text in the same way that the literary text attempts to cure the ground. If poetry is the impossible possible cure of the ground, criticism is the impossible possible cure of literature.[29]

Criticism takes its sense and possibility from the truth of literature, a truth it recalls, preserves, and displays as best it can. Its task is above all to know—to force the knowledge of—that which we would mostly deny: the literature that names our nothingness and our isolation, the weight of our freedom. "Criticism" thus becomes relay within a "philosophical anthropology" that takes literature as a "primary source of knowledge." With admirable rigor de Man disclaims in his forward "any attempt to contribute to a history of modern criticism" as well as any attempt to contribute to

> a science of criticism that would exist as an autonomous discipline. My tentative generalizations are not aimed toward a theory of criticism but toward literary language in general. The usual distinctions between expository writing *on* literature and the "purely" literary language *of* poetry or fiction have been deliberately blurred. (*Blindness*, p. viii)[30]

One of the seminal works in critical theory of the past twenty years—and *Blindness and Insight* is at least that—cannot acknowledge itself as such. This is, I think, a failure that has to be taken seriously. What has emerged as "deconstructive criticism" is unable to pose for itself the question of criticism except by passing immediately beyond criticism toward the twin truths of literature and philosophy, confusing the defeat of knowledge with the achievement of criticism, a prolongation of what literature has always already known.

With this we return to our starting point, "The Resistance to Theory." The propositions with which that article concludes—that theory is itself the resistance to theory, that theory is the theory of its own impossibility—should now show themselves as belated repetitions of the theses we have seen in *Blindness and Insight* about criticism and about modernity. It is, I think, important to see that this repetition is belated, pressured, figuring in and responsive to a historicity it would nonetheless deny. The very fact and shape of de Man's career fly in the face of the propositions that attain their most radical formulation at the close of the essay on Shelley—continuity, self, theory, are the permanent facts of a thought that would volatilize them utterly. I take this contradiction to lie behind the astonishing intellectual violence not only of "The Resistance to Theory" and "Shelley Disfigured" but also of de Man's late work on Kant and Hegel. Such self-resistance—a resistance erecting itself on a radical denial of self—forecloses in advance upon anything that could count as radical self-criticism or as acknowledgment of self.

—But to point this as an objection to the work of Paul de Man is to point out also how long it has been since criticism has conceived of itself as anything other than, precisely, the knowledge of literature (and we can let this ambiguous genitive stand). It was, after all, de Man who set out to indicate "some reasons . . . for considering the conception of literature (or literary criticism) as demystification the most dangerous myth of all" (*Blindness*, p. 14). And it is de Man who, more than anyone else, has shown the inevitability of this myth. To fault him for prolonging it is simply to recognize the way in which his work, with and against its own grain, does belong to the history of criticism and is a contribution to something that would exist as an autonomous discipline—even though this recognition is precisely what de Man closes for himself as he inscribes criticism within the truth of literature.

I have suggested that Derrida's philosophic contribution has been, in some measure, to free fiction and theory to one another (to enable the reading and writing of philosophy). This sounds as if it could serve directly as a means to criticism—but taken over thus directly it ends only in a renewed submission of literature to its truth and to that of philosophy—a solution to the question "What is literature?" To insist on some other autonomy of criticism is to insist that criticism appropriate this freeing of fiction and theory to one another as its own—that it see in this the means to its own achievement, recognize itself as its "own" activity. To do this is to begin by asking not "What is literature?" but "How is there criticism?" And the first step in answering this question is to see that its fullest form is "How is there criticism in this instance?" The question is neither methodological nor epistemological; it is critical. (Criticism owns itself anasemically.)

Chapter 5
Psychoanalysis, Criticism, Self-Criticism

Freud is hardly mentioned in *Blindness and Insight*, and the few scattered references to him in *Allegories of Reading* seem aimed at assimilating psychoanalysis to literature. Here is de Man discussing Paul Ricoeur's work on Freud:

> The part here played by Freud (and we are not now concerned with the "validity" of this interpretation with regard to Freud) could be equally assigned to literary texts, since literature can be shown to accomplish in its terms a deconstruction that parallels the psychological deconstruction of selfhood in Freud. The intensity of the interplay between literary and psychoanalytical criticism is easy enough to understand in these terms.[1]

This is, I think, a profoundly curious statement, taking note as it does of an interplay that otherwise has no place in de Man's own work and doing so in a way that reduces that interplay immediately to parallelism or identity, voiding it of any particular interest in either case.

To the extent that it is right to see in de Man's work a faith in the clarity of consciousness and a concomitant impulse to moral judgment rather than psychoanalytic diagnosis, such a setting aside of psychoanalysis is hardly surprising; the surprise lies rather in de Man's effort to stake out any place for psychoanalysis at all. What place does psychoanalysis in fact have within the field organized by the formulations of *Blindness and Insight*? What interplay between psychoanalysis and criticism does that book open, and what is the nature of that opening?

These are difficult questions to pose, depending as they do on our taking an apparent simple absence or neglect or lack of interest and turning it into something more determinate: a distinctive feature, a denial of interest. Two observations may help justify pushing our reading in this direction.

First, the criticism we have made of de Man's work is close to the critique Derrida makes of Lacan—both depend on a claim that the work in question ends by enclosing itself away from its conditions of possibility and so allowing a certain resistance to theory (a certain rejection of metalanguage) to become itself a mode of theoretical mastery (as, for example, a certain rejection of theatricality can itself become the most theatrical of gestures). The deepest moments of theoretical self-criticism can come only with its admission; the claim simply to read—a little and slowly—is itself, finally, theoreticist in a way that more overt admissions of theory are not. This suggests a complex affinity between de Man's work and Lacan's—a sharing both of theory and of the denial of theory.[2]

Second, there has been in the wake of *Blindness and Insight*, growing out of its theoretical terms, an intense interplay between psychoanalysis and literary criticism. The issue of *Yale French Studies* entitled "Literature and Psychoanalysis: The Question of Reading: Otherwise" is perhaps the most visible epitome of this interplay, containing two powerful and interesting explorations of the relations between psychoanalysis and criticism, Barbara Johnson's "The Frame of Reference: Poe, Lacan, Derrida" and Shoshana Felman's "Turning the Screw of Interpretation."[3] I will be suggesting that these explicit meditations on psychoanalysis arising in the wake of de Man's work are positive counterparts to de Man's avoidance of it, that all three belong to a single, necessarily divided theoretical field. The field is necessarily divided precisely by a complex entanglement with psychoanalysis—an entanglement in which de Man's theory would on the one hand deny or evade what it would on the other hand more simply subsume: as if what it does not—cannot—permit is an independent psychoanalysis and psychoanalytic criticism (and so also cannot permit itself to recognize its own dependence on psychoanalysis). This meditation cannot but finally lead back to the suspicion that, whereas Lacan and Derrida are locked in controversy by their interest in maintaining the autonomy of psychoanalysis, the de Manian interest in that controversy can lie only in depriving it of that central stake, turning it into a matter of good and bad faith, the truth of literature.

Our object in this chapter is to explore this entanglement of de Manian deconstruction with psychoanalysis. Our interest here continues to be in making a distinction between one aspect or tendency of this position that is caught up in a disabling and theatrical epistemologism, and another that is more nearly (that is, more powerfully) critical. But now we want to make this distinction more concretely, not as a theoretical point but as one responsive to the experience of criticism itself.

Johnson's "The Frame of Reference: Poe, Lacan, Derrida" is explicitly concerned with the relation between Lacan and Derrida and its relevance for criticism; Felman's "Turning the Screw of Interpretation" is not. Both assume a central continuity between Lacan and Derrida—but this assumption counts differently in the different instances. Both unfold within a shared theoretical framework derived from *Blindness and Insight*, and both exemplify the peril and promise, strength and weakness, of this adaptation of deconstruction to criticism.

Johnson's essay "The Frame of Reference" is one of the most influential works of recent deconstructive criticism. Yet its conclusions simply cannot be right as they stand:

> If at first it seemed possible to say that Derrida was opposing the unsystematizable to the systematized, "chance" to psychoanalytical "determinism," or the "undecidable" to the "destination," the positions of these oppositions seem now reversed: Lacan's apparently unequivocal ending says only its own dissemination, while "dissemination" has erected itself into a kind of "last word." . . . And "Symbolic determination" is not *opposed* to "chance": it is precisely that which emerges as the *syntax* of chance. But "chance," out of which what repeats springs, cannot in any way be "known," since "knowing" is precisely one of its *effects*. . . .
>
> As a final fold in the letter's performance of its reader, it should perhaps be noted that, in this discussion of the letter as what prevents me from knowing whether Lacan and Derrida are really saying the same thing or only enacting their own differences from themselves, my own theoretical "frame of reference" is precisely, to a very large extent, the writings of Lacan and Derrida. The frame is thus framed again by part of its content; the sender again receives his own message backwards from the receiver. And the true otherness of the purloined letter of literature has perhaps still in no way been accounted for. (*YFS* 504-5)

We should have no difficulty picking out the main slips and troubles in the passage: the slippage, for example, of an argument that seems to emerge crucially in time (between an "at first" and some later time, between "chance" and its transformation into its own "syntax") into a simple and simply reversible spatial confrontation—the folding of a letter (a matter of "positions" then, not "moments"); the presentation of both Lacan and Derrida as self-betraying allegories of reading against the ground of the revealing-and-concealing, sending-and-withdrawing, truth of literature; the theatricalization of the *mise-*

en-abîme into the timeless contradiction of the double bind; the recession of the text read behind its defeat of knowledge.

But our business here is complex: what we must see in Johnson's essay—and this is not easy—is both the wrongness of its conclusions and the persuasiveness of its itinerary, its apparent critical power and sense (perhaps the opposition we want is between the strength of its being in time and the ridiculousness of its evasion thereof). We must see also—and this is still harder—how very close Johnson's conclusion is to something else, something that does count, both for Derrida and for literary criticism.[4]

The obvious problem is that Johnson appears to have maneuvered herself into a position such that she forgets—or is, at any rate, no longer able to tell—the difference between phallogocentrism and its critique. But if, as we suggested long ago now, Derrida's critique of the tradition—the event he marks as having the "exterior form of a rupture and redoubling"—has the interior form of an acknowledgment of that tradition, that critique is, even in its most radical moments, a means also of access to or recovery of that tradition. (When we write later of "the achievement of criticism," one of the senses intended will be just this access or recovery.) The interchangeability of Heidegger's projects of "destruction" and "retrieve" is already packed into the Derridean portmanteau of "deconstruction."[5] The difference between the tradition and its critique is as thin and subtle as the difference between the tradition and itself, as obvious and elusive as the difference between a shell and its kernel, a kernel and its shell: Is this then what "the letter . . . prevents me from knowing whether Lacan and Derrida are really saying the same thing" means to say—that criticism is in the end always a mode of acknowledgment?

If this is right, if this gets to the real work and substance of Johnson's essay, we have to say that her theoretical commitments (her unacknowledged commitment, in particular, to theory) have led her instead, in spite of herself perhaps, to a position from which she can, precisely, not say what she means—must mean—to say: a position from which she can, among other things, no longer recall or recognize the terms that underlie those commitments—and so also no longer recognize or recall the way in which those terms are everywhere caught up in a project of recognition, recall, and acknowledgment (recalling, for example, psychoanalysis, in Lacan and out, from itself, to itself). What keeps Johnson from knowing whether or not Lacan and Derrida are really saying the same thing is just her insistence on *knowing that*, on making of their controversy an object of knowledge in relation to a specific truth (of literature). What keeps her from knowing is just her refusal to acknowledge the controversy as such. That the knowledge in question turns out to be impossible and that the truth— "the true otherness . . . of literature"—remains unaccounted for changes nothing in the structure of things here.

Johnson facing the argument between Derrida and Lacan is distinctly reminiscent of Lacan facing his string of odds-and-evens—in both cases the initiating events, the events that have aroused our interest and presented some claim on us, end by being lost behind the truth they are compelled to bear. If we say that the Unconscious persists in the seam of controversy between Lacan and Derrida, Johnson's essay is an undoing of that seam (as Lacan's reading of his Markov chain game undoes the seam between chance and its syntax).[6] The transformational critique of "Le Facteur de la vérité" can be brought to bear as fully upon this position as upon Lacan's. We can say:

> La littérature, à supposer, se trouve.
> Quand on croit la trouver, c'est elle, à supposer, qui se trouve.
> Quand elle trouve, à supposer, elle se trouve—quelque chose.
> Se contenter de déformer ici la grammaire, comme on dit, générative, de ces trois ou quatre énoncés.

> Let us suppose there is literature.
> When you think that you have got it, it is—to be supposed that literature evidences itself.
> When it is evidenced—to be supposed—it evidences itself—something.
> To limit oneself here to deforming the generative grammar—as it is called—of these three or four statements.[7]

To see this is to see how de Man's deconstruction is in both competition and complicity with psychoanalysis—how psychoanalysis and de Manian criticism have been able to crisscross in ways sometimes enabling and sometimes self-defeating but always powerful. Stanley Cavell has described contemporary French thought as "a reception or appearance of Freud" and the reception of French thought by American literary criticism as in its turn "a displacement of Freud." These passing remarks seem increasingly and uncannily apt.[8]

The central lines of the matrix that results from the encounter of psychoanalytic and literary allegories are sketched by Felman in her introduction to "Literature and Psychoanalysis: The Question of Reading: Otherwise." This field is organized by two centers, each of which appears as a locus of truth—a subject supposed to know and a subject of knowledge.

> It could be argued that people who choose to analyze literature as a profession do so because they are unwilling or unable to choose between the role of the psychoanalyst (he or she who analyzes) and the role of the patient (that which is being analyzed). Literature enables them not to choose because of the following paradox: (1) the work of literary analysis resembles the work of the psychoanalyst; (2) the status of what is analyzed—the text—is, however, not that of a patient, but rather that of a master: we say of the author that he is a master; the text has for us authority—the very type of authority by which Jacques

Lacan indeed defines the role of the analyst in the structure of the transference. Like the psychoanalyst viewed by the patient, the text is viewed by us as 'a subject presumed to know'—as the very place where meaning, the *knowledge* of meaning, reside. With respect to the text, the literary critic occupies thus at once the place of the psychoanalyst (in the relation of interpretation) *and* the place of the patient (in the relation of transference). (*YFS* 7)

These statements set out the relation of critic and text in terms of a (complicated) epistemological field. At this level, psychoanalysis and literature appear to face each other as competitive truths for or masters of criticism. And each is able to read the other's allegory as its own:

Psychoanalysis tells us that the fantasy is a fiction, and that consciousness is itself, in a sense, a fantasy-effect. In the same way, literature tells us that authority is a *language effect*, the product or the creation of its own *rhetorical* power: that authority, therefore, is likewise a fiction. (*YFS* 8)

Within this system of mutual convertibility, the critic has no place to call his or her own and seems condemned to be the simple spectator of the reciprocal undercutting of literature by psychoanalysis, psychoanalysis by literature. This is, more or less, the position occupied by Johnson in her account of the argument between Derrida and Lacan—which she implicitly reenvisions as an argument between literature and psychoanalysis. In this position Johnson, the critic, cannot choose sides—except by choosing not to choose, asserting the impossibility of choice: this defeat of knowledge then appears as the achievement of criticism and the conclusion of the critic's work.

But we can work our way out of Felman's statements another way – a way that lies as if concealed within or behind the grain of their intention. Say that what appears as an inability to choose between the role of analyst and the role of patient is the negative statement of a positive commitment to self-criticism, and that the central object of this self-criticism must be its imputation of truth and mastery to other subjects – its desire for knowledge – especially insofar as this imputation works as an avoidance of the labor of analysis and acknowledgment.

What appears as a certain inability to choose now reappears as a refusal to choose—and as a refusal that is burdened by the knowledge that, sooner or later, it will choose (as Johnson chooses Lacan—a choice she cannot acknowledge). Here the dream of criticism is no longer epistemological but ontological, a dream of some ultimate coincidence of text and critic, of each with itself, a moment of pure and self-conscious surface, in which what is felt is perhaps the simple repose of the text within itself, free of hierarchy, schematism, thematic or structural or other subdivision. (It is a dream in the tradition of New Criticism: a poem should not mean but be; criticism is not an explanation of meaning but a showing forth of being, a moment of pure apophansis.) The fact of criticism remains otherwise; we are in the end obliged to knowledge. Criticism cannot avoid saying something, somehow blocking the view it would enable. Sooner or later the truth will out.

Sooner or later: between, for example, the twinned allegories of psychoanalytic and literary truths, criticism would not choose but hover, playing the one against the other; and it will, inevitably, finally, choose, submit itself to the automatism of one allegory or another. It is allegory that delivers criticism from itself and from time (as the Symbolic delivers chance from itself)—delivers it bound hand and foot to knowledge. The truth that criticism obtains is but the measure of its failure.

Sooner or later: it is then only in time that the movement of allegoresis is seamed to texts and things, open to heterogeneity—as, for example, psychoanalysis and literature are seamed to one another in their heterogeneity only in the time of criticism and the time of their self-criticism. Psychoanalysis names this seam, inevitably, in its own terms (and so unstitches it as it goes):

> We would like to suggest that, in the same way that psychoanalysis
> points to the unconscious of literature, *literature, in its turn, is the
> unconscious of psychoanalysis*; that the unthought-out shadow in
> psychoanalytical *theory* is precisely its own involvement with litera-
> ture; that literature *in* psychoanalysis functions precisely as its
> 'unthought': as the condition of possibility *and* the self-subversive blind
> spot of psychoanalytical *thought* (*YFS* 10).

* * *

As the reader drowns under the ever-accumulating flood of criticism, he is justified in asking, why is there criticism rather than silent admiration? If every literary text performs already its own self-interpretation, which means its own self-dismantling, why is there any need for criticism? . . . Why must there be literary criticism at all, or at any rate more literary criticism? Don't we have enough already? What ineluctable necessity in literature makes it generate unending oceans of commentary, wave after wave covering the primary textual rocks, hiding them, washing them, uncovering them again, but leaving them, after all, just as they were?[9]

The question Miller seems to want to pose here slides away from itself in the very act of being posed—a question about criticism ends as a question about literature (it drifts into theory). If we reset it to ask "How is there criticism rather than silent admiration (and so on)?" our response must begin by an appeal to the fact of criticism, the wash and ebb of wave over rock. (We don't thereby say that Miller's literary truth is wrong—it's good enough; it can get certain work done—it just isn't interesting to criticism except incidentally and inevitably.) It is just the possibility of this alternate question we have tried to show counterpointing Felman's remarks.

What is the fact of criticism? —That it is, always, essentially, too late. That what will suffice will suffice without the help of the critic. That whatever necessity we may finally claim for the activity of criticism, in the beginning we can find it only gratuitous. The condition of criticism is essentially temporal—this has to be what it means to talk about the "priority" of the work over the critic; the moral over- and undertones are just that (Samuel Johnson and Matthew Arnold are the proof)—and the time in which criticism finds itself is first of all discontinuous. This is a time that is not only already more complex than allowed by any opposition of flow and evasion but is also distorted by it. It has lain behind our attempt to describe the "event" of modernism in terms of rupture and redoubling and in terms of an act of acknowledgment structured and limited by its inner ellipsis—and has lain as well behind our account of Derrida and our focus on the difficulties of *Beyond the Pleasure Principle*, the rhythmic structure of psychoanalytic theory and posteriority. It is or would be describable as a "retemporalization" of de Man's troping of modernism into the truth of literature, and it is what I would recall in using—even to abuse—the full range of tense and mood open to our language.

How is this time? Complex. Broken. Bent back on itself here and forward there. Welded to itself and filled with language. Seamed: with itself and with the world for the time that we are in it and to the extent that we can maintain ourselves within an element that is everywhere so differed from itself, so interfered with by itself. The time perhaps of deferred action—or of Deferred Action; the time that is already ruptured in our acknowledgment of it and our being in it.

For us it is enough that it is above all the time of criticism—the time a deconstructive criticism would acknowledge in recovering itself for itself. Felman's "Turning the Screw of Interpretation" can serve as a paradigm.

What is a 'Freudian reading' (and what is it *not*)? What in a text *invites*—and what in a text *resists*—a psychoanalytical interpretation? In what way does literature *authorize* psychoanalysis to elaborate a discourse about literature, and in what way, having granted its authorization, does literature disqualify that discourse? A combined reading of *The Turn of the Screw* and of its psychoanalytical interpretation will here concentrate, in other words, not only on what psychoanalytical theory has to say about the literary text, but also on what literature has to say about psychoanalysis. In the course of this double reading, we will see how both the possibilities and limits of an encounter between literature and psychoanalytical discourse might begin to be articulated, how the conditions of their meeting, and the modalities of their not meeting, might begin to be thought out. (*YFS* 102)

These opening questions and the project they propose follow clearly from the same understanding of literature and unfold very much in the same space as the opening remarks of "The Frame of Reference."[10] The concluding paragraph of Felman's very long essay seems also to echo Johnson's conclusion:

The deeply involved and immersed and more or less bleeding participants [Felman is quoting James here] are here indeed none other than the members of the "circle around the fire" which we ourselves have joined. As the fire within the letter is reflected in our faces, we see the very madness of our own art staring back at us. In thus mystifying us so as to demystify our errors and our madness, it is we ourselves that James makes laugh—and bleed. The joke is indeed on us; the worry, ours. (*YFS* 207).

And yet, Felman's reader will by now have found the first-person plural she has used throughout to have been deeply earned—the temptation to a certain solipsism, a skepticism about other minds seems to have been implicitly overcome (showing by contrast a curious isolation in Johnson's final claim to bewilderment). A certain "we" has been constituted or reconstituted—brought to a recognition of how it has always existed in and across the conflicting readings of *The Turn of the Screw* and of how its unity and division from itself has always already been acknowledged and anticipated in the text.

Felman's essay is long and complex. "The circle around the fire" is but one of its elements, one of the many threads that appear and disappear as she ravels her way through the text and its readings. It receives its most explicit and extended handling in the sections entitled "The Turns of the Story's Frame: A Theory of Narrative" and "The Scene of Writing: Purloined Letters."[11] These sections accomplish the central transition of the essay, from its opening treatment of the "merely external" controversies over *The Turn* to Felman's "own" reading of the text "itself." They do so by picking up the frame the story gives itself, its internal account of its reception. And in doing so the essay makes of the circle of listeners around the fire a critical tradition in which we too will come to have a place—it displays James's circle as a major means by which James creates his reader and allows us to recognize ourselves as so made—as caught up by James in just that way. Our access to the work and to its criticism are the same access: this is what I want to call the achievement of criticism. It is an achievement that leads us to take up a place in a history that we may want to say that we have, in some measure, debunked or demystified, but that we have also acknowledged as our own. In the end we have to say also that this history is not simply ours, but also James's—since it is Henry James who has shown us this interlocking of mystification and demystification in our critical and uncritical selves. The last words are thus not finally ours: whereas Johnson found herself alone within the ever-receding arch of a certain epistemological

stage from which literature itself has always already withdrawn, we find ourselves here at a moment in which what we most need to say for ourselves is what
James has to say to us. —There is no other participant, of course, than each of
the real, the deeply involved and immersed and more or less bleeding participants. We repeat this: acknowledging how we are James's, how he is ours.

I want, however, to be careful here. When Felman writes, just a paragraph
earlier, that

> literature (the very literality of letters) is nothing other than the
> Master's death, the Master's transformation into a ghost, insofar as
> that death and that transformation define and constitute, precisely,
> *literality* as such; literality as that which is essentially impermeable to
> analysis and to interpretation, that which necessarily remains unac-
> counted for, that which with respect to what interpretation does
> account for, constitutes no less than *all the rest* (*YFS* 207),

she is saying in fact just what Johnson said so much more simply with: "And
the true otherness of the purloined letter of literature has perhaps still in no way
been accounted for." Worse still: both are saying just exactly what the worst
of antitheoretical humanists tell us over and over again—the richness escapes;
theory only kills. It may still be hard to see that this is all right, and that it does
not touch the critical questions. We are not looking for truths about literature,
new or old; we are looking for criticism, for reading—responsibility to and contestation of a canon, of literature, of criticism.[12] This is a matter of time and of
detail. For criticism, "indecidability" is not a thesis but a fact—the fact that is
no longer acknowledged, is no longer even recognized, by "richness."

I am claiming "Turning the Screw of Interpretation" as a critical achievement. This does not mean that I find it to do away with—correct or replace—the
earlier criticism of this text. Indeed one of the criteria implicit in the phrase
"achievement of criticism" points in just the other direction—toward the
renewal of earlier work, toward showing the way that work has counted and
continues to count, or toward showing the way that its controversies are, finally,
the text's as well.

Nor do I mean that I find Felman to have spoken any sort of last word, to
have accomplished some sort of synthesis or other overcoming of the opposition
between psychoanalytic and more literary approaches to *The Turn of the Screw*,
because she has not. In fact, Felman is committed to the psychoanalytic reading;
that this might well escape her reader's notice is not without interest for us.

This commitment becomes explicit only at one point in her essay. The two
sections that move us from the controversies over *The Turn* more nearly into the
text itself lead first of all into a discussion of the way in which the governess
acts as a reader in search of the truth behind the obscure text that her wards are,
and of the way in which her search for a crux, a moment of absolute decidability,

eventuates in the death of little Miles. The next section, "A Child Is Killed," attempts "to discover the meaning of this murderous effect of meaning; to understand how a child can be killed by the very act of understanding" (*YFS* 161). It is in this section that Felman offers her own psychoanalytic analysis of a passage from the text:

> her attention is divided between Miles and the ghost at the window, between a conscious signifier and the unconscious signifier upon which the latter turns, between a conscious perception and its fantasmatic double, its contradictory extension toward the prohibited unconscious desire which it stirs up. Thus divided, her attention fails to "grasp" the child's reaction. The failure of comprehension therefore springs from the "fierce split"—from the *Spaltung*—of the subject, from the *divided state* in which meaning seems to hold the subject who is seeking it. (*YFS* 164-65)

One way of restating my remark that criticism cannot avoid saying something, and so somehow blocking its own view, would be to say that no reading can avoid the institution of a crux—which is then the mark of its failure to be purely reading, the trace left by the insistence of theory, the understanding that kills.[13] The passage I have cited is perhaps the crux instituted by Felman's reading: the place at which her grasp of the truth and that of the governess, Felman's primary critical adversary, cross: a chiasmus of blindness and insight, grasp and division—as it is also the seam along which Derrida and Lacan struggle within her work. One could no doubt graft a further deconstruction onto the critical chain at this point.

Felman's reading is developed to a very large extent by letting one or another feature of the text organize the whole, stand as its dominating figure: letters, turns, grasps, the Master, and so on.[14] Each of these is capable of generating theory—theories of narrative, theories of literary sense or nonsense—and each inevitably will as it theorizes its text. What matters is that these theories are properly critical, bound in their innermost being to particular texts and generalizable beyond them only through their grafting into the body of other texts. That is how, for criticism, fiction and theory are freed to one another.

In the passage just cited this rhetoricity comes to a halt. The division in the governess's attention is precisely and literally a division in her attention, the truth of which is psychoanalytically accessible and which is, in fact, a particularly Lacanian sort of truth. A limit is necessarily imposed on the circle of allegoresis; literature and psychoanalysis coincide. Something has after all been said: the governess is mad. But this is not what matters and counts for nothing. What we value in Felman is not this thesis but the time it took to say it, the willingness to say it in time. And this we can say of Johnson's essay as well. It is what we will say when we assent to de Man's Pascalian motto for *Allegories of Reading*, "Quand on lit trop vite ou trop doucement on n'entend rien" ("When one reads too fast or too gently, one understands nothing").

I have taken it that "Turning the Screw of Interpretation" is compelling criticism. Although I could no doubt go on at greater length about its virtues and its flaws, comparing it more or less favorably with one or another piece of criticism, I would still come round in the end to asking your assent in my conviction. I could, in time, be proved wrong; Felman's letter could go undelivered. (I could, for all that it matters and means, be right in everything I say; Felman's letter might still get simply but finally lost.) There are no guarantees for criticism outside the experience of criticism. This we tell ourselves often enough. What we say less often is that criticism can be its own model, needs nothing from philosophy or science (except itself). Theory we may well want to call bad or false can (and often does) give rise to good criticism—work that we want, in any case, to call criticism; good theory, theory we want to call true, can (and probably very often does) give rise to terrible criticism, work that fails to be criticism at all (and some of the very best theory may have failed to be criticism at all: *Blindness and Insight*, for example).

With good and bad, critical and extracritical, de Manian and anti-de Manian, all so jumbled up with one another, how are we to tell what counts for us?—Just the way we do. How are we to know what is and isn't criticism, who is and is not a literary critic, what does and does not make criticism possible? —What makes us think we have to know these things? These are short answers; for a fuller response we must turn once more to "The Rhetoric of Temporality."

* * *

For de Man "irony" names the tropological structure of the novel as "allegory" does that of the romantic lyric. While the poem gives itself as an act of transcendence that inevitably betrays its own failure, the novel appears as a narrative that continually gives away its inability to keep faith with itself. Allegory and irony are complementary modes of demystification:

> Essentially the mode of the present, [irony] knows neither memory nor prefigurative duration, whereas allegory exists entirely within an ideal time that is never here and now but always a past or an endless future. ("Rhetoric," p. 207)

> The act of irony, as we now understand it, reveals the existence of a temporality that is definitely not organic, in that it relates to its source only in terms of distance and difference and allows for no end, no totality. Irony divides the flow of temporal experience into a past that is pure mystification and a future that remains harassed forever by a relapse within the inauthentic. It can know this inauthenticity, but never overcome it. . . . The temporal void that it reveals is the same

void we encountered when we found allegory always implying an unreachable anteriority. Allegory and irony are thus linked in their common discovery of a truly temporal predicament. They are also linked in their common demystification of an organic world postulated in a symbolic mode of analogical correspondences or in a mimetic mode of representation in which fiction and reality could coincide. ("Rhetoric," pp. 203-4)

De Man is here reconstructing for the novel the analysis we have already seen for lyric poetry. We should recognize in it the notion of time as either flow or punctual break within that flow which cooperates with a certain epistemological insistence so as to land us before a void we can only know, over and over again. But what we need more importantly to see is similar to what we needed to see in considering Johnson's essay on Lacan and Derrida: how this passage is its own block to what it wants to say—how, in particular, this passage cannot forge for itself a notion of acknowledgment as the means by which we manage our being in time because it cannot imagine for itself the complexity of that being in time.

De Man's notion of irony is derived from Friedrich Schlegel and is definable as "parabasis"—the intrusion of an author or narrator on his narrative (as in Fielding or Sterne, for example). Such ironic intrusions, overt markers of fictionality, work to disrupt any promise of realism or of totality, sundering the narrative from itself (at the extreme, as in *Tristram Shandy*, the unity of the work can come profoundly into question—a problem for Wayne Booth but more nearly a paradigm for de Man). One can imagine the permanent parabasis of a narrative, its ironization at every point of its progress (this might recall our remarks about the way modernism finds itself and its precipitating event at work wherever it looks). For de Man such a radical ironization would be the creation of an allegory of irony, a novel of novels, reduced to telling itself only emblematically. This highest achievement of the novel would be "to seal, so to speak, the ironic moments within the allegorical duration" ("Rhetoric," p. 208)—a species of supreme fiction, having the same moral, cast into an inverted form, that de Man attributes to Shelley's *The Triumph of Life*. De Man offers Stendhal's *Charterhouse of Parma* as a candidate for this position, sketching an immensely powerful view of that novel in the closing pages of his essay.

We can think of the radical ironization de Man describes as "permanent parabasis" as if it were, in effect, the placing of every word of a given text in quotation marks, marking each word with an ironic "I say." "Marking" "each" "word" "with" "an" "ironic" " 'I' " " 'say' ": a palpably suspicious proceeding uncannily reminiscent of much recent criticism (and clearly related to Derrida's talk of "writing under erasure" and his insistence on "iterability" in his work on Austin and Searle). Its effects, beyond parody, are various: the quotation marks can be said to ironize the words they bracket but also to attribute to them or enforce upon them an appearance of deeper intentionality; they work as well to level out the emphasis given in the usual and casual reading of the phrase, offering the possibility that each word could become emblematic of, could organize, the whole. Overall, we might say that the quotation marks "aerate" the sentence and open it to critical occupation. We might also say that the imposition of quotation marks has the effect of repeating the sentence for us as its own rule, recalling its content, its message, to its particularity—its meaning to its being. "The sentence becomes autonomous."

Working through these possible variations on the notion of permanent parabasis should show how de Man's formulations work to recover the text as an object of criticism and as an object that is at once autonomous and heterogeneous, pure and impure—ruling itself only through its difference from itself. It is just this kind of autonomy that Felman is exploring and exploiting as she lets one or another feature of the text enfigure the whole—and it is just this heterogeneity she would acknowledge as "the Master's death," "the very literality of letters," and "that which is essentially impermeable to analysis and interpretation." This recovery is one in which the text appears, as it does for philosophic deconstruction, as its own absolute homonym and as its radical recession from itself—seamed by (in a now perhaps vaguely Jamesian phrase) the insistent thing. Criticism finds itself not in its defeat as knowledge but in the anasemic complexity that marks its attachment to literature as neither wholly internal to that literature nor simply an external addition to it—a primary supplement, a fact.

It is this difficult fact of criticism that is recognized and denied—betrayed, then—in Miller's attempt to pose a question of criticism that too quickly collapses back into the question (and answer) of literature. In the previous chapter we set this fact of criticism out as the fact of belatedness, of the "priority" of the text. But here we want to set out its inverted corollary: there always will have been criticism. (And now de Man's theories about the literary text and literary language will point powerfully to the way the fact of criticism can always be pursued into the text itself; they are theories that make the text visible as at once object and condition of possibility of criticism.)

There always will have been criticism. It is within the complex temporality this statement would register that we articulate the achievement of criticism. We can begin from a few programmatic questions and responses.

Can we deconstruct a given literary text?

—No. (Nor can those who claim to: the entire complex of issues that constitutes the picture of deconstruction as a demystifying achievement of the truth of the text is radically misleading and a submission to the temptation to epistemology that is precisely what deconstruction contests. To the very large extent that Booth, Abrams, and Bové [but also de Man and Miller] work from such a picture, their remarks and criticisms [or programs] have no interest for deconstructive criticism.)

Can we speak of a literary text's "self-deconstruction"?

—Not coherently and not without falling into the epistemologism we hope to sidestep—but at the same time some such locution is the inevitable consequence of our pursuit of criticism into the text, so we have to say: "not coherently and not without falling into the epistemologism we hope to sidestep—but also unavoidably." It is the way we will have to say "literary" when we feel compelled to say it. Truth will out. (And so we cannot be rid of our Booths and Abramses and Bovés [and de Mans and Millers and selves] as neatly and finally as we wish; we will inevitably put ourselves in the position of being accountable to them. We need then to understand the kind of community to which we are bound.)

Can we deconstruct criticism? Can we speak of criticism's "self-deconstruction"?

—Certainly. To do so at length and in detail is to do criticism and to do it as radical self-criticism, to acknowledge the way in which criticism finds itself, and to admit the complicity of criticism and modernism that works de Man's chapter "Crisis and Criticism." The achievement of criticism is just that—letting it be free to itself. This achievement does and does not have the structure of an event; it stands in need of repetition, of acknowledgment—a double movement of rupture and redoubling (the complex relation in which Felman would stand in relation to *The Turn of the Screw* and its criticism: the relation as well in which we will come to stand to her—to call her work paradigmatic is to recognize it as an achievement of criticism that will itself be in need of repetition, acknowledgment, betrayal—and not to set it forth as methodologically sound or epistemologically and metaphysically correct. Except, of course, that it is that too.)

Can we keep these questions and answers isolated from one another?

—No, of course not.

The impulse to criticism is the impulse to make of or find in finitude a positive achievement. It is because of this that it insists on being in time—and because of this that it is condemned to be too early and too late, so that to find itself in time is to find itself dispersed through the entire complexity of tense: past, present, and future, but also future perfect, pluperfect, imperfect—and also the play of mood that works this dispersion of tense and animates it with desire.

There always will have been criticism. The future perfect lets us comprehend a stretch of time, a fact of time, across its internal discontinuity. It allows us to acknowledge our being in time and can serve as an emblem of what we might mean by acknowledgment: a projection or imagination that would let the discontinuities and finitudes in which we find ourselves be. Such acknowledgment is the revelation not of some temporal void, but of the way in which we live between temptations to the void and to plentitude—in a universe of traces—just as the critical acknowledgment of the text reveals it as neither a meaningless nothingness nor a plenum of meaning and being, but as something more like the imprint these two terms leave on each other—a writing that hovers between the logocentric dream of presence, of the coincidence of being and sense, and its simple reversal into nothingness and absence. "Allegory" and "irony" are terms that would work this structure of trace and internal ellipsis as the "future perfect" would work it in time. All of these terms aim to enforce upon criticism its achievement and recognition of itself—even as they would enforce also the acknowledgment that this achievement is itself traversed by the finitude it would attain. It is thus that the arguments I have and do not have with de Man are arguments only in time—matters of sooner and later, first and second, questions of itinerary and not truth: critical and self-critical.

The conclusions to which this book inclines are susceptible to a variety of formulations. I have argued, for example, that the philosophic interest in deconstruction lies in forcing philosophy to acknowledge explicitly its implication in and dependence on literature; and that this counts for criticism only insofar as it enables a moment of self-recognition and self-criticism. I have argued that deconstruction offers criticism a means to acknowledge and assert its autonomy—an a-thetic autonomy set up in opposition to or against the grain of the reciprocal play through which philosophy and literature claim to find their truth in one another. The work of criticism is, on this view, one that takes place crucially in time, in complexes of rupture and continuity with its traditions. It is, in this sense, a paradigmatically modernist discipline; and where criticism cannot acknowledge modernism—not as a literary historical program, field, or canon but as a fact of our inhabitation of time—it fails as well its deepest self-recognition as criticism. Criticism—radical self-criticism—is a central means through which the difficult facts of human community come to recognition (and in this lies the particular privilege of psychoanalysis for criticism now). I am arguing for criticism as an activity intimately bound to the ways in which we do and do not belong in time and in community.

These may not seem on their face terribly Derridean conclusions. Derrida does not, for example, seem to address such matters as "community"—a term we are more likely to associate with Wayne Booth. But to speak of selves in a deconstructive vein is precisely to unfold their absolute sociability, their constitutive entanglement in alterity and difference. We might then want to say that Booth's "community" stands in need of deconstruction, in need of acknowledgment. Similarly, my insistence on the temporal situation of criticism and the "priority" of literature may seem to fall back directly into phonocentrism—but here it would be a mistake to think the essential claim for criticism could be made apart from such an admission (as if, for example, the goal of deconstruction were to promote writing to the place and value of voice rather than to transform that place and value precisely by relying on and working through such terms as "trace" and "secondariness"). Criticism gains its (proper) autonomy only through an acknowledgment of its essential impropriety, its inherent submission to . . . (But only criticism can show us that to which it is submitted; the "priority" of the work is neither epistemologically nor ontologically guaranteed; it is an effect and not an origin.)

Behind this general worry about how far the consideration of de Man's work has led us toward and how far away from Derrida, lies, I think, an understandable and inevitable desire to assure something very much like the purity and integrity of the Derridean position—as indeed a version of such a desire underlies the general movement of the present work. Given the overarching subversive force of Derrida's writings, it seems that such an assurance ought to take the form of a guarantee of that force—a keeping clear of the terrain that separates the various "-centrisms" from their critique. But neither acknowledgment nor critique can stand apart from one another, and the desire to guarantee something that would be pure subversion, pure play, and so on is simply incoherent. Deconstruction does indeed invite and encourage us to talk nonsense; this is a major and genuinely risky philosophic move, but it would be a mistake to think that it offers a general license to nonsense. *That* maneuver has no claim upon us at all. So the risks deconstruction runs include the making of sense and the recovering of sense, the chance that part of what we will come to will be not so terribly different from what we have left behind. This returns us to the deepest points registered in the best work of de Man, Johnson, Felman, and others working in this vein: as I have tried to put it earlier, "if . . . Derrida's critique of the tradition . . . has the interior form of an acknowledgment of that tradition, that critique is, even [and, I would now add, most especially] in its most radical moments, a means also of access to or recovery of that tradition. . . . The difference between the tradition and its critique is as thin and subtle as the difference between the tradition and itself, as obvious and elusive as the difference between a shell and its kernel, a kernel and its shell."

The desire to protect Derrida from a betrayal into the hands of his enemies is of a piece with a desire to see the passage from Derrida to literary criticism somehow guaranteed—and here again a version of such a desire underlies the present work. But we have seen that there are strong senses in which there is no such passage—such passage as there is lies solely in writing and in reading. De Man here regains his exemplary force, offering us such passage in the guise of a critique that we, reading, take, also as an acknowledgement. If then I have seemed to argue that in his writing de Man is somehow wrong, the proper note to strike is that of *mere* wrongness,[15] a wrongness that is not to be corrected, but understood, which is to say criticized, which is, I would have you say, acknowledged. There is no more positive vision of theory (and indeed the frequent object of our critique is precisely *theoria*, the interlocking of theory and vision) for us to arrive at beyond or in separation from the more various facts of our writing, our reading, and our readings.

This book itself aspires to criticism and attempts to maintain itself in time, refusing—to the extent possible—the temptation to speak a truth of literature or of philosophy or of literary criticism. Its ambition is perhaps to say nothing— nothing, in any case, that does not belong to and vanish with the time of its saying; it asks that we recognize in this aspiration to silence an established ambition of criticism. It would itself be a-thetic—even as it argues for criticism as an a-thetic and autonomous discipline. It would have its conclusions be radically self-reflexive, anticlimactic, and without thesis; it would be aware of its own failure and finally justificatory only of its own writing—its grammar and rhythms and style.

That it succumbs to thesis and theory after all is simply a fact about the condition of criticism—that it (and we) are no more free to time than we (and it) are free from time. Our time and our community are marked and marked inwardly by our finitude. It is because they—we—are so marked that they— we—need always to be recalled, recollected, reopened to criticism, its inevitabilities and impossibilities.

Notes

Notes

Preface

1. Also useful are Heckman, "Introduction" to Hyppolite, *Genesis and Structure of Hegel's Phenomenology of Spirit*; Hughes, *The Obstructed Path;* and Poster, *Existential Marxism in Postwar France*. Poster begins his account by reviewing the effect of Alexandre Kojève's arrival in Paris in the early 1930s and in doing so goes a long way toward sketching out a vision of recent French intellectual history rather different from Hughes's. Alan Montefiore's *Philosophy in France Today* (which includes an interesting reflection by Derrida on the course of his career, "The Time of a Thesis: Punctuations") is a collection that serves as a companion volume to Descombes's *Modern French Philosophy*.

2. Richman, *Reading Georges Bataille*, includes a very useful selected bibliography and directions to still fuller lists. My own reading of Bataille emphasizes his interest in sacrifice while Richman takes pretestation to be central.

3. Other works of interest include Lemaire, *Jacques Lacan*; Juliet Mitchell, "Introduction I," and Jacqueline Rose, "Introduction II," to Jacques Lacan and the *école freudienne, Feminine Sexuality*; Muller and Richardson, *Lacan and Language*; and Schneiderman, *Jacques Lacan*.

4. Recent—somewhat overlapping—translations of Blanchot's criticism include *The Gaze of Orpheus, The Sirens's Song,* and *The Space of Literature*. Lydia Davis and Station Hill Press have also brought out translations of the *récits Death Sentence* and *The Madness of the Day*.

Chapter 1. On Modernism

1. Derrida, "Structure, Sign and Play," p. 247. Reprinted, in a slightly modified translation, in Derrida, *Writing and Difference*.

I have in general tried to avoid bibliographical complexity, citing English translations where they are available (and what I take to be the most accessible version if there is more than one). Otherwise unattributed translations from the French throughout the text are my own.

2. The first short quotation in the paragraph is from Derrida's "Où commence et comment finit

159

un corps enseignant?" the second from "Differance" in *Margins of Philosophy*. The short quotations in the following paragraph are likewise from "Où commence."

3. Greenberg, "Modernist Painting," p. 67. Otherwise unattributed short quotations in chapter 1 are from this essay, which was first published in 1965.

4. Richard Rorty's recent writings on Derrida seem to set him in just this context; see *Consequences of Pragmatism*.

5. I take the central formulation of Fried's book to be the statement that "it seems clear that starting around the middle of the eighteenth century in France the beholder's presence before the painting came increasingly to be conceived by critics and theorists as something that had to be accomplished or at least powerfully affirmed by the painting itself; and more generally that the existence of the beholder, which is to say the primordial convention that paintings are made to be beheld, emerged as problematic for painting as never before" (*Absorption*, p. 93).

6. I mean with this formulation to suggest that Fried's account is open to a variety of psychoanalytic parsing—in which we would speak of denial in a strong sense, of a certain resultant fetishism of the aesthetic, and of the history of (modern) art as organized by a complex play of temporalities that invite formulation in terms of deferred action. This play between history and psychoanalysis will become explicit in our discussion of Derrida.

7. See Fried's essays "Thomas Couture" and "Manet's Sources."

8. Fried, "The Beholder in Courbet." The short quotations in the next paragraph are from this essay (pp. 116-17), as also the concluding statement about Manet (p. 121). Fried has recently published several further essays on Courbet, notably "Representing Representation" and "Painter into Painting."

9. Rosalind Krauss can thus—within and against the "same" formalist tradition—make the very works Fried would reject central to her account of modern sculpture. See, e.g., her books *Terminal Iron Works* and *Passages in Modern Sculpture*. For more on this general topic—with particular reference to claims to "postmodernism"—see my "Notes on the Reemergence of Allegory."

10. This paragraph should afford a glimpse of how or why talk about and theories of modern art are haunted by the possibility that art is "nothing more" than whatever gets hung on museum walls (as, e.g., George Dickie's institutional theory of art) and so also why certain claims to "postmodernism" are accompanied by an attack on or revision of the idea of the museum. See, e.g., Crimp, "On the Museum's Ruins."

11. I suspect that anyone with even a superficial acquaintance with the vagaries of contemporary psychotherapy can feel the force behind "theatricality" here—and perhaps so sense the acuity of Greenberg's remark that art fears losing itself first as entertainment and finally as therapy. It might also be remarked that much of the performance art of the late sixties and seventies can appear as a radical realization of just this psychotherapeutic theater.

12. Greenberg, *Art and Culture*, pp. 7, 62.

13. "This is the essential reason that redefinitions and borderline cases are irrelevant here. For the question raised for me about these new objects is exactly whether they are, and how they can be, *central*. If they are not, if I cannot in that way enter their world, I do not know what interest, if any at all, I would have in them. It *may* turn out to be one which would prompt me to think of them as borderline cases of art; or I might think of them as something which replaces (which replaces my interest in) works of art." Cavell, *Must We Mean What We Say?* (henceforth abbreviated "*MWM*"), p. 215.

14. Fried, *Three American Painters*, pp. 50-51.

15. Austin, *Philosophical Papers*, pp. 195-97.

16. Derrida, "Fors," pp. 90-91.

17. Cavell, "Existentialism and Analytical Philosophy," p. 969. The ensuing quotation is from the same essay, p. 963.

18. " . . . 'voluntarily' and 'involuntarily,' in spite of their apparent connexion, are fish from

very different kettles. In general, it will pay us to take nothing for granted or as obvious about nega-tions and opposites. It does not pay to assume that a word must have an opposite, or one opposite, whether it is a 'positive' word like 'willfully' or a 'negative' word like 'inadvertently.' Rather, we should be asking ourselves such questions as why there is no use for the adverb 'advertently.' For above all it will not do to assume that the 'positive' word must be around to wear the trousers; com-monly enough the 'negative' (looking) word marks the (positive) abnormality, while the 'positive' word, *if* it exists, merely serves to rule out the suggestion of abnormality." Austin, *Philosophical Papers*, pp. 191-92. (The affinity of this kind of empirical attention for Derrida's systematic critique of binarism bears remarking.)

19. This problem of forgery, of counterfeiting, of the signature and the propriety of the name that is signed in "one's own hand" organizes the two texts Derrida has devoted to the writings of J. L. Austin ("Signature Event Context" in *Margins of Philosophy*) and to John Searle's "defense" of Austin ("Limited Inc") as well as a variety of later texts.

20. Derrida, "Où commence," p. 64.

21. Ibid., p. 67.

Chapter 2. A Context for Derrida

1. The term "double bind" was coined by Gregory Bateson in his work on schizogenesis and is defined by him as "a primary negative injunction. . . . A secondary injunction conflict with the first at a more abstract level, and like the first enforced by punishment or signals which threaten survival. . . . A tertiary negative injunction prohibiting the victim from escaping the field" (*Steps to an Ecology of Mind*, pp. 206-7). A shorter definition might be: heads I win, tails you lose.

2. These quotations are from a two-part interview of Derrida published in the journal *Digraphe*, "Entre crochets" (1976) and "Ja, ou le faux-bond" (1977).

3. Hegel, *Hegel's Philosophy of Right*, pp. 12-13.

4. Derrida, "Entre crochets," p. 110.

5. Hegel, *Hegel's Phenomenology of Spirit*. All references in the text to the *Phenomenology of Spirit* will use the abbreviation *PG* (*Phänomenologie des Geistes*) followed by the paragraph number as given in Miller's translation. Derridean texts of special pertinence to our discussion include "The Ends of Man" in *Margins of Philosophy*, "Outwork" in *Dissemination*, and "From Restricted to General Economy: A Hegelianism without Reserve" in *Writing and Difference*.

6. This challenge is taken up again, in a way very different from Hegel's and yet very close to it, by Stanley Cavell in his essay "Knowing and Acknowledging" (in *MWM*) and at greater length in *The Claim of Reason*.

7. It will become apparent that Derrida moves between a logic of "determinate negation" and a certain abyssal imagery (notably that of the *mise-en-abîme*). To his detractors, he appears then to throw everything into the same empty abyss, but such Derridean terms as "trace" would hold them-selves between the content Hegel can attribute to his determinate negations and the emptiness of a merely abstract abyss. (It is interesting to remark in the preface to the *Phenomenology* Hegel's state-ment that "in a Spirit that is more advanced than another, the lower concrete existence has been reduced to an inconspicuous moment; what used to be the important thing is now but a trace [*eine Spur*], its pattern is shrouded to become a mere shadowy outline" (*PG* 28).

8. See Abrams, *Natural Supernaturalism*, pp. 225-37.

9. Hegel, *The Logic of Hegel*, vol. 1 of *The Encyclopedia of the Philosophical Sciences*, para. 13. Future references will use the abbreviation *EL* (Encyclopedia-Logic) followed by the paragraph number.

10. One can, of course, speak of a Coherence Theory of Truth in Hegel: "Truth, then, is only possible as a universe or totality of thought. . . . Each of the parts of philosophy is a philosophical whole, a circle rounded and complete in itself. . . . The idea appears in each single circle, but at the same time the whole Idea is constituted by the system of these peculiar phases, and each is a

necessary member of the organization" (*EL* 14-15). But what matters is that this Coherence Theory emerges when a certain notion of objectivity as adherence to the articulatory structure of the object is, in effect, fitted inside an apparently simple propositional truth—the Absolute Syllogism—and that this theory then meshes with Hegel's historical claims in such a way as to give the bare notion of "post-Hegelian philosophy" resonance throughout the system.

11. Queneau, "Premières confrontations avec Hegel," p. 697.

12. Heidegger, *Hegel's Concept of Experience* and *Identity and Difference*. References to the latter text will be abbreviated *ID*.

13. Heidegger, *Being and Time*, p. 43. Future references will be abbreviated *BT*.

14. "In the woods are paths which mostly wind along until they end quite suddenly in an impenetrable thicket.

"They are called 'woodpaths.'

"Each goes its peculiar way, but in the same forest. Often it seems as though they were like one another. Yet it only seems so.

"Woodcutters and forest-dwellers are familiar with these paths. They know what it means to be on a woodpath." Heidegger, *Holzwege*, as cited by Krell in his introduction to Heidegger, *Early Greek Thinking*, pp. 3-4. On the lime-twig passage, see Heidegger's discussion in *Hegel's Concept of Experience*, pp. 29-31.

15. Kant, *Critique of Pure Reason*, A 158, B 197. See also Heidegger, *Kant and the Problem of Metaphysics*, pp. 118-29, especially p. 123. Two useful books on Heidegger and Kant are Sherover, *Heidegger, Kant and Time*, and Declève, *Heidegger et Kant*.

16. Kant, *Critique of Pure Reason*, A 138, B 177.

17. Ibid., A 141, B 180-81.

18. Heidegger, *Poetry, Language, Thought*, pp. 213-29. Heidegger's reading of Hölderlin, of which this essay is the keystone, was of central interest to de Man in the mid-fifties and gave rise to three of his most important early essays: "Les Exégèses de Hölderlin par Martin Heidegger," "Tentation de la permanence," "Le Devenir, la poésie." The continuity of vision between these works and de Man's late work is overwhelming.

19. Derrida, "The *Retrait* of Metaphor," p. 14. It is not accidental that this statement arises when Derrida is concerned to articulate his distance from Heidegger.

20. Lacan, *Ecrits*, p. 181.

21. Ibid.

22. Lacan, *The Four Fundamental Concepts*, p. 195. For "getting sucked" the French text has "se faire sucer." Serge Leclaire in his *Psychanalyser* has taken this view one step further to argue that the erogenous zone must be understood as a letter inscribed upon the surface of the body.

23. And from here we can begin to take account of Heidegger's valorization of the poet and see something of the peculiar, deep risks that valorization opens for philosophy—risks with which Derrida is profoundly engaged.

24. See Marx, *Reason and World*, especially chapter 2, "Reason and Language," and his *Hegel's Phenomenology of Spirit*.

25. Queneau, "Premières confrontations avec Hegel," p. 700.

26. Bataille, *Oeuvres Complètes*, V: 56. Henceforth cited in the text as *Oeuvres*, followed by volume and page number.

27. Bataille, "Hegel, la mort et le sacrifice," p. 21. Subsequent references to this work are given in the text as "Hegel."

28. The second citation is from *Sur Nietzsche* as cited by Charles Larmore in "Bataille's Heterology," p. 100.

29. Hubert and Mauss, *Sacrifice*.

30. This is perhaps usefully set against Lévi-Strauss's statements on ritual: "On the whole, the opposition between rite and myth is the same as that between living and thinking, and ritual repre-

sents a bastardization of thought, brought about by the constraints of life. It reduces, or rather vainly tries to reduce, the demands of thought to an extreme limit, which can never be reached, since it would involve the actual abolition of thought. This desperate, and inevitably unsuccessful, attempt to re-establish the continuity of lived experience, segmented through the schematism by which mythic speculation has replaced it, is the essence of ritual, and accounts for its distinctive characteristics" (*The Naked Man*, p. 675). But this settles all the issues Bataille wants to raise—about the persistence of possibility—and allows no room for his comic sense.

31. The essential heterodoxy of Bataille's Marxism lies in his assumption of a fundamental situation of luxury rather than scarcity. It qualifies as a Marxism, if it does, largely through its emphasis on labor as alienation.

32. Such formulations seem to me to approach the sense in which Cavell wants to meet the skeptic. "Only what is there to point or gesture towards, since everything I know you know? It shows; everything in our worlds shows it. But I am filled with this feeling—of our separateness, let us say—and I want you to have it too. So I give voice to it. And then my powerlessness presents itself as ignorance—a metaphysical finitude as an intellectual lack" (*MWM*, pp. 262-63). What is at stake here is the full complexity of the act of acknowledgment.

33. Goodheart, *The Failure of Criticism*, p. 5. Abrams's charge against J. Hillis Miller is also worth recalling in this context: "As a Deconstructive Angel, Hillis Miller, I am happy to say, is not serious about deconstruction, in Hegel's sense of 'serious'; that is, he does not entirely and consistently commit himself to the consequences of his premises. He is in fact . . . a double agent" (Abrams, "The Deconstructive Angel," p. 437).

Chapter 3. Psychoanalysis and Deconstruction

1. Derrida, "Freud and the Scene of Writing," in *Writing and Difference*, pp. 196-97.

2. Freud, *The Interpretation of Dreams*, in *The Standard Edition*, V:517. All references to Freud will be by volume and page number in *The Standard Edition*.

3. Freud, *Beyond the Pleasure Principle*, XVIII:22.

4. Although "The Seminar on 'The Purloined Letter' " has been published in an English translation (in *Yale French Studies* 48), this version includes none of the introductions and postscripts that accompany it in *Ecrits*. The "Points" edition of *Ecrits* includes an additional preface addressing Derrida explicitly. The original (year-long) seminar from which "The Seminar" was drawn has been published as *Le Moi dans la théorie de Freud*, volume 2 in *Le Séminaire*, the series of Lacan's seminars: chapters 15 and 16 are of particular relevance to our discussion.

5. Freud, *The Psychopathology of Everyday Life*, VI, chap. 12. We might note also the lovely conjunction (in "Further Remarks in the Technique of Psychoanalysis") that lets Freud write: "The first symptoms or chance actions of the patient . . . have a special interest and will betray one of the governing complexes of the neurosis" (XII:239-79).

6. For Lacan, this imputation of knowledge defines the position of the analyst as, precisely, "the one who is supposed to know"—the story of an analysis is then in large measure the story of the defeat of this supposition.

7. The *a-lethic* play of revealing and concealing implicit here is a part of the Heideggereanism that Derrida attacks in Lacan. (See the related discussion on phenomenology and anasemy in the "*Contre-bande*" section of this chapter.)

8. Derrida, "Freud and the Scene of Writing," *Writing and Difference*, pp. 196-97.

9. Ibid., pp. 198-99.

10. Derrida, "The Purveyor of Truth," pp. 65-66.

11. For copyrights, see Derrida, "Limited Inc"; for footnotes and margins, "Tympan" in *Margins of Philosophy*; for shoelaces; "Restitutions" in *La Vérité en peinture*, pp. 291-436 (the shoelaces are painted).

12. This is an irony that Booth works to stabilize (in *A Rhetoric of Irony*) and that Derrida would

reveal as uncontrollable, as capable of deconstructing the philosophic claims of the text, in "Plato's Pharmacy" in *Dissemination*, pp. 61-171.

13. Kant, *Critique of Pure Reason*, A 4-5, B 8-9. This is a passage both Booth and Abrams have wanted to cite against deconstructive criticism—on the assumption that something like "fixed meanings" are the medium of literary criticism. It is important to see that Derrida is working already very deeply within the Kantian frame and is concerned above all with determining that medium in which philosophy does fly—and always has (even if, with Hegel, too late, spreading her wings only at dusk). What deconstruction would then seem to have to offer to literary criticism would be a way to its own acknowledgment of its proper medium—and this does not necessarily mean a "theory of literature." (The gist of our argument with de Man will be that he makes the mistake—the very sophisticated and compelling mistake—of taking from deconstruction something like a theory of literature rather than a question about the medium of criticism; the gist of an argument with Booth would then be that he is in some sense unable to conceive of criticism as having—as having always had—a medium.)

14. The contrast we are setting up here between Heidegger and Derrida is the same contrast we drew within Clement Greenberg's writings and arises likewise as first of all a contrast within Kant— turning, perhaps, on the differences between taking Kant's project to be a purifying correction of past philosophic excess or more nearly an attempt at acknowledging and making explicit the grounds of philosophic success. The explicitly Kantian line in Derrida's work is relatively recent and develops through readings of the third *Critique* especially opening into Heidegger's aesthetics as well. See *La Vérité en peinture* and "Economimesis."

15. Bataille's "materialism" is essentially critical—a way of examining and criticizing the restricted economies within which one lives, rather than a theory of what (economic) matter is and how it should be changed. It is as this sort of materialist (one who has, as Andrew Parker has put it, Marx in protective custody) that Derrida criticizes Lacan's notion of the "materiality of the letter" (in "The Purveyor of Truth," pp. 86-87). See Parker's "Of Politics and Limits."

16. This is the core formulation through which Derrida's essay on Blanchot turns and on which it plays out its variations; the interlacing within it of *pas* as step and as negation (and as other than negation, split particle of negation) works Derrida's writing on *Beyond the Pleasure Principle* as well. See Derrida, "Pas."

17. These formulations may be somewhat easier to follow if one keeps in mind that for Derrida there is no "mere" appearance, but neither is there some fully present truth. "Merely appearing" is, as it were, a central way in which the world manages to be—and coming to grips with the world then demands a certain careful dancing in and on this business of appearing. Is the "logocentric enclosure" merely an appearance or does it really exist? Why not say that it "really appears" or that it "merely exists"? We might say that the logocentric enclosure insists—makes such presence as it has felt—precisely in these difficulties and questions. To follow out this line of inquiry would be to bring Nietzsche, and especially his short, pointed fable "How the World Became an Error," very much into the foreground. See Pautrat, *Versions du soleil*.

18. Miller, "Stevens' *Rock*," p. 11.

19. "Envois," "Le Facteur de la vérité," "Spéculer—sur 'Freud,' " and "Du tout" are published together as *La Carte postale*. (The English translation of "Le Facteur de la vérité," "The Purveyor of Truth," appeared in *Yale French Studies*; parts of "Spéculer" have been translated in the *Oxford Literary Review* and in *Psychoanalysis and the Question of the Text*, edited by Geoffrey Hartman.) An English translation of "Fors" appeared in *The Georgia Review*. "Me—Psychoanalysis" and Abraham's "The Shell and the Kernel" both appeared in "The Tropology of Freud" issue of *Diacritics*.

20. Abraham and Torok, *L'Ecorce et le noyau*, pp. 337-39, p. 386.

21. Abraham's direct critique of Lacan is thus quite straightforward: "The Lacanian error consists in putting 'castration' at the origin of language when it is only its universal *content*. And the question anasemic clarification should resolve is this: what is the function and, eventually, the gene-

sis of the intrapsychic falsehood insofar as it is the source of the significance of language?" (*L'Ecorce et le noyau*, pp. 386-87).

22. The problems of theory and legacy we are exploring here unfold as well into questions of practice. For more on this, see Derrida's discussion of "la tranche" (literally, a slice), an attempt to register within the practice of psychoanalysis its necessary heterogeneity, in "Du tout," in *La Carte postale*, pp. 525-49.

23. The working of this "grandfather law" (I take the phrase from Walter Friedlander) can be seen clearly enough in, for example, our own presentation of the relations between Kant, Hegel, Heidegger, and Derrida. One might want to say here that the idea of "grandpaternity" is needed to anchor the idea of "generations"—much as the future perfect is needed to anchor the apparently simpler and more obvious idea of the future.

24. Abraham and Torok, *L'Ecorce et le noyau*, p. 350.

25. Written by two of Lacan's colleagues, Jean Laplanche and Jean-Baptiste Pontalis, *The Language of Psychoanalysis* is an extraordinarily useful glossary of psychoanalytic concepts. It is also the basis for Laplanche's *Life and Death in Psychoanalysis*.

26. Abraham, "The Shell and the Kernel," p. 17.

27. Freud, "Observations on 'Wild' Psychoanalysis," XI:222.

28. This phrase echoes the terms in which we earlier described the Heideggerean project of a hermeneutic retrieve of the question of Being as the living kernel beneath the sclerosis of the tradition.

29. Abraham, "The Shell and the Kernel," pp. 18-19.

30. Ibid., pp. 19-20.

31. It is this *décramponnement* that allows the passage from the metapsychological considerations with which we are engaged here to the more properly psychological aspects of the work of Abraham and Torok on dual unity, mourning, the crypt, and the phantasm. Derrida's introduction to this material will be found in "Fors"; these writings are also addressed in "Ja, ou le faux-bond" and "Entre crochets."

32. The "-*sans*-" structure carries over into English very nicely, since "without" plays so naturally on Derrida's favorite topic of inside and outside.

33. Derrida, "Me–Psychoanalysis," p. 5.

34. Here, then, we can begin to acknowledge explicitly the way in which a certain language of purity can be at once inevitable and inadequate—how it could belong in, for example, a larger grammar of modernism.

35. We might note that if the "law of the Father" is always complicated by the fact and prospect of grandpaternity, so also is it complicated by the insistence of the (grand-)child and its theories. Abraham's writings assume the existence of "child-theories" within the logic of psychoanalysis.

36. Derrida, "Living On/Border Lines," p. 171.

37. Derrida, "Me–Psychoanalysis," p. 5.

38. Derrida, "The *Retrait* of Metaphor," p. 23.

39. "It is the word 'between,' whether it names fusion or separation, that thus carries all the force of the operation. . . . This tip advances according to the irreducible excess of the syntactic over the semantic. The word 'between' has no full meaning of its own. *Inter* acting forms a syntactical plug; not a categorem, but a syncategorem: what philosophers from the Middle Ages to Husserl's *Logical Investigations* have called an incomplete signification" (Derrida, *Dissemination*, pp. 220-21).

40. Derrida, *Speech and Phenomena*, p. 130.

41. Derrida, *Dissemination*, p. 3.

42. Derrida, "Pas," p. 197.

43. Derrida, *Positions*, p. 54.

44. Derrida, "The *Retrait* of Metaphor," p. 20.

46. Derrida, "The *Retrait* of Metaphor," p. 33.

47. It is tempting to suggest that Derrida has reinstalled Heidegger's "ontological difference" at the heart of every being—so that this difference (*différance*) is that which accomplishes the uniqueness of each being in its being. This difference allows no room for a hypostasized "Being."

48. Derrida, "Pas," p. 187.

49. Ibid., pp. 138-39.

50. Derrida, *La Carte postale*, p. 433—as also the citation immediately following.

51. *MWM*, p. xxi. Cavell closes his recent book *The Claim of Reason* with the following (he has been discussing *Othello*): "So we are here, knowing they are 'gone to burning hell,' she with a lie on her lips, protecting him, he with her blood on him. Perhaps Blake has what he calls songs to win them back with, to make room for hell in a juster city. But can philosophy accept them back at the hands of poetry? Certainly not so long as philosophy continues, as it has from the first, to demand the banishment of poetry from its republic. Perhaps it could if it could itself become literature. But can philosophy become literature and still know itself?" (p. 496).

52. Johnson, "The Frame of Reference," p. 505.

Chapter 4. Paul de Man: The Time of Criticism

1. There is an old story about a man who tries on a coat that doesn't fit him at all. The salesman tells him to bend over this way, hold his arm just so, hunch up here, and everything will be just fine. So the man buys the coat and wears it, as instructed, home. Two women pass him—one says, "Oh, look at that poor deformed man!" and the other answers, "True, but his coat fits beautifully!" This may become a parable about contemporary literary criticism.

2. The influence of this book is still more extraordinary when one considers that it was out of print for most of the past decade and has only recently been reissued, with additional material, by the University of Minnesota. (Henceforth referred to as *Blindness*.)

3. De Man's early work is in general little known (it is characteristic, perhaps even essentially so, that de Man almost never refers back to earlier work). A complete bibliography can be found in Arac, Godzich, and Martin, eds., *The Yale Critics*.

In lieu of any detailed reading of this work, I offer a sampling from some of the more important of the essays. It will be readily apparent that they already hold the positions associated with "deconstructive criticism," although without the linguistic and rhetorical sophistication of de Man's work of the late sixties and seventies. The center of de Man's interest in most of these essays lies in Heidegger on poetry (on Hölderlin especially); Blanchot is a constant, if fugitive, presence in them.

"Le Devenir, la poésie":

Far from being a knowledge with a positive and determinate contest, becoming is thus essentially the knowledge of a non-knowledge, of the persistent indeterminacy that is historical temporality. (P. 114)

The poetic consciousness of becoming thus maintains itself insofar as it is self-consciousness. This poetry knows itself entirely and accounts for its own existence. (P. 117)

It seems then that, no matter how we look at the return Hölderlin calls for, it promises nothing but aridity, dryness, and lack. Such is, perhaps, in its beginnings, the climate of our truth. (P. 124; this is the concluding paragraph of the essay.)

"Tentation de la permanence":

Far from being anti-historical, the poetic act (in the general sense that includes all art) is the historical act par excellence: that through which we become conscious of the divided charac-

ter of our being and consequently the need to achieve it, to make it, in time instead of undergo it in eternity. (P. 53)
Our age seems indeed an age of fatigue. One sees manifold examples of that collapse of the spirit taking refuge in the earth. However, because these signs often give themselves as what they are not and because we all suffer from this fatigue, this collapse may appear to us in the opposite form of a promise, a lightening. If one wants to avoid being duped, one must strive to see it for what it is. (P. 51; one might want to set this alongside the closing lines of his "The Resistance to Theory.")
Historical poetics can be spoken of only in the conditional, for it exists but in scattered form. Strictly speaking, Marxist criticism is not historical for it is bound to the necessity of a reconciliation scheduled to occur at the end of a linear temporal development, and its dialectical movement does not include itself as one of its terms. A truly historical poetics would attempt to think the divide in truly temporal dimensions. . . . Poetic consciousness, which emerges from the separation, *constitutes* a certain time as the noematic correlate of its action. Such a poetics promises nothing except the fact that poetic thought will keep on becoming; will continue to ground itself in a space beyond its failure. Although it is true that a poetics of this kind has not found expression in an established critical language, it has, nevertheless, presided over certain great poetic works, at times even consciously. (P. 241-42)

"Les Exégèses de Hölderlin par Martin Heidegger":
In conclusion, this hymn suggests a conception of the poetic as an essentially open and free act, a pure intention, a mediated and conscious prayer that achieves self-consciousness in its failure; in short, a conception diametrically opposed to Heidegger's. . . . In the works of his madness, the complexity gives way to a childlike simplicity, coupled, one suspects, with a terrifying lucid irony. Who will dare say whether this madness was a collapse of the mind or Holderlin's way of experiencing totally, absolute skepticism? (P. 263)

It should be noted that de Man approaches his Heideggerean concerns with a significantly Sartrean vocabulary and vision of clear consciousness and pure intention; an essay on Mallarmé ("Le Néant poétique") brings to the fore de Man's ethical interest in the choice (between history and occultism, Hegel and Eliphas Lévi, the facts of separation and their wishful overcoming) imposed by the confrontation with "le néant poétique." The Sartrean vocabulary and moral pathos is a persistent feature of de Man's writing; Frank Lentricchia argues for its centrality in *After the New Criticism*.
 4. See Marshall, "History, Theory, and Influence."
 5. Felman, "Turning the Screw of Interpretation."
 6. Derrida, *Signsponge*, p. 2.
 7. Other, less compelling, efforts to understand our current use of this word include Jonathan Culler, *On Deconstruction*, and Elizabeth Bruss, *Beautiful Theories*.
 8. De Man, "Resistance to Theory," p. 20.
 9. Bové, *Destructive Poetics*, pp. ix, 32, 46, 48.
 10. De Man, "The Intentional Structure of the Romantic Image," p. 77. Henceforth referred to as "Intentional Structure."
 11. Bloom, *Poetry and Repression*, p. 270. Christopher Norris's small introduction, *Deconstruction*, is notable for its willingness to recognize this uncanny fit between de Man and Bloom. It is a subthesis of the argument of this chapter that the Yale School, insofar as it is organized by its central reference to de Man, does not well understand its own alliances and oppositions, intersections and divergences; in particular, the fundamental internal distinction between demystifiers (de Man, Miller) and revalorizers (Hartman, Bloom) seems to me untenable and misleading.
 12. The radical skepticism about other minds so casually thrown up in the first sentence of this passage should not escape the reader's notice. Neither should the breakdown of parallelism that it

causes: the invention of fictional emotions to create the illusion of recollection is not on the same footing as the invention of fictional subjects to create the illusion of the reality of others.

13. De Man, "Introduction," *Studies in Romanticism* 18, p. 498. The resurgence of Sartrean terms in this piece is quite remarkable.

14. De Man's statement of the problem locates these questions not only in response to specific modernist devaluations of romanticism but also precisely at the place—in the play of Enlightenment and reaction—that Greenberg and Fried found their account of modernism.

15. See Abrams, *Natural Supernaturalism,* and Miller, "Tradition and Difference."

16. The word "seam" has for me a quasi-technical sense that, whether I have actually derived it from Cavell or not, I take to be close to at least some part of what he means by it. I think its use here is clear enough as it stands, but the reader might want to look at the last part of *The Claim of Reason,* pp. 424-25 especially.

17. Abrams, *Natural Supernaturalism,* p. 13.

18. "The Rhetoric of Temporality" adumbrates a theory of the novel as well. De Man has not gone on to develop it systematically; I will touch on some aspects of it in the next chapter.

19. Here we should be able to glimpse the way in which de Man's Sartrean commitments unsurprisingly preclude any psychoanalytic approach to the literary text from the outset. We will be exploring the difficult relation between de Man's deconstructive criticism and psychoanalysis in more detail in the next chapter, but it can be remarked here that there are important ways in which the debate between Lacan and Derrida, with its overriding concern—on both sides—for psychoanalysis and for some sort of realism of the Unconscious, takes place entirely outside the space of de Man's problematic. There is a clear sense in which any de Manian effort to grapple with this argument (as, for example, Barbara Johnson's "The Frame of Reference") is determined in advance as an attempt to fold it back into a space organized by (self-)knowledge, truth, clear consciousness, and good or bad faith. (It is interesting then that both Johnson and de Man speak of features in Derrida's arguments that they take to betray "a pattern too interesting not to be deliberate" and make a portion of their argument turn on this refusal of psychoanalytic construal.)

20. "Thus generalized, allegory rapidly acquires the status of the trope of tropes, representative of the figurality of all language, the distance between signifier and signified, and, correlatively, the response to allegory becomes representative of critical activity *per se*." Fineman, "The Structure of Allegorical Desire," p. 48. Joel Fineman's essay and companion essays by Craig Owens ("The Allegorical Impulse," pts. 1 and 2) offer an interesting counterpoint to de Man's formulations.

21. In a recent essay on the work of H. R. Jauss (the introduction to Jauss's *Toward an Aesthetic of Reception*) de Man plays the literary historical notion of "reception" off against the Benjaminian notion of "translation" (as developed in Benjamin's "The Task of the Translator," in *Illuminations*) precisely in order to reabsorb the moment of reception into the temporal dialectics of the work's rhetoricity.

22. See Lacoue-Labarthe and Nancy, *L'Absolu littéraire.*

23. De Man's tendency has been to avoid the German romantics and their explicit philosophic involvements as "aestheticist" ("Introduction," *Studies in Romanticism* 18, p. 469). His last work however presents itself precisely as a critique of aestheticism and led him to focus on Kant, Schelling, and Hegel.

24. De Man's valorization of allegory has led to a more general interest in allegory as central to the phenomenon of "post-modernism." For more on this topic, see the work by Craig Owens and Douglas Crimp listed in the bibliography (and Hal Foster's recent anthology, *The Anti-Aesthetic*). I discuss this position in my "Notes on the Reemergence of Allegory."

25. See "Intentional Structure," especially the discussion of "origination."

26. Christopher Fynsk has begun exploring this web of relations in a series of essays and lectures to appear under the title *The Cast of Heidegger's Early Thought.*

27. Much of the argument I have to offer in this chapter can be condensed around Miller's state-

ment that "literature, however, has always performed its own mise-en-abyme" (Miller, Stevens' *Rock*, II," p. 330). I can make no sense of this statement as it stands; the best I can manage is the assertion that literature will have always performed its own *mise-en-abyme* (that is, will always be found to have done so)—but this is a statement about criticism and how it inevitably stands to its texts, and not about what literature is. Everything is right in Miller's statement—except that it cannot be said coherently.

28. De Man, "Shelley Disfigured," p. 69. De Man's insistence on the sheer fact of randomness here can be plausibly viewed as the inversion of Lacan's insistence on random order. Both function as statements of the Symbolic law to which we are submitted and both refuse the question of the seam between or within the essential oxymoron.

29. Miller, "Stevens' *Rock*, II," p. 331.

30. With this "deliberate blurring" we are brought back to Fried's assertion that "whatever lies between the arts is theater"—the same may be said of disciplines (and this would not be an argument against interdisciplinary work but a measure of its difficulty and its risks).

Chapter 5. Psychoanalysis, Criticism, Self-Criticism

1. De Man, *Allegories of Reading*, pp. 174-75.

2. It is interesting in this respect to speculate on the way in which the word "aporia" came to its current place in critical theory; it seems to have passed, as nearly as I can tell, from Lacan (see "The Direction of the Treatment and the Principles of Its Power" and "The Signification of the Phallus" in *Ecrits*) to de Man and thence to Derrida.

3. *Yale French Studies* 55/56 (1977). All otherwise unidentified page references in this chapter are to this volume (abbreviated as *YFS*). It should be clear that the distinction I will be trying to draw between these two articles is one I take to be internal to and constitutive of the common field in which they both arise. Similar distinctions could thus be drawn between, for example, Johnson's essay discussed here and her essay on *Billy Budd*, or between the latter essay and her work on Mallarmé and Austin (see Johnson's *The Critical Difference*), or even between the first and the last sections of Felman's *Le Scandale du corps parlant*. In each case the object of the critique is to bring out the problematic structure of the field in which the work unfolds. Johnson's own remarks on differences "between" and "within" in her *Billy Budd* essay are very much to the point; see *The Critical Difference*, pp. 105-6.

4. I am offering a characterization of Johnson's work and its interest for us parallel to Cavell's characterization of the nature and force of the skeptic's claim in "Knowing and Acknowledging" (in *MWM*) and *The Claim of Reason*.

5. The complexity of Derrida's position "between" rupture and acknowledgment, destruction and retrieve, repetition and radicality, is interestingly reflected in his remarks on the historical attitudes of some of the work being done in his wake—see, for example, *La Carte postale*, pp. 163-65 or p. 285.

6. This means that Johnson's "nonchoice" is ultimately a choice for Lacan—for the Lacan who is capable of forgetting the Unconscious; that is, for Johnson, Lacan comes to stand in for de Man as the paradigm of deconstruction. It is as such that Lacan emerges as the central figure in Johnson's fine study of the prose poem in Baudelaire and Mallarmé, *Défigurations du langage poétique*.

7. These lines repeat, with a simple change of subject from "la psychanalyse" to "la littérature" the opening lines of "Le Facteur de la vérité" (*La Carte postale*, p. 441).

8. Cavell, *The Claim of Reason*, p. xiv.

9. Miller, "Stevens' *Rock*, II," p. 330. This question interests Booth and Abrams as well as Miller and de Man: all four stand together in a fundamental uneasiness with the ungrounded fact of criticism, although they diverge in how they finally deal with it.

10. "A literary text which *both* analyzes itself *and* shows that it actually has neither a self nor any neutral metalanguage with which to do the analyzing, calls out irresistibly for analysis. And

when that call is answered by two eminent French thinkers whose readings emit an equally paradoxical call-to-analysis of their own, the resulting triptych, in the context of the question of the act-of-reading (-literature), places *its* would-be reader in a vertiginously insecure position" (*YFS*, p. 457).

11. At this point Felman's path crosses Johnson's. The contrast between the temporality emphasized by Felman's linking of "framing" to narrative and the transmission of narrative, and the spatiality of Johnson's implicitly pictorial frame is striking and instructive.

12. I am reminded of Cavell's statement that "a standing discovery of *auteur* theory was of the need for a canon of movies to which any remarks about "the movies" should hold themselves answerable" (*The World Viewed*, p. 9). However transgressive our criticism becomes, it cannot do without some notion of canon (although it certainly can do without a fixed canon).

13. If understanding can kill—and it can, particularly (this is not unrelated to the case of little Miles) when someone claims (even rightly) to understand us better than we understand ourselves—then it is not always the case that "whenever [understanding] is achieved, our life is enhanced" (Wayne Booth, *Critical Understanding*, p. 349). The interlocking of vitality, justice, and understanding within criticism can be complex.

14. What we may want to say here is that Felman's reading lets "the work . . . be its own rule-maker" and "is open to makings in all modes, without surrendering to complete relativism" (Wayne Booth, *A Rhetoric of Irony*, p. 276). But it will take a considerable revision in our understanding of our critical field, its divisions and controversies, before we can be comfortable with this confluence of critical modes.

15. I owe this felicitous formulation to Donald Marshall.

Bibliography

Bibliography

The reader is referred to the following bibliographies:

"French and English Bibliography of Jacques Derrida," compiled by John Leavey and David B. Allison, and appended to Derrida, *Edmund Husserl's Origin of Geometry: An Introduction*, translated by John P. Leavey and David B. Allison, pp. 181–93. Stony Brook, N.Y.: Nicolas Hays, 1978. This bibliography also appears in *Research in Phenomenology* 8 (1978): 145–60.
"Deconstructive Criticism: A Selected Bibliography," by Richard A. Barney, *SCE Reports* 8, supplement (1980). This includes material on a number of figures in addition to Derrida, including Paul de Man, Barbara Johnson, and J. Hillis Miller.
"Bibliography," compiled by Wallace Martin. In Arac et al., *The Yale Critics* (1983), pp. 203–12.
"Bibliography" to *Textual Strategies*, edited by Josue V. Harari, pp. 443–63. Ithaca: Cornell University Press, 1979. This bibliography is broken down into sections on "Structuralism," "Post-Structuralism," "Literary Criticism," "Philosophy," "Psychoanalysis," "Anthropology," "Linguistics, Semiotics, and Related Subjects," and "Periodicals."

Of more specialized interest are:

"Bibliographie," translated by Lee Hildreth. *Semiotexte* 2 (1976): 121–33.
This is a special issue devoted to Georges Bataille.
"Maurice Blanchot: A Bibliographical Check-list," by Steven Ungar. *Sub-Stance* 14 (1976): 142–59.

Abraham, Nicholas. "The Shell and the Kernel." Translated by Nicholas Rand. *Diacritics* 9 (Spring 1979): 16–28.
Abraham, Nicolas, and Maria Torok. *L'Ecorce et le noyau (Anasémies II)*. Paris: Aubier-Flammarion, 1978.
Abrams, M. H. "Coleridge, Baudelaire, and Modernist Poetics." In *New Perspectives in German Literary Criticism*, edited by Richard E. Amacher and Victor Lange, pp. 150–81. Princeton: Princeton University Press, 1971.

——. *Natural Supernaturalism: Tradition and Revolution in Romantic Literature*. New York: W. W. Norton & Co., 1971.

——. "The Deconstructive Angel." *Critical Inquiry* 3 (Spring 1977): 425–38.

Agacinski, Sylviane, et al. *Mimesis désarticulations*. Paris: Aubier-Flammarion, 1975.

Arac, Jonathan, Wlad Godzich, and Wallace Martin, eds. *The Yale Critics: Deconstructionism in America*. Minneapolis: University of Minnesota Press, 1983.

Austin, J. L. *Philosophical Papers*. Edited by J. O. Urmson and G. J. Warnock. Oxford: Oxford University Press, 1970.

Bataille, Georges. "Hegel, la mort et le sacrifice." *Decaulion* 5 (1955): 21–43.

——. *Oeuvres complètes*. Paris: Gallimard, 1970–.

Bateson, Gregory. *Steps to an Ecology of Mind*. New York: Chandler Publishing Co., 1972.

Beaujour, Michel. "Eros and Nonsense: Georges Bataille." In *Modern French Criticism: From Proust and Valery to Structuralism*, edited by John K. Simon, pp. 149–74. Chicago: University of Chicago Press, 1972.

Benjamin, Walter. *Illuminations*. Translated by Harry Zohn. New York: Schocken Books, 1969.

Blanchot, Maurice. *The Gaze of Orpheus and Other Literary Essays by Maurice Blanchot*. Edited by P. Adams Sitney. Translated by Lydia Davis. Barrytown, N.Y.: Station Hill Press, 1981.

——. *The Sirens's Song: Selected Essays of Maurice Blanchot*. Edited by Gabriel Jospovici. Translated by Sacha Rabinovitch. Bloomington: Indiana University Press, 1982.

——. *The Space of Literature*. Translated by Ann P. Smock. Lincoln: University of Nebraska Press, 1982.

Bloom, Harold. *Poetry and Repression: Revisionism from Blake to Stevens*. New Haven: Yale University Press, 1976.

Booth, Wayne C. *The Rhetoric of Fiction*. Chicago: University of Chicago Press, 1961.

——. *A Rhetoric of Irony*. Chicago: University of Chicago Press, 1974.

——. " 'Preserving the Exemplar': or, How Not to Dig Our Own Graves." *Critical Inquiry* 3 (Spring 1977): 407–23.

——. *Critical Understanding: The Power and Limits of Pluralism*. Chicago: University of Chicago Press, 1979.

Bové, Paul. *Destructive Poetics: Heidegger and Modern American Poetry*. New York: Columbia University Press, 1980.

Bruss, Elizabeth. *Beautiful Theories: The Spectacle of Discourse in Contemporary Criticism*. Baltimore: The Johns Hopkins Press, 1982.

Cavell, Stanley. "Existentialism and Analytical Philosophy." *Daedelus* (1964): 946–74.

——. *Must We Mean What We Say?* Cambridge: Cambridge University Press, 1976.

——. *The Claim of Reason: Wittgenstein, Skepticism, Knowledge, and Morality*. Oxford: Oxford University Press, 1979.

——. *The World Viewed: Reflections on the Ontology of Film*. Enl. ed. Cambridge, Mass.: Harvard University Press, 1979.

Crimp, Douglas. "On the Museum's Ruins." *October*, no. 13 (Summer 1980): 41–57.

Culler, Jonathan. *On Deconstruction: Theory and Criticism after Structuralism*. Ithaca: Cornell University Press, 1982.

Declève, Henri. *Heidegger et Kant*. The Hague: Martinus Nijhoff, 1970.

de Man, Paul. "Les Exégèses de Hölderlin par Martin Heidegger." *Critique*, no. 100/101 (1955): 800–819. English translation in 2d ed. rev. of *Blindness and Insight: Essays in the Rhetoric of Contemporary Criticism*. Minneapolis: University of Minnesota Press, 1983.

——. "Le Néant poétique." *Monde nouveau*, no. 88 (1955): 63–75.

——. "Tentation de la permanence." *Monde nouveau*, no. 93 (1955): 49–61.

——. "Le Devenir, la poésie." *Monde nouveau*, no. 105 (1956): 110–24.

——. "Impasse de la critique formaliste." *Critique*, no. 109 (1956): 483–500. English translation in 2d ed. rev. of *Blindness and Insight: Essays in the Rhetoric of Contemporary Criticism.* Minneapolis: University of Minnesota Press, 1983.

——. "La Critique thématique devant le thème de Faust." *Critique*, no. 120 (1957): 388–404.

——. "Symbolic Landscape in Wordsworth and Yeats." In *In Defense of Reading*, edited by Reuben Brower and Richard Poirier, pp. 22–37. New York: E. P. Dutton & Co., 1960.

——. "The Rhetoric of Temporality." In *Interpretation: Theory and Practice*, edited by Charles S. Singleton, pp. 173–210. Baltimore: The Johns Hopkins Press, 1969.

——. "The Intentional Structure of the Romantic Image." In *Romanticism and Consciousness: Essays in Criticism*, edited by Harold Bloom, pp. 65–77. New York: W. W. Norton & Co., 1970.

——. *Blindness and Insight: Essays in the Rhetoric of Contemporary Criticism.* New York: Oxford University Press, 1971. 2d ed. rev. with an introduction by Wlad Godzich. Minneapolis: University of Minnesota Press, 1983.

——. *Allegories of Reading: Figural Language in Rousseau, Nietzsche, Rilke, and Proust.* New Haven: Yale University Press, 1979.

——. "Introduction." *Studies in Romanticism* 18 (Winter 1979): 495–99.

——. "Shelley Disfigured." In *Deconstruction and Criticism*, by Harold Bloom et al., pp. 39–73. New York: Seabury Press, 1979.

——. "The Resistance to Theory." *Yale French Studies*, no. 63 (1982): 3–20.

——. "Introduction." In *Toward an Aesthetic of Reception*, by Hans Robert Jauss, translated by Timothy Bahti, pp. vii–xxv. Minneapolis: University of Minnesota Press, 1982.

Derrida, Jacques. "Structure, Sign and Play in the Discourse of the Human Sciences." In *The Structuralist Controversy: The Languages of Criticism and the Sciences of Man*, edited by Richard Macksey and Eugenio Donato, pp. 247–72. Baltimore: The Johns Hopkins Press, 1970. Reprinted in *Writing and Difference*.

——. *Speech and Phenomena and Other Essays on Husserl's Theory of Signs.* Translated by David B. Allison. Evanston: Northwestern University Press, 1973.

——. *Glas.* Paris: Galilée, 1974.

——. "Economimesis." In *Mimesis désarticulations*, by Sylviane Agacinski et al., pp. 57–93. Paris: Aubier-Flammarion, 1975.

——. "The Purveyor of Truth." Translated by Willis Domingo, James Hulbert, Moshe Ron, and Marie Rose-Logan. *Yale French Studies*, no. 52 (1975): 31–113. French text in *La Carte postale*.

——. "Entre crochets." *Digraphe* 8 (April 1976): 97–114.

——. *Of Grammatology.* Translated by Gayatri Chakravorty Spivak. Baltimore: The Johns Hopkins Press, 1976. (*De la grammatologie.* Paris: Minuit, 1967.)

——. "Où commence et comment finit un corps enseignant?" In *Politiques de la philosophie*, edited by Dominique Grisoni, pp. 60–89. Paris: Bernard Grasset, 1976.

——. "Pas." *Gramma: Lire Blanchot I* 3-4 (1976): 111–215.

——. "L'Age de Hegel." In GREPH. *Qui a peur de la philosophie?*, pp. 73–107. Paris: Flammarion, 1977.

——. "Fors." Translated by Barbara Johnson. *Georgia Review* 31 (Spring 1977): 64–116. (French text published as the introduction to Nicolas Abraham and Maria Torok, *Le Verbier de l'homme aux loups* [*Anasémies I*]. Paris: Aubier-Flammarion, 1976.)

——. "Ja, ou le faux-bond." *Digraphe* 11 (March 1977): 83–121.

——. "Limited Inc abc . . . " Translated by Samuel Weber. *Glyph* 2, pp. 162–254. Baltimore: The Johns Hopkins Press, 1977. (French text issued as supplement to *Glyph* 2.)

——. "The *Retrait* of Metaphor." *Enclitic* 2 (Fall 1978): 5–33. (French publication in *Poésie* 7 [1978].)

——. *Writing and Difference.* Translated by Alan Bass. Chicago: University of Chicago Press, 1978.

——. "Living On/Border Lines." Translated by James Hulbert. In *Deconstruction and Criticism*, by Harold Bloom et al., pp. 75–176. New York: Seabury Press, 1979.

——. "Me–Psychoanalysis: An Introduction to the Translation of 'The Shell and the Kernel' by Nicolas Abraham." Translated by Richard Klein. *Diacritics* 9 (Spring 1979): 4–12.

——. *Spurs/Eperons*. Translated by Barbara Harlow. Chicago: University of Chicago Press, 1979.

——. *La Vérité en peinture*. Paris: Flammarion, 1979.

——. *La Carte postale: de Socrates à Freud et au-delà*. Paris: Aubier-Flammarion, 1980. Partial translations of the essay "Spéculer–sur 'Freud' " have appeared before. As (1) "Speculations–on Freud." Translated by Ian McLeod. *Oxford Literary Review* 3 (1978): 78–97. As (2) "Coming Into One's Own." Translated by James Hulbert. In *Psychoanalysis and the Question of the Text*, edited by Geoffrey Hartman, pp. 114–48. Baltimore: The Johns Hopkins Press, 1978.

——. *Dissemination*. Translated by Barbara Johnson. Chicago: University of Chicago Press, 1981. (*La Dissemination*. Paris: Seuil, 1972.)

——. *Positions*. Translated by Alan Bass. Chicago: University of Chicago Press, 1981. (*Positions*. Paris: Minuit, 1972.)

——. *Margins of Philosophy*. Translated by Alan Bass. Chicago: University of Chicago Press, 1982. (*Marges de la philosophie*. Paris: Minuit, 1972.)

——. "The Time of a Thesis: Punctuations." Translated by Kathleen McLaughlin. In *Philosophy in France Today*, edited by Alan Montefiore, pp. 34–50. Cambridge: Cambridge University Press, 1983.

——. *Signéponge/Signsponge*. Translated by Richard Rand. New York: Columbia University Press, 1984.

Descombes, Vincent. *Modern French Philosophy*. Translated by L. Scott-Fox and J. M. Harding. Cambridge: Cambridge University Press, 1980.

Donato, Eugenio. "Ending/Closure: On Derrida's Edging of Heidegger." *Yale French Studies*, no. 67 (1984): 3–22.

Felman, Shoshana. "Turning the Screw of Interpretation." *Yale French Studies*, no. 55/56 (1977): 94–207.

——. *Le Scandale du corps parlant: Don Juan avec Austin ou la séduction en deux langues*. Paris: Seuil, 1980.

Fineman, Joel. "The Structure of Allegorical Desire." *October*, no. 12 (Spring 1980): 47–66.

Les Fins de l'homme: à partir du travail de Jacques Derrida. Paris: Galilée, 1981.

Fish, Stanley. "With the Compliments of the Author: Reflections on Austin and Derrida." *Critical Inquiry* 8 (Summer 1982): 693–721.

Foster, Hal, ed. *The Anti-Aesthetic: Essays on Postmodern Culture*. Port Townsend, Wash.: Bay Press, 1983.

Freud, Sigmund. *The Standard Edition of the Complete Psychological Works of Sigmund Freud*. 24 vols. London: Hogarth Press, 1961.

Fried, Michael. *Morris Louis*. New York: Abrams, 1971.

——. *Three American Painters*. Cambridge, Mass.: Fogg Art Museum, 1965.

——. "Shape as Form: Frank Stella's New Paintings." *Artforum* 5 (1966): 18–27.

——. "Art and Objecthood." In *Minimal Art*, edited by Gregory Battcock, pp. 116–47. New York: E. P. Dutton & Co., 1968.

——. "Manet's Sources: Aspects of His Art, 1859–65." *Artforum* 7 (1969): 28–82.

——. "Thomas Couture and the Theatricalization of Action in 19th Century French Painting." *Artforum* 8 (1970): 36–46.

——. "Toward a Supreme Fiction: Genre and Beholder in the Art Criticism of Diderot and His Contemporaries." *New Literary History* 6 (Spring 1975): 543–85.

——. "Absorption: A Master Theme in 18th Century French Painting." *Eighteenth Century Studies* 9 (1975–76): 139–77.

——. "The Beholder in Courbet: His Early Self-Portraits and Their Place in His Art." *Glyph* 4, pp. 85–129. Baltimore: The Johns Hopkins Press, 1978.

——. *Absorption and Theatricality: Painting and Beholder in the Age of Diderot.* Berkeley and Los Angeles: University of California Press, 1980.

——. "Representing Representation: On the Central Group in Courbet's 'Studio.' " *Art in America* 69 (September 1981): 127–33, 168–73. Reprinted in *Allegory and Representation: Selected Papers from the English Institute, 1979–80*, edited by Stephen Greenblatt. Baltimore: The Johns Hopkins Press, 1981.

——. "Painter into Painting: On Courbet's 'After Dinner at Ornans' and 'Stonebreakers.' " *Critical Inquiry* 8 (Summer 1982): 619–49.

——. "How Modernism Works: A Response to T. J. Clark." *Critical Inquiry* 9 (September 1982): 217–34.

Fynsk, Christopher. "A Decelebration of Philosophy." *Diacritics* 8 (Spring 1978): 80–90.

——. "The Self and Its Witness: On Heidegger's *Being and Time*." *boundary 2*, no. 10 (Spring 1982): 185–207.

——. *The Cast of Heidegger's Early Thought: Difference and Self-Affirmation.* Forthcoming.

Gaschè, Rodolphe. "Deconstruction as Criticism." *Glyph* 6, pp. 177–216. Baltimore: The Johns Hopkins Press, 1979.

——." 'Setzung' and 'Übersetzung': Notes on Paul de Man." *Diacritics* 11 (Winter 1981): 36–57.

——. "Du trait non adéquat: la notion de rapport chez Heidegger." In *Les Fins de l'homme: à partir du travail de Jacques Derrida*, pp. 133–61. Paris: Galilée, 1981.

——. "Joining the Text: From Heidegger to Derrida." In *The Yale Critics*, edited by Jonathan Arac et al., pp. 156–75. Minneapolis: University of Minnesota Press, 1983.

Gearhart, Suzanne. "Philosophy *before* Literature: Deconstruction, Historicity, and the Work of Paul de Man." *Diacritics* 13 (Winter 1983): 63–81.

Goodheart, Eugene. *The Failure of Criticism.* Cambridge, Mass.: Harvard University Press, 1978.

Greenberg, Clement. *Art and Culture: Critical Essays.* Boston: Beacon Press, 1961.

——. "Modernist Painting." In *The New Art*, edited by Gregory Battcock, pp. 66–77. New York: E. P. Dutton & Co., 1973.

Heckman, John. "Introduction." In *Genesis and Structure of Hegel's Phenomenology of Spirit*, by Jean Hyppolite, pp. xv–xli. Evanston: Northwestern University Press, 1974.

Hegel, G. W. F. *The Logic of Hegel.* Vol. 1 of *The Encyclopedia of the Philosophical Sciences.* Translated by William Wallace. Oxford: Oxford University Press, 1892.

——. *Hegel's Philosophy of Right.* Translated by T. M. Knox. Oxford: Oxford University Press, 1952.

——. *Hegel's Phenomenology of Spirit.* Translated by A. V. Miller. Oxford: Oxford University Press, 1977.

Heidegger, Martin. *Being and Time.* Translated by John Macquarrie and Edward Robinson. New York: Harper & Row, 1962.

——. *Kant and the Problem of Metaphysics.* Translated by James S. Churchill. Bloomington: Indiana University Press, 1962.

——. *Identity and Difference.* Translated by Joan Stambaugh. New York: Harper & Row, 1969.

——. *Hegel's Concept of Experience.* New York: Harper & Row, 1970.

——. *Poetry, Language, Thought.* Translated by Albert Hofstadter. New York: Harper & Row, 1971.

——. *Early Greek Thinking.* Translated by David A. Krell and Frank A. Capuzzi. New York: Harper & Row, 1975.

Hubert, Henri, and Marcel Mauss. *Sacrifice: Its Nature and Function.* Translated by W. D. Halls. Chicago: University of Chicago Press, 1964.

Hughes, H. Stuart. *The Obstructed Path: French Social Thought in the Years of Desperation, 1930–1960*. New York: Harper & Row, 1969.

Hyppolite, Jean. *Genesis and Structure of Hegel's Phenomenology of Spirit*. Translated by Samuel Cherniak and John Heckman. Evanston: Northwestern University Press, 1974.

Johnson, Barbara. "The Frame of Reference: Poe, Lacan, Derrida." *Yale French Studies*, no. 55/56 (1977): 457–505.

——. *Défigurations du langage poétique*. Paris: Flammarion, 1979.

——. *The Critical Difference: Essays in the Contemporary Rhetoric of Reading*. Baltimore: The Johns Hopkins Press, 1980.

Kant, Immanuel. *Critique of Pure Reason*. Translated by Norman Kemp Smith. London: Macmillan & Co., 1929.

Kojève, Alexandre. *Introduction to the Reading of Hegel*. Translated by James H. Nichols, Jr. New York: Basic Books, 1969.

Krauss, Rosalind E. *Passages in Modern Sculpture*. New York: Viking Press, 1977.

——. *Terminal Iron Works: The Sculpture of David Smith*. Cambridge, Mass.: The M.I.T. Press, 1979.

Krupnick, Mark, ed. *Displacement: Derrida and After*. Bloomington: Indiana University Press, 1983.

Lacan, Jacques. *Ecrits*. Paris: Seuil, 1966.

——. "Seminar on 'The Purloined Letter,'" translated by Jeffrey Mehlman. *Yale French Studies*, no. 48 (1972): 39–72.

——. *Télévision*. Paris: Seuil, 1973.

——. *Encore*. In *Le Séminaire livre 20*. Paris: Seuil, 1975.

——. *Ecrits: A Selection*. Translated by Alan Sheridan. New York: W. W. Norton & Co., 1977.

——. *The Four Fundamental Concepts of Psycho-Analysis*. Translated by Alan Sheridan. New York: W. W. Norton & Co., 1978. (This is a translation of *Le Séminaire livre 11*.)

——. *Le Moi dans la théorie de Freud et dans la technique de la psychanalyse*. In *Le Séminaire livre 2*. Paris: Seuil, 1978.

Lacan, Jacques, and the *école freudienne*. *Feminine Sexuality*. Edited by Juliet Mitchell and Jacqueline Rose. Translated by Jacqueline Rose. New York: W. W. Norton & Co., 1982.

Lacoue-Labarthe, Philippe, and Jean-Luc Nancy. *L'Absolu littéraire: théorie de la littérature du romantisme allemand*. Paris: Seuil, 1978.

Laplanche, Jean. *Life and Death in Psychoanalysis*. Translated by Jeffrey Mehlman. Baltimore: The Johns Hopkins Press, 1976.

Laplanche, Jean, and Serge Leclaire. "The Unconscious: A Psychoanalytic Study." *Yale French Studies*, no. 48 (1972): 118–78.

Laplanche, Jean, and Jean-Baptiste Pontalis. *The Language of Psychoanalysis*. Translated by Donald Nicholson-Smith. New York: W. W. Norton & Co., 1973.

Larmore, Charles. "Bataille's Heterology." *Semiotexte* 2 (1976): 87–104.

Leclaire, Serge. *Psychanalyser*. Paris: Seuil, 1968.

Lemaire, Anika. *Jacques Lacan*. Translated by David Macey. London: Routledge & Kegan Paul, 1977.

Lentricchia, Frank. *After the New Criticism*. Chicago: University of Chicago Press, 1980.

Levi-Strauss, Claude. *The Elementary Structures of Kinship*. Translated by James Harle Bell, John Richard von Sturmer, and Rodney Needham. Boston: Beacon Press, 1969.

——. *The Naked Man*. Translated by John Weightman and Doreen Weightman. New York: Harper & Row, 1981.

Marshall, Donald. "History, Theory, and Influence: Yale Critics as Readers of Maurice Blanchot." In *The Yale Critics*, edited by Jonathan Arac et al., pp. 135–55. Minneapolis: University of Minnesota Press, 1983.

Marx, Werner. *Reason and World: Between Tradition and Another Beginning*. The Hague: Martinus Nijhoff, 1971.

———. *Hegel's Phenomenology of Spirit: Its Point and Purpose—a Commentary on the Preface and Introduction*. Translated by Peter Heath. New York: Harper & Row, 1975.

Mauss, Marcel, and Henri Hubert. *Sacrifice: Its Nature and Function*. Translated by W. D. Halls. Chicago: University of Chicago Press, 1964.

Melville, Stephen. "Psychoanalysis Demands a Mind." In *Aesthetics Today*, rev. ed., edited by Morris Philipson and Paul Gudel, pp. 434–55. New York: New American Library, 1980.

———. "Notes on the Reemergence of Allegory, the Forgetting of Modernism, the Necessity of Rhetoric, and the Conditions of Publicity in Art and Criticism." *October*, no. 19 (Winter 1981): 55–92.

Miller, J. Hillis. "Tradition and Difference." *Diacritics* 3 (Winter 1972): 6–13.

———. "Stevens' Rock and Criticism as Cure." *Georgia Review* 30 (Spring 1976): 5–31.

———. "Stevens' Rock and Criticism as Cure, II." *Georgia Review* 30 (Summer 1976): 330–48.

Montefiore, Alan. *Philosophy in France Today*. Cambridge: Cambridge University Press, 1983.

Muller, John P., and William Richardson. *Lacan and Language: A Reader's Guide to the Ecrits*. New York: International Universities Press, 1982.

Norris, Christopher. *Deconstruction: Theory and Practice*. London: Methuen & Co., 1982.

Owens, Craig. "The Allegorical Impulse: Toward a Theory of Postmodernism (Part 1)." *October*, no. 12 (Spring 1980): 67–86.

———. "The Allegorical Impulse: Toward a Theory of Postmodernism (Part 2)." *October*, no. 13 (Summer 1980): 59–80.

Parker, Andrew. "Of Politics and Limits: Derrida Re-Marx." *SCE Reports*, no. 8 (Fall 1980): 83–104.

Pautrat, Bernard. *Versions du soleil: figures et système de Nietzsche*. Paris: Seuil, 1971.

Perniola, Mario. *L'Instant éternel: Bataille et la pensée de la marginalité*. Paris: Méridiens/Anthropos, 1982.

Poster, Mark. *Existential Marxism in Postwar France: From Sartre to Althusser*. Princeton: Princeton University Press, 1975.

Queneau, Raymond. "Premières confrontations avec Hegel." *Critique*, no. 195–96 (August–September 1973): 694–700.

Ray, William. *Literary Meeting: From Phenomenology to Deconstruction*. Oxford: Basil Blackwell, 1984.

Richman, Michele H. *Reading Georges Bataille: Beyond the Gift*. Baltimore: The Johns Hopkins Press, 1982.

Ricoeur, Paul. *The Rule of Metaphor: Multidisciplinary Studies of the Creation of Meaning in Language*. Translated by Robert Czerny. Toronto: University of Toronto Press, 1977.

Riddel, Joseph N. "A Miller's Tale." *Diacritics* 5 (Fall 1975): 56–65.

Rorty, Richard. *Philosophy and the Mirror of Nature*. Princeton: Princeton University Press, 1979.

———. *Consequences of Pragmatism: Essays (1972–80)*. Minneapolis: University of Minnesota Press, 1982.

Schneiderman, Stuart. *Jacques Lacan: The Death of an Intellectual Hero*. Cambridge, Mass.: Harvard University Press, 1983.

Searle, John R. "Reiterating the Differences: A Reply to Derrida." *Glyph* 1, pp. 199–208. Baltimore: The Johns Hopkins Press, 1977.

Sherover, Charles M. *Heidegger, Kant, and Time*. Bloomington: Indiana University Press, 1971.

Staten, Henry. *Wittgenstein and Derrida*. Lincoln: University of Nebraska Press, 1984.

Turkle, Sherry. *Psychoanalytic Politics: Freud's French Revolution*. New York: Basic Books, 1978.

Weber, Samuel. "It." *Glyph* 4, pp. 1–31. Baltimore: The Johns Hopkins Press, 1978.

Wilden, Anthony. *The Language of the Self*. Baltimore: The Johns Hopkins Press, 1968.

Index

Index

Differance is neither a *word* nor a *concept.*
—Jacques Derrida

Abraham, Nicolas: 85, 110; break with "psychologism," 23; critique of Lacan, 164–65 n21; and Maria Torok, opposed to Lacan by Derrida, 97–106; *L'Ecorce et le noyau*, 98–99, 101; "The Shell and the Kernel," 101, 102, 103

Abrams, M. H.: 120, 152, 153; and medium of criticism, 164 n13; and "seriousness," 163 n33; "Coleridge, Baudelaire, and Modernist Poetics," 135; "The Deconstructive Angel," 135; *Natural Supernaturalism*, 42, 122, 123, 135

Absorption: 10; pure, 13; and theatricality, dialectic of, 11. *See also* Theatricality

Abyss: in Hegel, 72, 73, 75, 78, 161 n7; in Heidegger, 57, 109; and imagination in Kant, 56. *See also* Mise-en-abîme

Acknowledgment: 104, 105, 112, 116, 117, 118, 127, 142, 146, 151, 153, 155; of beholder in Manet, 14; in *Blindness and Insight*, 137; and denial, 25; and disciplinarity, 27; of double necessity, 35; as event in history of painting, 14; failure of,

and negation, 25; as having past as problem, 136; of indecidability, 148; of literature, by philosophy, 154; of modern as impossible, 131; of positionality in Hegel, 38; and reconception of skepticism, 20; and repudiation, 40; and rupture, 116; and temporality of language, 128; transformative of history, 15; in *The Turn of the Screw*, 147; and voice in writing, 26–27

Action, deferred. *See* Deferred action

Allegory: 124–28, 135, 141, 144, 145, 154; and irony in de Man, 150; limits of, in Felman, 149; and postmodernism, 168 n24; as trope of tropes, 168 n20

Anasemy/*anasémie*: 99, 101–6, 108, 110; and *aufhebung*, 112; and criticism, 138, 152

Andre, Carl, 29

Aporia, 169 n2

Arnold, Matthew, 146

A-thetic, 101, 104, 106, 107, 156

Aufhebung: 38; and *anasémie*, 112; Cavell on, 25; and "step back," 55, 56, 57–58, 93. *See also* Negation; *Pas*; Step

Austen, Jane, 8
Austin, J. L.: 21, 107, 132, 151; on binary
    oppositions, 160-61 n18
Autonomy: of philosophy, 27; and purity, 9,
    10

Bad faith, 132, 140, 168 n19
Barth, John, 29
Barthelme, Donald, 29
Bataille, Georges: 43, 46, 47, 60, 71-82, 92,
    103; economics of, 79-81; materialism of,
    163 n31, 164 n15; and self-reflection, 96;
    sovereignty in, 78-79; "Hegel, la mort et
    le sacrifice," 74-78, 82; Oeuvres com-
    plètes, 47, 72, 74, 76, 79, 80, 81
Bateson, Gregory, 161 n1
Baudelaire, Charles: Le Peintre de la vie
    moderne, 132-34
Belatedness: 54, 95, 107, 113, 138; and criti-
    cism, 146, 152; and facticity in Heideg-
    ger, 54; and recognition, 108. See also
    Deferred action; Temporality; Tense
"Between," 37, 39, 107, 109, 165 n39, 169
    n3, 169 n5
Blanchot, Maurice, 99, 106, 107, 117, 126,
    128-29
Bloom, Harold, 120
Booth, Wayne: 151, 152, 153, 154; and
    irony, 163 n12; and medium of criticism,
    164 n13; on understanding and vitality
    (Critical Understanding), 170 n13; on
    work as rule-maker (A Rhetoric of Irony),
    170 n14
Boucher, François, 8
Bové, Paul, 152, 153; Destructive Poetics,
    119

Capitalization, 102. See also Designification
Cavell, Stanley: 17-33, 36, 38, 40, 54, 85,
    119; on borderline cases, 160 n13; on
    canons, 170 n12; on criteria, 21; on fini-
    tude, 163 n32; on fraudulence, 28-30; on
    Freud and French thought, 143; on Hegel,
    25, 35-36; on literature and literary criti-
    cism, 19, 166 n5l; on the modern, 17-33;
    on ordinariness, 21, 24; on psychology
    and psychologism, 21-22; on "seams,"
    168 n16; on skepticism, 21-27; "Existen-
    tialism and Analytical Philosophy," 24;

Must We Mean What We Say?, 17-18, 19,
    20, 21, 22, 25-26, 29-30, 33, 35, 113
Community, 154-56
Contingency: in Fried's dialectic, 12, 15; in
    Hegel, 78; of human separateness, 22; and
    materiality, 83; and Real in Lacan, 87-89
Convention, 9, 13, 23-24
Courbet, Gustave, 13-14, 15, 16
Couture, Thomas, 12, 14

Dasein: defined, 49
David, Jacques-Louis, 12, 14
Deconstruction: as revision of Heideggerean
    Destruktion, 4
Deferred Action/deferred action: 105, 146.
    See also Belatedness; Temporality; Tense
de Man, Paul: 115-38, 152, 153, 155; on
    allegory, 124-28; early work cited,
    166-67 n3; and medium of criticism, 164
    n13; on modernity, 128-38; and other
    minds, 167-68 n12; and psychoanalysis,
    139-41, 143, 168 n19; on randomness,
    169 n28; and Sarte, 168 n19; Allegories of
    Reading, 124, 133, 139, 149-50; Blind-
    ness and Insight, 114, 116, 117, 119,
    120-21, 124, 128-38, 139, 140, 141, 150,
    153; "Intentional Structure of the Roman-
    tic Image," 120, 122-23, 133; "Introduc-
    tion" (Studies in Romanticism), 121; "The
    Resistance to Theory," 118, 138; "The
    Rhetoric of Temporality," 120, 121, 124,
    125, 126, 130, 150-51; "Shelley Dis-
    figured," 133, 138; "Symbolic Landscape
    in Wordsworth and Yeats," 136
Demystification, 54, 95, 119, 120-22, 123,
    127, 132, 134, 135, 137, 147, 150, 152
Denial: 11, 40, 140; of modernism in de
    Man, 130; as organizing a history, 15;
    and psychoanalysis, 160 n6; as radical
    failure of acknowledgment, 25-26; and
    recognition, 9; of self in de Man, 138; as
    supreme fiction, 13; of theory in de Man
    and Lacan, 140
Derrida, works cited: La Carte postale, 112;
    "Differance," 4; "Dissemination," 97, 107;
    "The Double Session," 97; "Du tout," 97;
    "Entre crochets," 34, 97; "Envois," 98,
    99, 105; "Fors," 23, 97; "Freud and the
    Scene of Writing," 85, 92-93, 97; Glas,

98, 105; "Ja, ou le faux-bond," 35, 97; "Living On/Border Lines," 106; "Me—Psychoanalysis," 97, 104; *Of Grammatology*, 84; "Où commence et comment finit un corps enseignant," 4, 32; "Pas," 109, 111, 112; *Positions*, 97, 109; "The Purveyor of Truth," 32, 93, 97, 143; "The *Retrait* of Metaphor," 61, 109, 110–11; *Signsponge*, 117; "Spéculer—sur 'Freud,' " 97, 100–101; *Speech and Phenomena*, 108; *Spurs*, 106; "Structure, Sign and Play in the Discourse of the Human Sciences," 3; "White Mythology," 110
Designification: 3, 103–4, 106, 111. *See also* Capitalization; Erasure; Quotation marks
Dialectic: of absorption and theatricality, 11; Bataille's disruption of, 78–79; broken or limping, 60, 61, 112, 127; and contingency in Fried, 12; deconstruction as simulacrum of, 60; of desire in Hegel and Lacan, 64–66; and "double invagination," 61; Hegelian contrasted with Heideggerean, 43, 44, 55–56; of master and slave, 65–66, 76–78; of mind and nature in romantic poetry, 122; in psychoanalysis, 93; and purity, 7. *See also* Deferred action; Negation; *Pas*; Step
Diderot, Denis, 8, 10, 13, 14, 15, 16
Difference/Differance: 35, 55–56, 57, 104, 108, 127, 142, 152, 166 n47; and absolute sociability of self, 154
Disciplines/disciplinarity: acknowledgment or profession of, 27, 35–36; and criticism, 93, 115, 138, 154, 156; economics of, 104; in Hegel, 38–40, 43–44; and heterogeneity, 81, 95; limits as truth of, 20; and modernism, 6, 154; and philosophy, 24, 37, 43, 46, 68, 71; and psychoanalysis, 61-62, 71, 87, 104, 116; and purity, 24, 38
Domestication: 4, 37; of Negative in Hegel, 76
Double bind/*Double bande*: 3, 34–35, 37, 108, 142; Bateson's definition of, 161 n1
Durkheim, Emile, 80

Economics: 79–81, 113, 127; and mise-en-abîme, 96; of psychoanalysis, 104
Erasure: 3, 151; in Hegel, 69–70. *See also*

Capitalization; Designification; Quotation marks
Event/"event," 3, 4, 14, 17, 18, 31–32, 33, 105, 122, 146, 153
Exclusion, 13, 16, 26, 32, 70–71, 92, 100, 104

Faith, bad. *See* Bad faith
Felman, Shoshana, 116, 117, 140, 141, 143–50, 153, 155
Fichte, Johann Gottlieb, 38
Fiction, 104-5, 125, 138, 149
Fielding, Henry, 151
Forgetting, 23, 25, 48, 54, 56, 60, 84, 95, 109, 113, 114, 127, 131. *See also* Repression
Frege, Gottlob, 22
Freud, Sigmund: 25, 62, 85, 86, 95, 99–100, 101, 102, 104, 105, 139, 143, 163 n5; *Beyond the Pleasure Principle*, 100–101, 106, 112, 146; *The Interpretation of Dreams*, 86; *The Psychopathology of Everyday Life*, 90
Fried, Michael: 8–18, 127; *Absorption and Theatricality*, 8, 9; "The Beholder in Courbet," 13; "Manet's Sources," 14; *Three American Painters*, 18

Generations: as internal to theory, 165 n23, 165 n35
Gide, Andre, 96
Goodheart, Eugene, 83
Grammar: 3, 10, 15–16, 18–19, 26, 29, 30–31, 32, 36, 52, 165 n34; of this book, 156. *See also* "Between"; Designification; Dialectic; "Is"; Mere; Mood; Quotation marks; Tense
Greenberg, Clement, 4–8, 16, 17, 19, 20, 28, 29, 31, 38, 39, 127, 160 n11
GREPH, 40
Greuze, Jean-Baptiste, 11, 15
Gurvitch, G., 47

Hegel, G. W. F.: 25, 28, 34–83, 87, 92, 93, 103, 104, 116, 138, 161-62 n10; and Continental modernism, 28; critique of Kant, 37–40; and Heidegger, 55–56; history and discipline in, 43; as last professor of philosophy, 35–36; legacy of,

45–47; reception of, in France, 47; on skepticism and determinate negation, 40–42; speculative proposition in, 68–69; on truth and temporality, 43–44; and Wittgenstein, 25; *Encyclopedia of the Philosophical Sciences*, 42–43, 44, 45; *Phenomenology of Spirit*, 4, 38, 39, 41, 62, 64–65, 66, 67–70, 72, 74–75, 78, 82, 86, 112; *Philosophy of Right*, 36, 66, 72. *See also* Dialectic

Heidegger, Martin: 4, 27, 28, 29, 40–43, 45–60, 63, 71, 72, 78, 84, 94, 100, 106, 109, 110, 111, 127, 128, 134, 142, 162 n 14; in de Man's early work, 166–67 n3; and Hegel, 48, 54–60; and Kant, 48–54; and language, 3–4, 53, 58, 109–110; as reader of Hölderlin, 117, 129; *Being and Time*, 48–49, 53; *Hegel's Concept of Experience*, 48; *Identity and Difference*, 54–60; "Poetically Man Dwells," 53. *See also* Step

Hermann, Imre, 98, 99
Heterogeneity, 93, 95, 96, 103, 110, 127, 145, 152
Hitchcock, Alfred, 105
Hölderlin, Friedrich, 117, 122, 129, 166–67 n3
Hubert, Henri, 77, 80
Husserl, Edmund, 22, 47
Hyppolite, Jean, 47, 74

Imaginary (Lacan), 66, 71, 86, 88, 91
Imagination: in Kant, 50–52; radicalized by Heidegger, 52–54
Impossibility. *See* Possibility
Invagination, 61, 107
Irony, 150–52, 154, 163–64 n12
"Is," 3–4, 42, 48, 56, 57

James, Henry, 8, 146–50, 153
Johnson, Barbara, 8, 114, 116, 140, 141–43, 144, 148, 151, 155, 169 n3, 169 n6
Johnson, Samuel, 146
Joke, Harold's, 166 n1
Judd, Donald, 15

Kant, Immanuel: 20, 25, 28, 36, 39, 40, 50, 67, 68, 127, 138, 164 n14; and Hegel, 37–40; imagination in, 50–53; on medium

of philosophy, 164 n13; orientation of Heidegger toward, 48, 49; and the position of the philosopher, 37; and the post-Kantian 37–38; *Critique of Judgment*, 37; *Critique of Pure Reason*, 37, 49, 50, 51, 53, 94–95
Kernel, 5, 7, 58, 95, 102, 142, 155. *See also* Anasemy; Purity
Kojève, Alexandre, 47, 71, 74, 75. 76, 77
Krauss, Rosalind, 160 n9

Lacan, Jacques: 43, 46, 47, 60–71, 86, 99, 100, 103, 105, 109, 111, 114, 140, 142, 144, 151; controversy with Derrida, 84–114; and Hegel, 64–65; and Heidegger, 59, 163 n7; mirror-stage, 62, 63–64, 88; randomness in, 88–92; "Discourse of Rome," 47; *Ecrits*, 62, 63; *Four Fundamental Concepts*, 64; *Le Moi*, 88; "Seminar on 'The Purloined Letter,' " 106
Lacoue-Labarthe, Philippe, 127
Language: Bataille's, 76, 82–83; Derrida's, 3–4, 106–12; Hegel's, 67–71; Heidegger's, 3–4, 53, 56, 58, 109–11; remarkability and temporality of, 108, 128. *See also* Capitalization; Designification; Grammar; Mood; Quotation Marks; Tense
Laplanche, Jean, 101
Leclaire, Serge, 162 n22
Leiris, Michel, 96
Lévinas, Emmanuel, 47
Lévi-Strauss, Claude: 62; on ritual, 162–63 n30
Logocentrism: 87, 92–93, 154; exemplified in Heidegger, 58. *See also* Tradition
Louis, Morris, 15, 18

Mallarmé, Stéphane, 10, 128, 129, 136
Manet, Edouard, 12, 14, 16, 17, 18
Marshall, Donald, 117
Marx, Karl, 80, 95
Mauss, Marcel, 77, 80
Mere (merely, merest): ability to remark, 90; accident, 15, 92; act of reading, 68–69; appearance, 41, 164 n17; appetite, 65; beings, 55; decoration, 6, 9, 10; discipline, 104; entertainment, 6; epistemological regress, 20; existence, 45, 164 n17; fact, 45, 47; ideal, 96; idiolect, 106;

metaphoricity, 110; modernizing, 31; nothingness, 75; opposition, 38; possibility, 45, 79; preliminary, 67; rhetoric, 108; taste, 17; text, 67, 94; theatricality, 14; wrongness, 155
Metaphilosophy: refusal of, 20–21
Metaphysical enclosure. See Tradition
Miller, J. Hillis: 152, 153, 168–69 n27; "Stevens' Rock," 130, 137, 144; "Tradition and Difference," 122, 135
Milton, John, 121
Mirror-stage (Lacan), 62, 63–64, 88
Mise-en-abîme, 96–97, 141–42. See also Abyss
Modernism: 3–33, 122, 136, 146, 151, 154; in Blindness and Insight, 128–38; defined by Cavell, 17–18; defined by Greenberg, 4; and retrospection, 11–12, 17
Mood: 146, 153; in Cavell, 19; imperative, modernist, 32; subjunctive of last professor, 36

Nancy, Jean-Luc, 127
Negation/negative: 65, 75, 76, 77, 78, 82, 111, 125; abstract, 41; determinate, 40, 41, 42. See also Dialectic; Not/knot; Pas; Step
Nietzsche, Friedrich, 4, 6, 59, 61, 95, 106
Not/knot, 9, 10. See also Dialectic; Negation; Pas; Step
Novalis, 38

Old Masters, 17, 29

Pas, 55, 95, 11, 164 n 16. See also under Derrida; and Dialectic; Negation; Not/knot; Step
Phallocentrism, phallogocentrism, See Tradition
Phonocentrism, See Tradition
Plato/plato, 94, 105
Poe, Edgar Allen, 88, 100
Pollock, Jackson, 73
Ponge, Francis, 96, 106, 107, 126
Pontalis, Jean-Baptiste, 101
Position/positionality, 24, 37, 42, 45, 60, 73, 81–83, 107, 142
Possibility/(Im)possibility: and autonomy, 77; of choice in Barbara Johnson, 144; of

criticism, 152, 156; and double bind, 35; of fraudulence, 30; in game of odds-and-evens, 90; and impossibility, 79; of loss, failure, error, 7–8, 10, 14, 100; of the modern, 130; of philosophy after Hegel, 45, 59, 73–74; "real," 8; of self-reading, 129; of theory, 138; of transition or mediation, 116
Postmodernism, 7, 17, 160 n9, 160 n10, 168 n24
Poussin, Nicolas, 8
Psychoanalysis, 23, 24–25, 60–71, 84–114, 116, 139, 168 n19
Psychology/psychologism, 21–22, 23–24, 86, 89
"Purity," 5–6, 7, 10, 13, 16, 24, 38, 60, 80, 87, 93, 99, 131, 152, 155, 165 n34. See also Heterogeneity; Kernel; Mere; Quotation marks

Queneau, Raymond, 47, 71, 72
Quotation marks, 3, 85, 108, 151. See also Capitalization; Designification; Erasure

Real (Lacan), 91
Recognition. See Acknowledgment; Denial
Rembrandt van Rijn, 8
Repression/repression: 109; for Cavell, 26; read anasemically, 105; of writing, 84, 97, 107
Rhetoricity: defined by de Man, 129; halting of, in Felman's reading, 149
Rhythm, 69, 70, 100, 107, 112, 146, 156
Ricoeur, Paul, 110, 139
Robbe-Grillet, Alain, 29
Rousseau, Jean-Jacques, 84, 116, 121, 122, 124, 128, 129
Rupture: 116, 122; and acknowledgment, 116; and continuity, 16- 18, 31, 154; and redoubling, 3, 18, 36, 40, 49, 127, 136, 142, 146, 153; and repetition, 59; and reproduction, 33. See also Abyss

Sacrifice, 77–78, 80–81
Saint-Saëns, Camille, 30, 33
Sartre, Jean-Paul, 116, 127
Schelling, Friedrich, 59
Schlegel, A. W., 38, 151
Schlegel, F., 38, 151

Seam/seamless, 63, 122, 126, 127, 143, 145, 149, 152, 168 n16
Searle, John, 107, 151
Self-criticism, 4–6, 16–19, 37, 85, 118, 140, 144, 154
Self-reflection, 96–97
Self-resistance, 118, 138
Shelley, Percy Bysshe, 133, 138, 151
Sidney, Sir Philip, 132
Skepticism, 21–27, 40–42, 50, 75, 147
Smith, Tony, 15
Socrates, 105
Speculative proposition (Hegel), 68–69, 111–12
Stendhal, 151
Step: 111–12; back, in Heidegger, 55, 56, 57–58, 61; beyond philosophy, 95. See also Dialectic, broken or limping; Pas
Sterne, Laurence, 151
Stierle, Karlheinz, 136
Subject: of psychoanalysis, 70; subjectivity of, in Heidegger, 53
Supplement, 84, 95, 96, 105, 152
Symbolic (Lacan), 62, 64, 66, 86, 88, 91, 100, 145

Tasso, Torquato, 87
Temporality: 128, 170 n11; of criticism, 146, 154; in de Man, 125, 131–33; in Heideg-
ger, 52–54; and schematism in Kant, 51–53. See also Belatedness; Deferred action; Mood; Tense
Tense, 107, 140, 153
Text: emergence of, in Hegel, 66–71
Theatricality: 10, 11, 14–15, 18, 30, 118, 127, 141–42, 160 n11, 169 n30
Torok, Maria. See Abraham, Nicolas
Tradition: 17, 27, 28, 54, 58, 61, 93, 109, 142, 155; as anasemic homonym, 105; critical, 145; as forgetting, 48, 109; and Hegel, 43, 46; and Heidegger, 46, 60–61, 94–96
Trilling, Lionel, 8
Turkle, Sherry, 61

Unconscious: as post-Hegelian object, 62, 71
Unthought (Heidegger): 54; as criterion for conversation, 55

Wahl, Jean, 47
Wasserman, Earl, 122
Wimsatt, W. K., 12
Wittgenstein, Ludwig, 19, 22, 24, 25, 27–28, 39–40, 85
Wordsworth, William, 121, 124

Yale School, 167 n11
Yeats, William Butler, 121, 122, 124

Stephen W. Melville earned his Ph.D. in Comparative Studies in Literature at the University of Chicago in 1981; he is assistant professor of English at Syracuse University. During the 1985–86 academic year he served as Getty Foundation Fellow in the History of Art at Bryn Mawr College.

Donald Marshall is professor of English at the University of Iowa; he earned his Ph.D. in English at Yale University in 1971. He is also author of the introduction to a forthcoming book in the Theory and History of Literature series, Geoffrey Hartman's *The Unremarkable Wordsworth*.